Traditions and Reminiscences
of Concord Massachusetts,
1779–1878

Edward Jarvis (1803–1884), etching

Traditions and Reminiscences
of Concord, Massachusetts
1779–1878

EDWARD JARVIS

Edited by Sarah Chapin

Introduction by Robert A. Gross

Amherst

The University of Massachusetts Press

Library of Congress Cataloging-in-Publication Data
Jarvis, Edward, 1803–1884.
    Traditions and reminiscences of Concord, Massachusetts,
  1779–1878 / Edward Jarvis ; edited by Sarah Chapin ;
  introduction by Robert A. Gross.
    p.   cm.
Includes index.
ISBN 0–87023–849–3 (alk. paper)
1. Concord (Mass.)–Social life and customs.
I. Chapin, Sarah, 1931–   . II. Title.
F74.C8J33   1993   93–20179
974.4'4—dc20   CIP

British Library Cataloguing in Publication data are available.

Frontispiece: Edward Jarvis (1803–1884, etching)

CONTENTS

Contents

PREFACE

Sarah Chapin

On December 6, 1876, Dr. Edward Jarvis wrote to Rev. Grindall Reynolds, minister of the First Parish church, "It would be interesting to look into the houses and families of the last century, still more a hundred years earlier and see their manner of life, their furniture, their food, cookery, drinks etc." He continued,

> With such means, you could write a history of Concord, of the progress of the people, and show, to great extent, the debt we owe to our fathers, for their privations and labors, in order to put us in the dwellings and conditions of comfort that we now enjoy.
>
> If you could write such a History of Concord people, as Knight's *History of England*, Goodman's *Social History of Great Britain*, Macauley's 3d chap. vol. I, Macullochs Statistical account of the British Empire, etc., you would do an excellent work for humanity.

It is likely that Jarvis was taking advantage of Rev. Reynolds's receptive ear to advance a proposal he had every intention of fulfilling himself. He completed his autobiography in 1873 and began reflecting on his early years after suffering a mild stroke in 1874. In 1878, at age seventy-five, he was still musing—tidying up his work room, sorting the desk drawers, reexamining mementos, and squaring accounts; selecting, categorizing, itemizing, counting, always counting, as if only by applying the lens of statistical verification could he put his life into tolerable perspective. His reminiscences are not scrapbook recollections of good old days along the mill dam. These memories are all business.

Wearied by years of disappointed ambition, Jarvis decided to in-

vii

dulge himself by annotating the material presented in Lemuel Shattuck's *History of Concord*. It was a doubly gratifying task. He could finally correct Shattuck, whose career had paralleled his own in ways often too enviable for comfort, and he could carry on Concord's historical tradition with his own extensive recollections. It was never his intention to write another history of the town.

Many of Jarvis's papers are preserved in the Concord Library's archives. He donated most of them himself. There are small books and pamphlets (mainly treatises on medical subjects), his diary, a couple of volumes from his personal library (including his copy of Bigelow's *Plants of Boston*), and a few letters. "Traditions and Reminiscences," Jarvis's copy of Shattuck's *History*, and *Houses and People of Concord* (Jarvis's local gazetteer) are all thick, leather-bound volumes with gold lettering on the spine. Jarvis's copy of Shattuck's *History* is a miscellany of interlineations and insertions. In the beginning Jarvis's notes are neatly written in longhand at the bottom of Shattuck's pages; then, as he warmed to his task, he wrote all around the edges of the text, glued in newspaper clippings, and added pages numbered (and labeled with lowercase letters) to correspond to Shattuck's original pagination. When he came to the end, "there were other topics that seemed to require separate and longer treatment," so he kept on, "chapter after chapter," until it was clear that he had to bind his extra pages separately—all 663 of them. "Traditions and Reminiscences" is written in longhand on hand-numbered pages; the illustrations are limited to clippings from newspapers, with the exception of a photograph of Jarvis as a frontispiece. The book falls somewhere between an encyclopedia of nineteenth-century social history, an autobiographical essay, and the candid revelations of a proprietary cat. Jarvis escorts us through the family home, directing our attention first here, then there, occasionally pausing as he moves from room to room to make certain we understand not only the function but also the value of each aspect of the domestic scene. Then he is off to the neighbors, the schoolhouse, the church, the social clubs, the library, the post office, the town hall, and finally the tavern, where he unabashedly counts the townspeople's drinks. The town belonged to him as it could only to a person who lived in the place as a child. He knew its roads and bridges, and who lived on farms and who lived in town. He even knew where the wildflowers were.

He named names. He made lists. Who went to college? Only a few did not go to Harvard. Two dozen graduates stayed in Concord and "gave the people the advantage of their educated influence." Jarvis's list of European travelers—including Mr. and Mrs. Hawthorne; Mr. Emerson and his daughter; Mr. and Mrs. Edward Hoar and their daughter—defined Concord's aristocracy.

"Traditions and Reminiscences" has wide-ranging literary parallels. Aficionados of Charles Dickens will find themselves at home in Jarvis's Concord. Elijah Paige, the schoolmaster; drunken Breed and the prostitute Huldah Williams; Francis Jarvis (*père*); and the nameless maid-servant-cousin who lived with the family for twenty-six years and died with "a good little fortune"—all have counterparts in Dickens's stories. Mystery fans familiar with inhabitants of deceptively quiet English villages will easily focus their inventive fantasies on Thomas Healy, the wanton boy who turned out well; Ebenezer Hardy, the gouty, misanthropic farmer, victim of a malicious joke that could have been fatal; and whimpering Luther Osborne (who knows things), cowering before the bully Ben Stearns. Jarvis's own mother, "a bright, observing woman . . . inherited a great interest in all Concord matters, and carefully noticed whatever was going on around her. She was full of the traditions of the past and was fond of telling of what she had heard and had seen of the people of the town—their habits and manners, sayings and doings." Was she Miss Marple's great-aunt?

Gilbert White, the curate of Selbourne, wrote with elegant simplicity and wit about his parish one hundred years before Jarvis. Among other things of interest and significance to naturalists and historians he described, as an alternative to candles, rush (*juncus conglomeratus*), which was split and dipped into hot fat. "Each rush, before dipping, costs ⅓₃ of a farthing, and ⅟₁₁ afterwards." Jarvis continues the economic history of lighting: "Downes's kerosene . . . is sold by the barrel . . . for 15 cents a gal. . . . A gallon of whale oil, costing 60 cts., will burn in an ordinary lamp with two wicks 31–33 hours. A gallon of sperm oil, costing 120 cts., will burn 30–31 hours. A pound of tallow candles costing . . . 14 cts., will burn 48 hours and give only about ⅟₁₅ or ⅟₂₀ as much light as the kerosene."

Jarvis vigorously condemns the use of alcohol in Concord. His argument is noteworthy, not because of the conviction that rum (new rum, West Indies rum, toddy, flip) was the ruination of many good, and all bad, men—everyone knew temperance was in the air—but because Jarvis produced solid data to support his judgment. In Boston at about the same time, Dr. Oliver Wendell Holmes asserted that liquor worked its precarious charm exclusively on constitutions weakened by physical flaw, spiritual decadence, and moral turpitude. Though both men had a piece of the truth, and prestigious as Holmes was, it was Jarvis who had the facts and therefore the better claim to credibility.

In my opinion, a point-by-point past/present equation of Jarvis's work would dull the edge of its originality and risk reducing it to quaintness. Edward Jarvis's contribution to social history should not be so diminished. What does seem worth noting are subjects on which Jarvis is silent. "Traditions" lacks entries on topics just as significant for Concord's domestic history as intemperance and military tattoos. Environmental health (waste disposal and disease-producing contamination) and its corollaries (soap-making, bathing, and laundry) are missing from "Traditions and Reminiscences." How was laundry done in Jarvis's mother's kitchen? Was there a kettle for making soap as big as the one for making candles? A bathing pan (looking rather like a huge Aladdin's lamp with a broad brim) was advertised in Concord's newspaper in the 1840s. Did the Jarvises "enjoy the luxury and health ever attendant on those who practice daily ablution over the whole surface of the body," or did they make do with a Spartan sponge-off in cold water to diffuse accumulated nocturnal humors?

In the middle of the nineteenth century, the Concord Reformatory complex was discharging 150,000 gallons of wastewater per day into the Assabet River, thence into the Concord River, and ultimately under the North Bridge. This was mainly drainage from the dye works and gas works, roof runoff and sink waste from the houses on the periphery of the reformatory. This "grey water" mixed with the overflow from the prison's cesspools, and the whole odorous broth found its way into the river. Since plans to modernize the sewage disposal system at the prison were under way about the time Jarvis wrote "Traditions and Reminiscences," it would have been reasonable for him to comment on sanitation conditions in the town and opportunities for improving them. Jarvis's Puritan conscience might have forbidden discussion of excremental waste in anything except the most theoretical terms, but he was too good a scientist to underestimate the significance to Concord townspeople of a contaminated river flowing through the meadows.

Jarvis could not leave his important mortality statistics out of the book. Though they are neither traditions nor reminiscences, they *are* part of Concord's social history. Within them one meets head-on Jarvis's problems with "foreigners," by which he means the Irish. The Irish were a sickly lot, and they liked to drink, which made them sicker, and "their marriages are more productive than those of other races, of whom we have the records." He tries to sound objective—in fact, he would rather be objective than admit his bias—but it is clear where he stands when he regrets the necessity for counting American-born children of Irish parents who, "in a pathological or sanitary point of view . . . should be included in the class of foreigners, for they inherit the feebler constituency and the low vitality of their parents." Without them, he declares, his calculations would prove that Concord is one of the healthiest places to live in. Twenty years later, Concordians blamed Italian laborers for infecting the town with malaria. One wonders what statistics Jarvis would have offered to support or disprove this notion.

The original manuscript of "Traditions and Reminiscences" was copied out from dictation and notes by Dr. Jarvis's wife, Almira, and by his sister and niece in a labor born of great affection and respect. The changes of handwriting present an interesting challenge to the modern transcriber. One scribe's *S* sometimes appears to be another's *P*; Dr. Jarvis's *4* is another's *h*, and the double-*S*, often but not always written in the old way, causes a transcriber to ponder whether the word is "legs" or "less," "bags" or "bass." Although the figures in the statistical tables are not always mathematically accurate, it is unfair to blame these errors on the faithful ladies. Probably Jarvis, suffering from failing eyesight when he wrote "Traditions and Reminiscences," had difficulty copying his own notes. Since I believe Jarvis's argument has not been compromised by the errors, no effort has been made to correct the discrepancies.

Throughout the manuscript I have inserted "indecipherable" when all efforts at word recognition failed. Occasionally there are blanks, so noted, where the ladies were either inattentive or themselves confused by the Doctor's abbreviated notation. To aid the reader I have in some cases rearranged awkward sentences and eliminated (or relocated) commas and semicolons. Words in square brackets are my clarifying editorial additions. Curly brackets indicate Jarvis's original brackets. Some of the footnotes in part 1, the addenda to Shattuck's *History*, indicate the placement of Jarvis's comments in that volume. In part 2, the text proper of "Traditions and Reminiscences," footnotes include both Jarvis's original notes as well as my own comments (introduced by "Ed.").

"Traditions & Reminiscences" has been transcribed with the kind permission of the Concord Free Public Library Corporation, the li-

Almira Jarvis (1804–1884)

brary director, Barbara Powell, and the curator of the library archives, Marcia Moss. Joyce Woodman and Leslie Wilson contributed valuable research assistance. My thanks to them all.

Jarvis dedicated his book to his friend George Washington Hosmer, with an epigraph by Wordsworth. I would like to dedicate this edition of "Traditions and Reminiscences" to the memory of Almira Jarvis. She had a heart of gold—all of it pledged to Edward Jarvis. She endured childlessness, poverty, and separation from her beloved mother. She opened her house to her husband's mentally ill patients and transcribed his manuscripts. She nursed Jarvis through illness and accident. At the end, Almira, ill herself, worn down by work and stress, roused herself when Jarvis died, made the appropriate arrangements, went back to bed, and with magnificent loyalty (that had never failed him in life) followed her Edward forthwith into the next world. They were buried together, one casket covered with ivy, the other with ferns. The Reverend Andrew Peabody wrote of her in 1885, "She was [Jarvis's] faithful helper in his entire life-work, and [her] blended strength and beauty of character, veiled by modesty and reserve from the larger world, have left the most precious memories with all whose privilege it was to know her."

INTRODUCTION

Preserving Culture:
Edward Jarvis and the Memory of Concord

Robert A. Gross

In 1875, at a time of national uncertainty, the town of Concord, Massachusetts, set out to commemorate the moment that had established its enduring place in American history: the battle of April 19, 1775, between Minutemen and Redcoats at the Old North Bridge. Marking the start of the War for Independence—"the shot heard 'round the world"—the celebration launched the centennial of the American Revolution. This was no ordinary occasion for regional pride; though New Englanders were long accustomed to treat the event as "the national birthday," Concord was determined to turn the one hundredth anniversary into a focus "of national interest." It was an understandable impulse. The commemoration was taking place just ten years after the close of a bloody civil war and amidst a severe economic depression. Anxious about the future of the republic, Americans—or rather, Northerners—looked to the affair in Concord for assurance that in the course of national expansion and industrial revolution, they had not lost touch with the past.[1]

They were not disappointed. The centennial celebration proved to be a national jubilee, notwithstanding freezing weather and huge

1. *Proceedings at the Centennial Celebration of Concord Fight April 19, 1875* (Concord Mass.: published by the town, 1876), 5.

XV

crowds that swamped preparations for the event. Some sixty thousand persons streamed into the little town of twenty-four hundred souls; arriving in a constant procession of railroad cars, the friendly army of visitors was sixty times larger than the invading force of British Regulars a century before. President Ulysses S. Grant was there, accompanied by Vice President Henry Wilson, Massachusetts' native son, and by members of the Cabinet. So, too, were the governors of every New England state, a host of distinguished visitors, numerous companies of militia for the formal parade, and a multitude of ordinary people from every part of the Union, many returning to their ancestral home. So packed were the trains that some guests couldn't get anywhere near Concord. William Dean Howells and Samuel L. Clemens made the mistake of skipping the official car from Boston and seeking regular passage from Cambridge. "A swift procession of coaches, carriages, and buggies, all going to Concord," Howells reported, "passed us, inert and helpless, on the sidewalk in the peculiarly cold mud of North Cambridge. We began to wonder if we might not stop one of them and bribe it to take us, but we had not the courage to try."[2]

For those who prevailed, the festivities proffered a visible connection to the past. Concord had transformed itself into an outdoor museum of the American Revolution. Houses and stores were wrapped in bunting; flags decorated the graves of the "Revolutionary Heroes" atop Burial Hill; a replica liberty pole stood nearby; painted signs indicated the places associated with "the stirring events of the 19th of April." After a lapse of seventy-five years, the town had rebuilt the North Bridge over the Concord River, so that travelers could easily visit the statue of the Minuteman, commissioned for the occasion and designed by local sculptor Daniel Chester French. These were the tangible signs of the emotional bond between town and nation. The spirit of '75 still lived.

On a higher plane, the speakers for the day sounded a common theme: in the culture and institutions of the New England town lay the origins of the American republic. The official orator, George William Curtis, the reform-minded editor of *Harper's Weekly*, was forced to deliver his address above the noise of "twenty bands and unspeakable

2. David B. Little, *America's First Centennial Celebration: The Nineteenth of April 1875 at Lexington and Concord, Massachusetts*, 2d ed. (Boston: Houghton Mifflin, 1974); *Proceedings at the Centennial Celebration*, 63–64; Mildred Howells, ed., *Life in Letters of William Dean Howells*, 2 vols. (Garden City, N.Y.: Doubleday, Doran & Co., 1928), 1:202–3.

chaos," but as "an old soldier of mass meetings in the open air," he pressed on. The fifty-one-year-old Curtis, a native of Providence, Rhode Island, told a shivering crowd of six thousand, huddled in a cavernous tent, that the town meeting, "the true glory of Concord," was "the nursery of American independence." In that arena, the Puritan settlers learned the practice of self-government. Forced by frontier necessities to rely upon themselves, the inhabitants, "the rich and the poor, the good and the bad," met in common to lay out roads, establish schools and churches, levy taxes, and defend themselves, all by general consent. "Thus each town was a small but perfect republic, as solitary and secluded in the New England wilderness as the Swiss canton among the Alps." From that experience developed a political faith—a devotion to liberty and a heritage of civic duty—that inspired the Minutemen of 1775 and that remained vital to the American future. "The story of this old town," Curtis declared, "is the history of New England. It shows us the people and the institutions that have made the American republic."[3]

Such rhetoric was familiar to those who had attended previous commemorations of Concord Fight; invariably, the occasion became a tribute to the collective virtue of the Yankee farmer. But in the wake of the Civil War, Curtis directed his message to the experiences and anxieties of his audience. Before the late conflict, he suggested, the world of the Minutemen had grown "vague and unreal," and the few surviving veterans of Lexington and Concord appeared "venerable relics of a vanished age." No more. Having sacrificed their lives to preserve liberty and union, the Civil War generation recognized the men of '75 as contemporaries. "Now, if never before, we understand the Revolution." That lesson remained as pertinent as ever. As Curtis surveyed the nation in 1875, he discerned ominous signs ahead. America had entered "an age of consolidation," propelled by the twin engines of industry and government. The dominant forces of the era—the steam engine, the railroad, the telegraph—shattered the autonomy of local communities, gathering them up into an integrated, national network, centered in distant cities and subject to the "unscrupulous greed of power." "In New England, the characteristic village and local life of the last century perishes in the age of steam." At the same time, a huge national government, swollen by the demands of war, held sway

3. *Proceedings at the Centennial Celebration,* 30–37, 91–93; Little, *America's First Centennial Celebration,* 9–42; Gordon Milne, *George William Curtis & the Genteel Tradition* (Bloomington: Indiana University Press, 1956), 169.

over a defeated South and fell prey to corruption. Worse still, the United States was vulnerable to the growing power of ignorant, impoverished citizens—the immigrant Irish of the North and the emancipated blacks of the South—who had no grasp of self-government. Altogether, the prospect was unsettling: beset by concentrations of wealth and power without, besieged by aliens within, local communities, the foundation of the republic, were losing control of their destiny, thus opening the way to tyranny. The times demanded "minutemen of liberty" once more, ready to resist the latest foes.

> They do not come proudly stepping to the drum-beat, with bayonets flashing in the morning sun. But wherever party spirit shall strain the ancient guaranties of freedom; or bigotry and ignorance shall lay their fatal hands upon education; or the arrogance of caste shall strike at equal rights; or corruption shall poison the very springs of national life,—there, minutemen of liberty, are your Lexington Green and Concord Bridge; and as you love your country and your kind, and would have your children rise up and call you blessed, spare not the enemy![4]

The official orator knew his audience. He had lived in Concord as a young man back in the mid-1840s, after he had left the utopian community of Brook Farm, and he had retained ties to some of the town's leading men; indeed, he shared the platform that day with his longtime hero, the Transcendentalist Ralph Waldo Emerson, and his political friend, onetime U.S. Attorney General Ebenezer Rockwood Hoar, who was presiding over the entire commemoration. Abolitionist, supporter of women's rights, champion of nonpartisan government by the "best men," Curtis articulated the beliefs of the liberal Republican community that was host to his talk. In the face of the emergent realities of an interdependent, urban, industrial society, he looked back to the past, to the sturdy virtues of New England tradition. His celebration of the town meeting was hardly new; it resonated the theme of Emerson's own address at Concord's bicentennial in 1835 and harkened back to John Adams's view that New Englanders' love of liberty was rooted in the local institutions of town, church, school, and militia, all bound together in a common way of life.[5]

4. *Proceedings at the Centennial Celebration*, 90, 112–18; John McWilliams, "Lexington, Concord, and the 'Hinge of the Future,'" *American Literary History* 5 (Spring 1993): 1–29.
5. Milne, *George William Curtis & the Genteel Tradition*, 9–33, 99, 117, 135, 155–56; Ralph Waldo Emerson, "Historical Discourse at Concord," in *The Complete Works of Ralph Waldo Emerson*, ed. Edward Waldo Emerson, 12 vols. (Boston: Houghton Mifflin, 1903–04), 10:23–85; John Adams, *A Defence of the Constitutions of Government of the United States . . .* (1787), in *The Works of John Adams, Second President of the United States, with a Life of the Author, Notes, and Illustrations*, ed. Charles Francis Adams, 10 vols. (Boston: Little, Brown and Co., 1850–56), 5:494–96.

In the setting of 1875, speaking to national as well as local concerns, this outlook assumed a new tenor and purpose. In Curtis's telling, "Concord" became an abstraction, a timeless symbol more than a concrete place. Its institutions were sundered from time and circumstance and reified into an ideal model. Actually, any town would do—Concord, Lexington, a backwoods settlement in Maine, so long as it wasn't urban. Similarly, the heroes of Concord Fight entered the realm of myth as stock figures in a patriotic tableau. This simplification of history surely proved Curtis's point: the real world of Revolutionary Concord had vanished from view. It was now an object of nostalgia, onto which New Englanders could project feelings of loss, even as they seized the advantages of the modern world. The artifacts of that past—old plows and spinning wheels, ancient muskets and swords—were already on display in the museum the antiquarian Cummings Davis had established in the center of town.

Together, the memorials to the Revolution and the emblems of bygone times served to fix the identity of Concord in the wider world. Thanks to the centennial, the town gained popularity as an attraction for tourists, eager to venerate and to consume the icons of history. By the turn of the century, George William Curtis's tribute to Concord was a cliché of the popular press. Under the headline "Concord an Ideal Town," the *Boston Globe* informed potential visitors that "Concord, one of the oldest towns in the commonwealth, has retained through all the stress and strain of 275 years much of her pristine purity and most of her Puritan ideals." A "haven of rest," the town was a reminder of past glory and a refuge from care—but increasingly remote from the problems of an urban-industrial age.[6]

Nobody in Curtis's audience on that cold April morning loved Concord more than another official guest from the Boston area, the seventy-two-year-old Dr. Edward Jarvis, who, despite a recent stroke that rendered him partially paralyzed, made his way through the crowds to attend the ceremony. Born and raised in the town, Jarvis was a faithful scion of the community. His father, Deacon Francis Jarvis, had come there as a youth and become a successful businessman and pillar of the church; his mother was descended from generations of farmers, stretching back to the first English settlers. After attending local schools, Jarvis had gone off to Cambridge for college—in those days, Harvard and Cambridge were synonymous—and studied medi-

6. A. J. Philpot, "Concord—An Ideal Town," a newspaper clipping from the *Boston Globe,* April 1909, pasted up in volume one of the series of scrapbooks entitled "Events in Concord" and housed in the Special Collections of the Concord Free Public Library (CFPL).

cine in Boston; in the 1830s, he returned to marry his longtime fiancée, Almira Hunt, start a household, and practice his profession. But his stay in Concord proved short-lived. By early 1837, he had left in search of better prospects, never to return for good. Eventually, Jarvis put down roots in Dorchester, near Boston, and acquired a national reputation as a pioneer statistician, medical writer, and reformer of the insane. But he never lost his devotion to Concord, whose memories he cherished. During his five years' residence as a doctor, he had come up with the idea of celebrating the two hundredth anniversary of Concord in 1835, served on the organizing committee, and the next year helped to write the inscription on the first monument to the battle at the North Bridge. Ever since, as a pastime, he had periodically drawn on his own fund of local lore to inscribe marginal comments in a copy of the *History of Concord,* written by his onetime Concord colleague and friend Lemuel Shattuck to mark the town's bicentennial. Now, in the aftermath of the 1875 commemoration, he embarked upon a literary project to preserve the details of a time long gone by, the first two decades of the nineteenth century, when he was a boy growing up in the center of town.[7]

The product of that effort, "Traditions and Reminiscences of Concord, Massachusetts, or a Contribution to the Social and Domestic History of the Town, 1799 to 1878," offers a striking alternative to the official version of Concord history that was crystallized at the centennial. To Jarvis, Concord deserved all the admiration outsiders bestowed, but the community was, in his mind, not merely an ideal type. Years before, as a young doctor, he had helped to organize the celebration of the town's bicentennial in 1835, only to feel disappointed when the affair swelled into a grand extravaganza, at which a host of guests from far and wide paid fulsome tribute to the town. "It was an intellectual feast of high and honorable order, satisfactory to the ambitious," he recalled. "Yet almost all the speeches had no special reference to Concord or to her two hundred years of experience." Doubtless, he could have made the same complaint about the Centen-

7. Edward Jarvis, "Autobiography," 1873, Houghton Library, Harvard University, reprinted as *The Autobiography of Edward Jarvis (1803–1884),* ed. Rosalba Davico (London: Welcome Institute for the History of Medicine, 1992); Gerald N. Grob, *Edward Jarvis and the Medical World of Nineteenth-Century America* (Knoxville: University of Tennessee Press, 1978); Lemuel Shattuck, *A History of the Town of Concord; Middlesex County, Massachusetts, From Its Earliest Settlement to 1832 . . .* (Boston: Russell, Odiorne, 1835). Jarvis's addenda to Shattuck are reprinted in this volume; the interleaved copy is in Special Collections, CFPL.

nial of Concord Fight. For there was no inkling on that occasion that Concord was a real community, rooted in particular families and concrete institutions, which had undergone a remarkable transformation over time. If the speakers acknowledged that the "embattled farmers" of the Revolution inhabited a very different world from their own, the point was a mere bow to the past, soon lost in the fabrication of political myth. Jarvis had little regard for politics. Like a modern social historian, he demanded to know the social and material circumstances of everyday life. It was only through "the minutiae of the past," re-created with "feelings of love and reverence," that an authentic narrative of Concord could be written.

"Traditions and Reminiscences" enacted that purpose. Written and completed in the Gilded Age, it constitutes an extraordinary evocation of daily life and material culture in New England during the early republic. Jarvis took pride, and rightly so, in the keen habits of observation and the love of the past that both his parents had fostered in him as a child. Summoning up memories of boyhood, Jarvis recorded what his family ate and drank, how they kept warm and dressed, how they furnished their home. He recalled, with much distaste, his days in school and the brawls between the boys and the master. He conjured up the nasty pranks that grown men played on others and the numerous ways they cooperated to get the tasks of farming done. "Traditions and Reminiscences" sought to capture a way of life in the daily rhythms and the social routines of the town. As a compendium of details about houses, artifacts, and tools, as a storehouse of anecdotes and "traditionary" stories passed on by the Jarvis clan, the book is a literary museum of a lost way of life. It represents Jarvis's centennial gift to his successors in the rapidly expanding field of material culture.

But "Traditions and Reminiscences" is more than a treasure trove of curiosities and facts. It represents an important intellectual document in its own right. The book offers a classic statement of progress by a nineteenth-century intellectual who witnessed and recorded the great transformation of his society over the century. This was a story of improvement, of growing comfort and refinement, brought about by extending markets, expanding communications, and technological change. Work became more productive and less exhausting; it provided greater income and more leisure time. Manners and morals improved along with the standard of living. Deeply immersed in the wider world, the people of Concord filled their homes with books, paintings, and pianos as well as with sofas and stoves. Relations between parents and children lost formality and harshness; reason and affection now shaped the nurture of the young. An improving culture was evident as well in numerous voluntary societies—libraries, lyceums, farmers' clubs, and the like—and in the spread of temperance. Jarvis's Concord stood in contrast to the depiction by his former pupil and townsman Henry David Thoreau, who in *Walden* saw the neighbors leading lives of "quiet desperation." Jarvis found a community, where mental and material progress went hand in hand. His hometown became the model community of the Victorian middle class.[8]

Three principal influences shaped the presentation of Jarvis's "Traditions and Reminiscences." The first was the Federalist-Unitarian world view he had absorbed in boyhood at Concord's established church and during his education at Harvard. From Jarvis's earliest days, the town minister, Ezra Ripley, presided over the community as an old-style patriarch, superintending all aspects of his parishioners' welfare. A moderate in theology but a fierce partisan of Federalism, Ripley eschewed polemics in the pulpit and invested his energies in doing good. He served in a number of benevolent causes—education, temperance, Masonry, the Bible Society, the Peace Society—and never hesitated to intrude into the lives of "his people." In 1803, the year Jarvis was born, the fifty-two-year-old Ripley, a native of Connecticut and graduate of Harvard, was marking his twenty-fifth anniversary in Concord's pulpit. To the young Jarvis, the stately parson was a formidable figure who, in his dignified appearance (he was the last man in town to wear breeches, long stockings, and knee buckles and to don a wig) and formal manners, appeared to embody the old order of eighteenth-century America. Every Sabbath, in the forenoon and afternoon, Deacon Jarvis and his family went to meeting "as a matter of course, as if nothing else was desirable or possible, as we went to our meals or to our beds," and heard from the pulpit a forthright lesson in practical Christianity. Dr. Ripley prayed for the well-being of his flock, comforted the members in their trials and griefs, and set forth their many obligations to one another. "He took such a deep and constant interest in the affairs of his people,—of every class," Jarvis fondly remembered, "—he so watched the ways and manners of persons of all ages, he watched with such tender anxiety over their happiness and prosperity, that he made himself very highly acceptable, and was

8. Robert A. Gross, " 'The Most Estimable Place in All the World': A Debate on Progress in Nineteenth-Century Concord," *Studies in the American Renaissance* 2 (1978): 1–16.

universally respected and loved by the young and the old." The minister played a part in key moments of Jarvis's own life: he recommended the boy go to Harvard, officiated at his wedding, and urged him to set up medical practice in Concord. He remained a permanent force in Jarvis's thinking: a model of character, with remarkable "self-control and moral discipline" and a "tender sympathy and . . . conscientious regard to the happiness of others," and a source of inspiration. "Dr. Ripley had great confidence in the progress of society. . . . He thought each generation improved upon their fathers."[9]

The practical lessons inculcated in the Concord meetinghouse were enhanced by the formal education Jarvis received in Cambridge. In the first decades of the nineteenth century, the Unitarian faculty of Harvard forged a distinctive synthesis of Protestantism with the Enlightenment that shaped the social and political outlook of Boston's patrician class. Federalist in politics, capitalist in economics, elitist in society, the "moral philosophers" of Harvard instructed the future leadership of New England in its responsibilities for the common good. Drawing on the ideas of John Locke and on the Common Sense philosophy developed in eighteenth-century Scotland, they portrayed society as an organic entity, composed of interdependent parts, all working together for the larger whole. "Man is evidently made for living in society," they quoted the founding father of Common Sense, the philosopher Thomas Reid; hence, it was imperative to cultivate the "benevolent affections" that knit people together. To this end, the members of New England's educated elite bore a special responsibility. It was their duty not only to pursue a lawful calling, overseeing their countinghouses and carrying on their professions, but also to employ their wealth for higher intellectual and spiritual ends. Once a man achieved economic success, he would devote himself to improving his mind, refining his manners, supporting the church, and assisting those less fortunate than himself. The result of this conscientious, disin-

9. William B. Sprague, ed., *Annals of the American Pulpit; or Commemorative Notices of Distinguished American Clergymen of the Various Denominations, from the Early Settlement of the Country to the Close of the Year Eighteen Hundred and Fifty-Five. With Historical Introductions. Volume VIII: Unitarian Congregational* (New York: Robert Carter & Brothers, 1865), 112–25 (Jarvis's comments are on 121–25); Robert A. Gross, *Books and Libraries in Thoreau's Concord: Two Essays* (Worcester, Mass.: American Antiquarian Society, 1988), 146–48, 154–57; Ronald A. Bosco, " '[M]ercy to Pardon & Grace to Help': Ezra Ripley's Ordination Diary, 1778–1836," *Studies in Puritan American Spirituality* 2 (1991): 153–92; Edward Jarvis, Diary 1827–42, 1:11–19 and 2:93–95, 130, in Special Collections, CFPL.

terested leadership would be social and moral progress for all. In the moral philosophers' ideal, the individual and society advanced together.[10]

Edward Jarvis faithfully absorbed this message during his years at Harvard and applied it in the organizing framework of "Traditions and Reminiscences." The basic categories of his analysis were derived from the liberal, Unitarian synthesis. As he charted the course of material progress in Concord, Jarvis conscientiously tracked its consequences for moral and intellectual life. In his telling, the social changes that followed from the market revolution served both to strengthen social bonds and to uplift peoples' morals and minds.

Reinforcing the heritage of Unitarian moral philosophy was the scientific outlook Jarvis gained in the course of his medical training and practice. When the young Harvard graduate began studying to be a doctor in 1827, the profession was losing credibility with the general public and its own practitioners. In the Jacksonian age, the authority of experts clashed with democratic expectations. Responding to calls for "every man [to be] his own physician," state legislatures abolished licensing requirements and allowed a host of unconventional therapists and quacks free access to the profession. Not that the "irregular" doctors did any more harm than their "orthodox" rivals. The "heroic" medicine that had been widely adopted in the early republic—the free resort to bleeding, puking, and purging patients in the effort to restore their humors—surely killed as many as it "saved." Amidst this disarray, leading physicians began to look for another approach. Influenced by his teachers at Harvard Medical School, Jarvis shared the skepticism about traditional therapeutics; there seemed to be no relation between his remedies and the patient's recovery. "I almost daily find," he wrote in 1833, "that, from habit, I give things, & when I ask myself what good will they do? I cannot tell."[11]

Jarvis resolved this doubt by adopting a perspective more congenial to his moralistic temper. If he couldn't cure disease, perhaps he could prevent it by discovering "the laws of life." That approach focused attention on the social and physical environment. Recognizing that

10. Daniel Walker Howe, *The Unitarian Conscience: Harvard Moral Philosophy, 1805–1861* (Cambridge: Harvard University Press, 1970); quotation from Reid is on 126.
11. Thomas L. Haskell, *The Emergence of Professional Social Science: The American Social Science Association and the Nineteenth-Century Crisis of Authority* (Urbana: University of Illinois Press, 1977), 77–82; Grob, *Edward Jarvis and the Medical World*, 23–25, 30–39 (quotation on 31–32); Rosalba Davico, "Introduction," *The Autobiography of Edward Jarvis*, xxx–xxxix.

daily habits—diet, exercise, hygiene—were closely bound up with health, Jarvis probed the living conditions of his contemporaries. The issue was personal as well as professional. He had been subject to bouts of dyspepsia ever since he cared for his dying brother Charles back in 1825; they were to recur throughout his life. As a medical student, he had felt a "weakness in [his] lungs" and was considered frail by his friends, who plagued him "by saying in all times and places, 'How is your health?' " In quest for relief, Jarvis began investigating the subject of diet and was soon lecturing on "the Anatomy and Physiology of Vegetables." Talks on temperance quickly followed. Jarvis drew his ideas not merely from his own experience and observations but also from the systematic collection of empirical data. In so doing, he was influenced by a new statistical approach to medicine, pioneered by French scientists, which would give direction to his entire career.[12]

Quantitative study appealed to Jarvis's desire for moral and intellectual certainty. As a schoolboy, he had shown an early aptitude for mathematics, learning arithmetic at age eleven and geometry, trigonometry, and surveying at thirteen. "I got a considerable reputation as a mathematician," he would recall, "much to my father's joy. . . ." He had also spent many happy hours collecting plant specimens around Concord and classifying them in a botanical *herbarium*. This turn of mind was well suited to the intellectual trend of the times. At the very moment Jarvis was discovering the French approach to medical statistics, Americans were racing to count and measure virtually every aspect of social life. "Arithmetic, I presume," observed the Englishman Thomas Hamilton on a visit to New England in the early 1830s, "comes by instinct among this guessing, reckoning, expecting, and calculating people." As a doctor in Concord, Jarvis joined in the popular enthusiasm for numbers by collecting statistics on liquor sales and publicizing the connection between drinking and disease. (He would recycle the data in "Traditions and Reminiscences.") This public activity complemented his scientific studies and provided Jarvis a new intellectual identity. He would become a leader in the field of "social statistics," joining with Lemuel Shattuck to found the American Statistical Association, serving as president of the body for two

12. Jarvis, *Autobiography*, 8, 13, 20; Jarvis, Diary 1:178–82, 333–35; Grob, *Edward Jarvis and the Medical World*, 36–38; Barbara Gutmann Rosenkrantz, *Public Health and the State: Changing Views in Massachusetts, 1842–1936* (Cambridge: Harvard University Press, 1972), 8–47.

decades (1852–72), advising the U.S. government on the national census, and winning international recognition in European intellectual circles.[13]

The fusion of morals and numbers that defined Jarvis's science shaped his approach to Concord's past. Everywhere in "Traditions and Reminiscences" there are figures: measures of agricultural productivity; calculations of population, mortality, and expectation of life; tables of public spending on schools; the exact dimensions of schoolhouses and the volume of fresh air for the children; and, of course, the totals of liquor sales in stores and taverns that he had obtained back in 1834 and his estimates of the money and life lost to drink. This collection of numbers reflects a deliberate design. Jarvis was still obsessed with concerns about diet, drinking, and health. "Traditions and Reminiscences" is, in effect, Jarvis's last major contribution to medical statistics: a sanitary survey of Concord's physical and moral well-being.[14]

If the intellectual framework derived from Unitarian moral philosophy and the method from social statistics, the actual subject of "Traditions and Reminiscences" was history or, more precisely, *local history*, a genre that took shape in New England during the 1820s and 1830s and that represents the third major influence on Jarvis's work. The rise of local history was itself the product of social change. As the advance of capitalism and democracy transformed the social landscape, attentive New Englanders perceived that a way of life, carried on by their ancestors, it seemed, since Puritan times, was ending. Identifying themselves as "antiquarians," they hurried to preserve the customs, the memories, and the records of that past from oblivion.

13. Jarvis, Diary 1:7–10; Jarvis, *Autobiography*, 7, 16, 20, 98–105, 108–9; Grob, *Edward Jarvis and the Medical World*, 147–50, 160, 187–94, 195–200; Patricia Cline Cohen, *A Calculating People: The Spread of Numeracy in Early America* (Chicago: University of Chicago Press, 1982), 47–115 (quotation, 175); Rosenkrantz, *Public Health*, 41–47.

14. That investigation, a careful reader will discover, was rigged from the start. Jarvis was determined to find evidence of Concord's superior condition. Viewing the mortality rates of his hometown in comparative perspective, Jarvis boasts that "Concord is healthier than two-thirds of the towns of Massachusetts and healthier than every nation of Europe . . . except Norway." He is quick to note that Irish immigrants, with their "feeble constituency" and "low vitality," have sullied this record; once they are removed from view, "Concord is among the most healthy towns and . . . is now as healthy as and probably more healthy than it has been in the last hundred years." That happy conclusion is, however, undercut by an important calculation Jarvis completely overlooks. Comparing mortality rates by half-centuries, 1779 to 1828 and 1829 to 1878, Jarvis provided evidence of only a modest improvement in life expectancy. (The number of deaths per 1,000 for the first period is 16.0; the ratio for the second is 15.2.) Given that Irish immigrants began to arrive in large numbers only after 1845, it seems likely that Jarvis overrated the progress of health among the "American population." By his own reasoning, the gain in popular morals, stressed throughout the manuscript, must be overrated.

Through the act of retrieval, they might insure continuity between old and new and perpetuate the values of the forefathers.[15]

Edward Jarvis was a natural candidate for this movement. In his parents' home, the past was a living presence, conveyed in his mother's stories "of what she had heard and had seen of the people of the town—their habits and manners, sayings and doings" and in his father's "abundant anecdotes" about the neighbors, dead and alive. "He told so much of these people and these matters," Jarvis remarked at age seventy-four, "and he presented them with such graphic form to us, that it was afterward difficult for us the children, and is sometimes even now [difficult] for me, to discriminate between the events and persons that he described to us and those which we had seen ourselves." Books and companions deepened this unusual interest in the past. Growing up in a culture that made little provision for children's tastes, the youthful Jarvis contented himself with the adult fare in his father's library and in the town's collection of books. He soon passed from light tales—Defoe's *Robinson Crusoe*, Smollett's *Peregrine Pickle*—to solid works of history, finding particular pleasure in Charles Robertson's weighty accounts of Europe and America. It was thus appropriate that Jarvis would have as his roommate at Harvard and lifelong friend Richard Hildreth, who would win fame for his multivolume history of the United States.[16]

Ultimately, it was Lemuel Shattuck's *History of Concord* that gave focus and purpose to Jarvis's own forays into history. Shattuck's work may strike a modern reader as an uninspired chronicle of facts and events, but it was hailed upon publication in 1835 as a landmark of the genre. Distinguished by a comprehensive approach, the volume covered not only the public story of the town from its founding through the Revolution, but also ecclesiastical history, natural history, topographical history, statistical history, and social and official history. It quoted extracts from old documents, compiled a valuable set of tables on population, property holdings, and taxes, and provided genealogies and biographies of first families and prominent citizens. One reviewer was astounded by Shattuck's insatiable appetite for facts:

15. David J. Russo, *Keepers of Our Past: Local Historical Writing in the United States, 1820s–1930s* (Westport, Conn.: Greenwood Press, 1988), 9–61; David D. Hall, "Reassessing the Local History of New England," in *New England: A Bibliography of Its History. Volume Seven of Bibliographies of New England History,* ed. Roger Parks (Hanover, N.H.: University Press of New England, 1989), xix–xxxi.

16. Jarvis, *Autobiography,* 3–4; Gross, *Books and Libraries in Thoreau's Concord,* 153, 352; Richard Hildreth, *The History of the United States of America,* 6 vols. (New York: Harper & Brothers, 1851–52).

There is, and should be, no such thing as a dull prospect, or a failure, or a small return, to such men [said the critic for the *North American Review*]. There is no such thing as dismay or disappointment. Half a page of some old illegible or unintelligible manuscript, wherein the moths have had their will undisturbed perhaps for a century, found in the attic, may reward him generously for months of plodding toil or aching eyes. It supplies him, perchance, with a christian name . . . or with a single date, which completes some nice little congeries of genealogy, wrought out of the rubbish of buried records, like a statue restored from the ruins of Pompeii. It is a discovery to him. He smiles at the sight, and rushes from his dusty laboratory into the open air of the wide world, and cries out 'eureka.'

Unfortunately, the critic added, Shattuck's "dismal drudgery" left its imprint on every page. But the antiquarian community didn't mind; a number of local historians paid Shattuck the compliment of deliberate imitation.[17]

It comes as no surprise that Jarvis admired the thoroughness of Shattuck's *History* and relished its facts. But he discerned more in the book than dry details. In a memorial tribute to his former townsman, colleague, and fellow member of the New England Historical and Genealogical Society, Jarvis praised "the philosophy of history" that prompted Shattuck to become "a statistician."

> Mr. Shattuck was not content with learning and reciting the mere facts or events of the past, but was inclined to examine them as to their motives, their bearing, and the consequences that arose or would arise out of them. Hence he was led to analyze and classify facts, and ascertain the part they had in history—their value and their power. . . . The statistical part of the *History of Concord*, caused him the most mental labor, and gave the world the most satisfaction. It is the most valuable part of the book.[18]

Curiously, it is not Shattuck or any other local historian whom Jarvis holds out as a model. Rather, in a letter to Concord's Unitarian

17. Shattuck, *History of Concord*; B. B. Thatcher, "History of Concord," *North American Review* 42 (April 1836): 449–50; William Lincoln, *History of Worcester, Massachusetts, from Its Earliest Settlement to September, 1836: with Various Notices Relating to the History of Worcester County* (Worcester, Mass.: M. D. Phillips, 1837), vi. Not only did Lincoln imitate Shattuck's scheme, but he also urged its general adoption: "It would have been greatly desirable that the excellence of this model could have been more fully copied."

18. John Ward Dean, "Mr. Lemuel Shattuck," in *Memorial Biographies of the New England Historic Genealogical Society Vol. III, 1856–1859* (Boston: New England Historic Genealogical Society, 1883), 315. Jarvis submitted a testimonial to Shattuck for publication in this work (314–19). Perhaps thinking of "Traditions and Reminiscences," he observed the need for a history of Concord after 1835. "There is now a very general desire that some other investigator and writer like Mr. Shattuck would spring up to complete the History from 1835 to the present time, and, while correcting the mistakes of Mr. Shattuck, make such additions as subsequent discoveries have furnished the means of making." I am indebted for this reference and for a more general understanding of Shattuck to a seminar paper by Maria M. Farland, entitled "Lemuel Shattuck, Statist: A Puritan in a Transcendental Age" and written at Amherst College in 1985.

minister and local historian, Rev. Grindall Reynolds, written around the time he must have been planning "Traditions and Reminiscences," Jarvis invokes the example of contemporary historians of England, including the great liberal Thomas Babington Macaulay. To produce "a History of Concord people" on the scale and with the grandeur of the English historians would be "an excellent work for humanity." Whence the appeal of Macaulay and the others in Jarvis's list? These books took a large, sympathetic view of the human enterprise, tracing the movement of the age in the smallest details of existence and providing a stirring panorama of progress. Certainly, that was the case of Macaulay's *History of England from the Accession of James II*. In a brilliantly opinionated survey of the social and economic condition of the nation in 1685, just before James II would ascend the throne and precipitate "the Glorious Revolution" of 1689, Macaulay issued a manifesto of social history. "Readers who take an interest in the progress of civilization and of the useful arts," he wrote, "will be grateful to the humble topographer who has recorded these facts, and will perhaps wish that historians of far higher pretensions had some-times spared a few pages from military evolutions and political in-trigues, for the purpose of letting us know how the parlours and bedchambers of our ancestors looked." Such curiosity, Macaulay went on, reflects no nostalgia for olden times, no desire for escape into a golden age. Just the opposite. It is the course of progress itself that renders ancient ways of life outmoded, turns our grandparents and their grandparents before them into strangers, and makes the past into "a foreign country." By re-creating the customs and the culture of a distant time, Macaulay meant to discover the world he had lost—less for its own sake than to ascertain the value of the world he had gained. Jarvis's purpose in "Traditions and Reminiscences" was the same. "Concord has had its due relation to the rest of the country, in the progress of civilization," he explained. "It has passed through its coarser and less refined stages and manifested among its people some of the spirit that held and governed the people of other parts of the country." If the town had now achieved a superior "state of culture and wealth," the inhabitants needed to appreciate just how far they had come. He thus wrote "Traditions and Reminiscences" as a gift to future residents, to be kept in the public library "for anyone to exam-ine, read, or quote from it as he may desire."[19]

19. Thomas Babington Macaulay, *The History of England from the Accession of James II,* 5 vols. (Boston: Estes and Lauriat, 188?), 1:257–386 (quotations on 318); David Lowen-thal, *The Past Is a Foreign Country* (Cambridge: Cambridge University Press, 1985).

It is a measure of Jarvis's accomplishment that he does carry us back to a different time and place. That world was the Concord of his childhood: the central village of the early republic. "Traditions and Reminiscences" deserves notice in the literature of boyhood. There is a remarkable charm to the glimpses of Jarvis's youth that appear in the various anecdotes of the manuscript. Situated right in the center of town, fascinated by the sights and sounds of the busy life around him, the young Edward was exposed daily to the adult world. One moment he could be dispatched to pick up his father's newspaper at the tavern or to deliver Dr. Ripley the leftover communion bread and wine. The next he could watch the militia troop by and thrill to the sound of a bass drum, wander among the booths set up on the common during the annual Court Week, or hear rumors that a brothel was operating out of Huldah Williams's house nearby and that in the dark of night, a delegation of respectable citizens had ridden the prostitute out of town on a rail. Ne'er-do-well neighbors dropped by to beg "just a drop of your good cider" or to borrow a lighted coal from the Jarvis hearth when their own fires had died out. Drunks were a common sight on the street; so were the "jail birds" from the Concord prison, allowed to walk "the limits" of the village. Unlike middle-class youth today, Jarvis was shielded from neither the harshness nor the responsibilities of adults.

Jarvis imagined that the Concord of his boyhood was largely continuous with the community founded by his mother's Puritan forebears back in 1635. In his telling, the town had, through long, unremitting toil, achieved a modicum of comfort by the early nineteenth century but remained bound by the social customs and the economic arrangements of the past. The world he depicts was, indeed, driven by inheritance and necessity. Jarvis's reminiscence of meals at his parents' house is a vivid case in point. Day in, day out, the Jarvises ate the same boiled dishes of meat and vegetables on which their great-grandparents had dined a century and a half before. It was salt beef or salt pork on weekdays and salt fish on the Sabbath. Fresh meat was available for only brief periods after a hog or cow was slaughtered; fresh cod, the staple of New England's oceans, seldom traveled as far inland as Concord. The free bounty of nature's storehouse—the wild game in the woods and the abundant water fowl and fish in the rivers and ponds—went untouched, except by "thriftless" families. Jarvis estimated that local fish provided no more than one meal a year in most homes. As for fruits and vegetables, these were seldom consumed raw.

The cabbages, squash, beets, carrots, peas, parsnips, and cucumbers that were raised in kitchen gardens by the women of Concord were either boiled and stewed into a "garden sauce" or pickled as a relish. Beans underwent long cooking to become the standard midday meal and symbol of New England: baked beans. Apples, worm-ridden or not, were pressed together to make cider, which aged into a "hard" drink for children and adults alike. In sum, the foodways of New England were an epitome of the social order. In Deacon Jarvis's household, young Edward encountered a culture of preservation in a setting of constraint.[20]

Shaped by economic scarcity—limited markets and a shortage of cash—the inhabitants of Concord needed one another to get by. Theirs was an inclusive, interdependent community. Children were not sharply set off from adults: little boys drank tea, coffee, and cider at meals; teenagers joined in barn raisings and consumed grog—sweetened rum—with laboring men in the fields. Likewise, the poor could make claims on the better-off: Deacon Jarvis regularly loaned small sums, at no interest, to needy neighbors and forgave bad debts "by saying they were very poor." Nobody could be spared when work was to be done. Jarvis recounts the numerous forms of neighborly cooperation by which the people of Concord got their living. In all sorts of "bees"—apple bees, wood bees, quiltings, corn huskings, and barn raisings—"friends combined to help one [another] out of straits. . . ." These events became communal gatherings, where work and play were joined, and young people found time to court and the old to drink.

In Yankee lore and in recent social history, these forms of hospitality and exchange have become the object of nostalgia, emblems of an era when the rules of the market were subordinated to the needs of community. Jarvis had fewer illusions. The other side of neighborly cooperation, in his perspective, was imposition upon others. The good deacon felt obliged to supply hard cider to his drunken neighbor, no matter how much he disapproved. The rowdies and roughnecks of

20. In its devotion to boiled dishes, baked beans, brown bread, apple cider, boiled puddings, and pies, the Jarvis family was faithful to the ascetic foodways set down by the Puritan founders of Massachusetts Bay. See David Hackett Fischer, *Albion's Seed: Four British Folkways in America* (New York: Oxford University Press, 1989), 134–39. The imperatives of preservation touched additional aspects of the domestic economy. Before matches were invented, families took elaborate precautions to keep a fire going through the night; should they fail, it was necessary to borrow live coals from a neighbor—and risk a reputation as "careless."

Concord had no qualms about the practical jokes they perpetrated on the unsuspecting and the vulnerable. Across the distance of almost two centuries, we may be amused at the hazing that Ebenezer Hardy, an impatient, "irritable" farmer of "violent temper" once received. Late one night, a journeyman hatter tied a long rope to the fetlock of Hardy's horse and attached the other end to a post. When Hardy got in the saddle, he naturally did the expected: with not a second to waste, he lashed the horse into a canter, only to crash to a halt when rider and mount reached the end of their rope. Thus was impatience literally pulled up short. We might laugh, too, at the Monty Python antics of lawyer Thomas Heald and his "riotous" crew, turning up at Abel Davis's "indifferent tavern," poking about his bar and kitchen, and demanding whatever item was out of stock. But when they spied Davis's messenger about to arrive with the missing good, "they would plead great haste and the impossibility of waiting for the matter and leave the tavern." But surely all humor dissolves in Jarvis's account of the abuse inflicted upon "the weak, the odd, the unfortunate." Rough boys, even "rude" men, thought little of mocking the jerky walk of the simple glazier John Stone, whom they nicknamed "Hop Stone." They were just as cruel to Brister Freeman, "a passionate negro, profane and suspicious." It was evidently a great pleasure to stir him into a fury. "He was said to have once stolen a haddock and was therefore tormented and hooted by boys. Then he would swear and storm. This gathered boys and men about him who insulted and violated him to greater passion." Rudeness and insensitivity, Jarvis knew, were "contemporaneous" with "abundant kindness and pleasant feeling." In retrospect, we can see that cruelty and cooperation were the warp and woof that wove the premodern community of Concord together.

It was precisely this "rudeness," this insensitivity to the feelings of others, that prompted Jarvis to refuse nostalgia for the community of his youth. For all his tributes to the industry, the piety, the self-sacrifice of his parents' generation, in "Traditions and Reminiscences" Jarvis makes clear that he disliked much about that world and was glad to leave it behind. One incident in Jarvis's coming of age provides a clue to his sentiments. In 1823, at age twenty, he and several young women, including his future wife, Almira Hunt, proposed to become full members of the town's Congregational church. This was a traditional step in the progress of New Englanders to full adulthood in their communities. But Jarvis was unhappy with the public ceremony it entailed. It was customary for candidates to step forth in the "broad aisle" of the meetinghouse and be "propounded" before the congregation, saints

and sinners alike, for church membership. Claiming to be too "diffident" to "make so public a demonstration of their act," Jarvis and
friends petitioned Dr. Ripley for a private induction "before the church
alone." As Jarvis tells it, the ancient minister, who had presided over
Concord since 1778, sympathized with the plea, but could not consent. "This was the time honored custom," which he had no power to
change. Jarvis replied that he and his friends were not alone; a good
many others shared their sentiment and hesitated to join the church. In
the face of this feeling, Dr. Ripley, a moderate by nature, came up with
an ingenious compromise: instead of standing in view of the whole
congregation, Jarvis and his friends could rise in their high wooden
pews, shielded from the gaze of strangers, and accept the covenant of
the church.[21]

This semi-withdrawal from public scrutiny was a critical moment in
the transformation of Concord. Jarvis and his contemporaries were
eager to be free from the prying eyes of neighbors and to be independent of the entangling alliances that bound the inhabitants together,
like it or not. They resented the obligation to meet the customary
claims of others: to invite strangers to their parties and weddings, to
trade tools and exchange work on the farm, to loan money to the
unworthy, to supply cider to importunate neighbors and liquor to
laborers and guests. They demanded more respect for privacy and
greater freedom to choose associates and friends. Jarvis played an
important part in this reconstruction of community. We can trace the
steps through the diary he kept in the 1820s and 1830s. When his
mother died in the spring of 1826, he insisted that the family drop the
custom of supplying the pallbearers with spirits. And when he served
as master of ceremonies at the wedding of a kinsman, he abandoned
the usual public procession to the home of the betrothed: it would have
drawn, he complained, "the gaze of boys, young women, and gossips."
It was no wonder, then, that Jarvis was viewed by townspeople as
"aristocratic"—a charge he admitted. He was no more willing, as a
schoolmaster in the neighboring town of Acton, to make the rounds of
local families than to invite one and all in Concord to a ball he
managed at the Middlesex Hotel. Like the poet Emily Dickinson,
Jarvis believed the "soul selects her own society, then shuts the door."[22]

In "Traditions and Reminiscences," Jarvis depicts the transforma-

21. Jarvis, *Autobiography*, 19; Jarvis, Diary 1:210, 212–15.
22. Jarvis, Diary 1:32–33, 129–30, 336–38; Robert A. Gross, "Lonesome in Eden:
Dickinson, Thoreau and the Problem of Community in Nineteenth-Century New England,"
Canadian Review of American Studies 14 (Spring 1983): 1–17.

tion of Concord as an impersonal process—what Victorians called progress and twentieth-century social scientists would label "modern-ization." As markets grew for farm crops and craft goods, families no longer aimed to produce their necessities and resorted, instead, to trade. And with more money in circulation to facilitate daily exchange, there was no reason to " 'change works" with neighbors or invite them to huskings and raisings. One could simply hire the labor needed and get the work done. In Jarvis's estimation, efficiency counted more than conviviality. "It is better that each should do his own work, with his own hands or by such aid as he can compensate in the ordinary way. Those burdens that in past years required the cooperation of friends and neighbors are now but ordinary affairs and are met by the ordi-nary means and their own exertions. The wasted work is now as well and completely done as ever and people both individually and socially are as happy and more prosperous and are loving, generous and ready to aid in distress, poverty and sickness, whenever they shall present themselves in any family or neighborhood."

This process of economic change—the expansion of markets, the spread of money, the growth of specialized roles—was tied, in Jarvis's view, to the advance of civilization. Jarvis discerned in Concord a broad movement from rudeness to refinement. His interpretation re-flected the outlook of gentlemen and scholars on both sides of the Atlantic. Leading thinkers like Macaulay gauged the progress of the age through the spread of education and civility.[23] Hence, Jarvis's emphasis upon the proliferation of books, newspapers, and periodi-cals; the numbers of college graduates in town; the ever-greater immer-sion of Concord in a wider world of travel and communications; and the softening of manners and advance of culture in school and home, as evidenced by the many pianos in the town's parlors. To Jarvis, still faithful to the Unitarian moral philosophy he learned as a student, the key to this process was the influence of a cultivated elite. "The presence of families of high culture, the refinement of their social influence, the sympathy of the favored classes with the other—all these wrought a good work in the town and Concord gradually became what it now is, one of the most cultivated towns in New England."

Jarvis's narrative of change disguises a set of events that were, for him, intensely personal. The erosion of communal customs was not simply a response to market forces, but the product of individual will.

23. Macaulay, *History* 1:383–85.

It reflected a class-conscious assertion of gentility, which had originated in England, spread among the colonial elite in the eighteenth century, and become a defining feature of the middle-class culture that Jarvis and his contemporaries created. For Jarvis himself, gentility was a value he learned in college, a means by which he and his Harvard classmates affirmed their superiority to urban laborers and "country clowns." Gentility meant politeness, delicacy, and taste. It involved cultivation of the mind, acquisition of bodily grace, and sensitivity to the feelings of others. In practice, aspiring gentlemen like Edward Jarvis learned to talk and dance in the best company with dignity and ease. And they judged others clearly by this standard. Through Jarvis's diary, one can witness the process by which a country youth became genteel. Introduced into elite circles in Essex County, Massachusetts, a twenty-two-year-old Jarvis attended the Salem assembly, "a dance that eclipsed all that I had seen before." Anxious of a faux pas, "I was diffident and feared to commit myself an awkward country youth in presence of so fine a company." But he quickly adapted and was soon measuring others with all the zeal of a new convert to the religion of gentility. He deemed a female cousin, his coeval, whom he met for the first time in 1825, to be quite acceptable: "She is not beautiful but genteel and agreeable." The young men he taught in Concord's grammar school the next year were "exceedingly gentlemanly in their deportment. They had a nice sense of honour and propriety, and tried to make my situation as comfortable as they could." And when he looked for a place to practice medicine in spring 1830, he canvassed the social character of communities as carefully as he assayed their economic prospects. Concord, New Hampshire, was inviting, but "there was a want of literary air among [the people], a lack of polish which I was accustomed to see." Marblehead, Massachusetts, a town of fishermen and laboring folk, was "poor & ignorant, unpolished, rude." Jarvis wanted to go only where society was as elevated as his ambitions. His native town of Concord was the ideal.[24]

The youthful Jarvis was unbearably judgmental and something of a snob. But his fastidiousness involved more than mere pride of distinction. It reflected a broad, generational impulse to escape the constraints of the traditional New England community. Ralph Waldo Emerson, Jarvis's exact contemporary and his Concord neighbor, would give the

24. Jarvis, Diary 1:41–51, 58–59, 120, 415–26; Richard L. Bushman, *The Refinement of America: Persons, Houses, Cities* (New York: Knopf, 1992).

mood a philosophical label. "It is the age of severance, of dissociation, of freedom, of analysis, of detachment," he wrote toward the end of his life. "Every man for himself. . . . The social sentiments are weak . . . veneration is low; the natural affections feebler than they were. People grow philosophical about native land and parents and relations. There is an universal resistance to ties and ligaments once supposed essential to civil society." In old age, Emerson could stand back and take a disinterested view. In youth, Jarvis could not. Instead, he struggled to free himself from the many pressures that hedged in his choices and confined his life.[25]

The limitations set in early, in the home, and extended outward into society as Jarvis came of age. First, there was the problem of a calling. With his taste for reading, the boy, at age fifteen, aspired to college and "a literary profession," but that was out of the question. His older brother Charles was already at Harvard, and in a dilemma with which late twentieth-century parents can easily sympathize, Deacon Jarvis couldn't afford to send two sons to college at the same time. (He was also too proud to seek financial aid.) So, teenage Edward, having declined to follow his father into the family bakeshop, was apprenticed to a nearby woolen mill for training to be a manufacturer. Away from home for the first time in his life, lonely and resentful, he hated the place—"My hostess was a virago. My master a tyrant and conceited squire"—and was by turns withdrawn and impudent. Intentionally or not, he expressed his misery in rebellion; Deacon Jarvis had no choice but to remove him from the mill and pay the cost of another college degree.[26]

If it was not the deacon dictating his future, it was other family and friends. When Jarvis announced his ambition to be a minister like the idealized Dr. Ripley, his intimates were aghast. He would never succeed, they insisted, what with his speech impediment—he salivated excessively when he talked, and his voice was so "shrill and remarkable" that one casual acquaintance immediately recognized it with horror decades later—and his rigid character. No congregation would stand him. Jarvis resigned himself to the disappointment and despite a good many qualms, opted to study medicine. Even then, he secured little independence. Upon completing his training, he cast about for a place to start a practice, but wherever he looked, he was subject to

25. Emerson, "Historic Notes of Life and Letters in New England," *Lectures and Biographical Sketches*, in *The Works of Ralph Waldo Emerson*, ed. Edward Waldo Emerson, 14 vols. (Boston and New York: Houghton Mifflin, 1883), 10:308–9.
26. Jarvis, *Autobiography*, 4–5; Jarvis, Diary 1:7–10.

unwelcome offers. The Unitarians in Concord, New Hampshire, were eager for a physician of their denomination; the Whigs of Hallowell, Maine, were alienated by the politics of their current doctor and hoped to recruit a more congenial one. Jarvis wanted to be judged on his own merits alone. But in a society where business was still conducted along lines of kinship, religion, and even politics, Jarvis was pressed to conform. Once again other people sought to define his life without his consent.[27]

The breaking point came when Jarvis got the opportunity to start an office in his hometown. Even there, a group of orthodox Congregationalists, who had seceded from Dr. Ripley's church, tried to drive him out; Concord already had one Unitarian doctor, and that was enough. Jarvis stood his ground and achieved a measure of success. He was able, at last, to marry the ever-patient Almira Hunt after a seven-year engagement and to set up housekeeping. He won the acceptance of the local establishment, which selected him for the exclusive Social Circle and put him on important town committees. He enjoyed associating with parson Ripley at gatherings of Sunday school teachers. He was surrounded by family and friends. And yet, he was discontented. After five years, he remained the junior physician, always in the shadow of his former mentor, the popular Josiah Bartlett, and he was still struggling to make ends meet. "Was the fault in his professional character generally," he asked himself, "or in his relation to the people of his native town?" The unhappy truth was that too many people continued to view him as the boy they had known for years. Success was perhaps only a matter of time, but Jarvis couldn't wait. For all his love of Concord, he longed to be out on his own, in a community where he could make his way, untrammeled by the past, free from narrow prejudices and selfish alliances, and achieve his full potential. In a word, Edward Jarvis aimed to be a self-made man.[28]

But the restless doctor lacked the spirit of a pioneer. He left Concord for the thriving western city of Louisville, Kentucky, but in no time at all, he was pining for New England. Within a few years, he returned in hopes of securing a position as superintendent of an insane asylum, then considered an important opportunity for social and professional leadership. He made the short list everywhere, but was offered no job. Success would come eventually by an alternate route; Jarvis took

27. Jarvis, *Autobiography*, 16, 24–26; John S. Keyes, "Memoir of Edward Jarvis," in *Memoirs of Members of the Social Circle in Concord. Second Series: From 1795 to 1840* (Cambridge: privately printed, 1888), 353.
28. Jarvis, Diary 2:94–96, 115–20, 140, 147; Jarvis, *Autobiography*, 38–39.

emotionally disturbed patients into his new home in Dorchester and won a reputation for the sensitive care he and Almira offered. Without children of their own, the couple could give attention and sympathy to their charges. Jarvis had finally achieved his ideal. He headed his own household, with secure authority over dependents, in a town close enough to Concord for comfort but far enough away for an independent life. With that base, which he maintained for four decades, he would build his intellectual career as an independent writer and consultant. Stability, not adventure, suited his temperament.

No matter how much he admired Emerson, the idealistic Jarvis simply could not find his way into outright individualism. Occasionally, he could strain against the demands of others. He got engaged to Almira over his father's objections, and he rejected the name he was given at birth, Asa Edward. But these bids for independence were undercut by hesitation. The engagement lasted for years. And the name change is notable for its deference to authority. Ralph Waldo Emerson was known as Waldo to friends, Amos Bronson Alcott as Bronson; David Henry Thoreau reversed the order of his names and demanded that everybody respect this change. None of them worried about the legal consequences. Jarvis, ever-respectful of authority, went to court for approval to drop "Asa." So deeply had he learned the social code of Unitarian respectability, so fully had he imbibed the notion that "we lived not alone," so "intimately" had "the whole society, neighborhood, and town . . . [been] interwoven with the web of our existence," that he could never assert his ego or rebel in the name of a higher self. The emotional cost, evident in his dyspepsia, was too great. Indeed, he turned his own experience into a medical diagnosis of America as a whole:

> In this country [Jarvis wrote], where no son is necessarily confined to the work or employment of his father, but all the fields of labor, of profit and of honor are open to whomsoever will put on the harness and enter therein, and all are invited to join the strife for that which may be gained in each, many are in transition state from the lower and less desirable conditions. They are struggling for that which costs them mental labor and anxiety and pain. The mistake or the ambition of some leads them to aim at that which they cannot reach, to strive for more than they can grasp, and their mental powers are taxed to their utmost tension; they labor in agitation; and they end in frequent disappointment. . . . Insanity is, then, a part of the price which we pay for civilization.[29]

29. Gerald N. Grob, introduction to Edward Jarvis, *Insanity and Idiocy in Massachusetts: Report of the Commission on Lunacy, 1855* (Cambridge: Harvard University Press, 1971), 49–50.

Rejecting the route of self-reliance, Jarvis directed his ambitions and energies into reform. He would help to remake the traditional New England community by purging its conflicts, restraining its vices, and refining its character and morals. That was the agenda he pursued during the five years he spent in Concord from 1832 to early 1837. Enjoying the status of gentleman and professional, Jarvis threw himself into the numerous voluntary associations that aimed to improve the town. He became superintendent of the Unitarian Sunday school, curator of the Lyceum, an officer of the Social Library, a participant in the Ornamental Tree Society, and, as noted, a member of the elite Social Circle. He was perhaps most influential as an elected member and secretary of the town's school committee, where he promoted the same reform agenda as did Horace Mann on the level of the state. And along with Dr. Josiah Bartlett, the senior doctor in town, he set about promoting the cause of temperance. In sum, Jarvis devoted himself to the same causes—education, culture, and temperance—that he would identify as the mainsprings of social progress in "Traditions and Reminiscences." Written almost a half-century after he had departed the town, the book becomes, in this perspective, not merely the history of a community but the autobiography of a moral reformer and of the world he made.

Jarvis devotes his largest attention in the memoir to the disorder and violence that pervaded the schools and burst forth from the taverns into the streets. As a child, he had experienced the schoolhouse as a closed world, with a stagnant, oppressive air, where a changing set of masters, normally college students on vacation, struggled to impose their will on unruly farmboys and apprentices, many their own age. In the new republic, New Englanders may have imagined they were educating children for citizenship, but within the walls of the schoolhouse, the entire system of instruction was geared to enforcing rules. In blank copybooks, the students were taught to "rule the page"; in arithmetic, they memorized a sequence of rules; in grammar, they attended to the prescribed forms of sentences and the proper "relations of the several parts." Nonetheless, an unending battle raged between would-be rulers and restive subjects. A few masters won esteem through their dignity and learning, but others upheld authority only through force. The normal instrument of discipline was the ferule, a wooden rod some eighteen to twenty-four inches long, which was applied to the palm of the hand and "like the Turkish bastinade on the sole of the feet, inflicts great suffering." But ingenious masters found numerous other ways—flogging backs, boxing ears—to impose pain on the young;

Jarvis was particularly appalled by the practice of making boys sit upright under the master's desk—a torment that, as he calculated the distance between the bottom of a boy's seat to the level of the desk, threatened injury to the spine. Happily, young Edward Jarvis escaped all these punishments, though he was tempted from time to time to join in his classmates' periodic revolts. As a schoolmaster himself, Jarvis wielded the ferule sparingly, but whenever it was necessary. In retrospect, he doubted that corporal punishment was ever justified, and as a member of the school committee, he labored to ameliorate the regime. "Where physical force was used the least," he concluded, "where tact took the place of force, where the Masters appealed to the self respect of the scholars rather than their fears, when the scholars were treated with the most courtesy and affection . . . there was the best order, the greatest propriety of conduct, and the best development of character." Gentility worked for boys as well as for men.[30]

The cause of temperance takes up the greatest share of Jarvis's attention in "Traditions and Reminiscences." In his account of Concord in the early republic, it becomes clear that alcohol was ever present in social life. Laboring men drank on the job and after work; militia companies enjoyed toddy at their trainings; storekeepers sealed bargains with a glass of rum; householders offered wine and spirits when the minister came to call. The taverns of Concord were always full, inevitably spilling drunks out into the street, where passersby would try not to stumble over them. One unfortunate, John Breed the barber, was commonly found "laying dead drunk in the highway and if in the carriage path and in danger of injury, people would haul him to the grassy side, as they would a log or any other obstacle to travel, and then leave him to recover consciousness and power of motion sufficient to carry him home." But Concord was not unique for its alcoholic haze; the era of Jarvis's boyhood, the first two decades of the nineteenth century, witnessed an upsurge of drinking unlike anything ever seen in U.S. history. By 1830, the average American—man, woman, and child—was estimated to imbibe over five gallons of liquor a year, exactly the figure Jarvis calculated for Concord (5.4).[31]

30. Jarvis, *Autobiography*, 15–16; Jarvis, Diary 1:43. Jarvis's disparaging account of the common schools of Concord is of a piece with reminiscences by other reformers from the period. See Carl E. Kaestle, *Pillars of the Republic: Common Schools and American Society, 1780–1860* (New York: Hill & Wang, 1983), 13–23.

31. W. J. Rorabaugh, *The Alcoholic Republic: An American Tradition* (New York: Oxford University Press, 1979), 7–10, 228–30; Robert L. Hampel, *Temperance and Prohibition in Massachusetts 1813–1852* (Ann Arbor: UMI Press, 1982), 14–24.

In the face of all this drinking, Jarvis enlisted in the crusade to promote temperance in everyday life. That required a break with his own background. His father, the good deacon, had originally come to Concord as a youth to work in John Richardson's tavern; he later established his family and bakeshop in the old Wright Tavern, where on April 19, 1775, Major John Pitcairn had supposedly stirred "a bloody finger" in a glass of brandy and vowed "he should stir the damned yankee blood so before night." The Jarvis family was generally abstemious, but like many another college student before and since, Edward enjoyed an occasional glass of wine with his Harvard classmates and treated drinking at parties as a pleasant form of sociability. But by the early 1830s, he had changed his mind, joined up with like-minded neighbors, and begun warning people in Concord and elsewhere about the "First Steps to Intemperance." "Traditions and Reminiscences" charts the course of this campaign: the voluntary measures to remove alcohol from the workplace and the home, to persuade storekeepers to end liquor sales, and to put the tavern on the margins of the community. Thanks to these educational efforts, a "silent revolution" took place in public opinion, and the respectable families of Concord adopted the cause of temperance. By 1833, the per capita consumption of alcohol had fallen to a little more than three gallons. And in the place of liquor, families had taken up new stimulants, notably coffee and tea. A generation later, Jarvis could boast that virtually all the farmers of Concord were "abstemious" and that the town was nearly dry. But he couldn't claim complete success. When he sat down to write "Traditions and Reminiscences," he was forced to acknowledge that the use of wine had become popular among the "fashionable" folks who had traveled to "the great cities or to Europe." Even worse, Concord's record of temperance was blighted by the influx of Irish immigrants, who brought with them "a strong appetite for drink which many indulge and some very freely." Still, the high morals of the Yankee population had a purifying influence. "This class of people drink less in Concord than in some other towns. The moral influence of the rest of the citizens has reached even them and persuaded some of the Irish, many we trust, to touch and taste not, but to be as sober as the best American population."[32]

Jarvis's memoir is thus a vindication of the reform measures the youthful doctor set in motion during his brief career in Concord.

32. Robert A. Gross, *The Minutemen and Their World* (New York: Hill & Wang, 1976), 128; Jarvis, Diary 1:57–59, 115–18, 158–59; Jarvis, *Autobiography*, 150.

Through the growth of the market and the advance of civility and temperance, Concord had become a prosperous place of progressive farmers and comfortable commuters, who supported schools, library, and lyceums with enthusiasm and kept up with the advances of the age. In this happy estimate, Jarvis was at one with a good many other New Englanders who were assessing just what their generation had achieved in the wake of mass democracy, industrial revolution, and a civil war. A year after Concord's April 19 centennial, on the one hundredth birthday of American independence, the Reverend Henry Ward Beecher, a proud product of Yankee culture, offered an audience in Peekskill, New York, once the headquarters of the Continental Army, a cheerful prospect of "the Advance of a Century." Beecher noted the same material changes as did Jarvis—the great continental surge of population and the vast "augmentation" of industry and wealth; the impressive improvements in everyday life, as evidenced in better food, better clothes, better homes—and he applied the same test to assess their worth: "The value of our material growth is to be estimated by its effect upon the people." By that standard, Americans had gained as well. Books, newspapers, and periodicals had proliferated, providing easy access to the wider world; religious sentiment had spread beyond the churches to inspire practical philanthropy in the society at large; and within and beyond the household, women had grown in "intelligence," influence, and moral force. "Never before in any land," Beecher exulted, "has womanhood attained such authority and eminence as at the present day." Morally as well as materially, Americans had progressed beyond their ancestors, while remaining true to the founding ideals of the republic.[33]

If Beecher's address highlights the ideological consensus among Victorians to which Jarvis subscribed, it also alerts us to significant silences and misgivings on the latter's part. Surprisingly, in "Traditions and Reminiscences," Jarvis says very little about women's roles, domesticity, or sexuality. Once he finishes the survey of his mother's kitchen, he gives limited attention to women's experience and work. Even his itemization of clothing concerns primarily male apparel. For the most part, he ignores the active participation of women in voluntary associations and reform and, unlike the centennial speakers Beecher and George William Curtis, fails to mention or endorse wom-

33. Henry Ward Beecher, "The Advance of a Century," in *Democratic Vistas*, ed. Alan Trachtenberg (New York: George Braziller, 1970), 66–82.

en's suffrage. Jarvis also remained far more of an ascetic than Beecher. If the complacent clergyman, a popular after-dinner speaker, could take delight in the "better bellies" Americans had developed from their "better food," the disapproving doctor worried about the ill consequences of such indulgence of the flesh. The lavish evening entertainments that now accompanied meetings of Concord's Social Circle and Farmers' Club, with their ample servings of fresh oysters, fresh fruit, and elaborate cakes and pies, were a waste of time ("the housekeeper's") and money ("the husband's"), and they were "needless for nutrition." It is not clear what Jarvis thought of other pastimes in the 1870s. He is silent on the great popularity of baseball (after the Civil War, Concord's "Middlesex" team was famous throughout the state) and the fad for minstrel shows. But he would surely have been shocked, had he attended the 109th anniversary of the Battle of Concord in 1884, held six months before his death, and witnessed the numerous attractions designed to appeal to the popular culture he abhorred. The program consisted of booming cannons, a military parade, and a "grand minstrel entertainment." As part of the evening's fare, the respectable citizens of Concord could enjoy a "Dime show," which was "very funny and included such rare specimens as the 'Albino girl'—the 'Living skeleton'—the 'Fat boy'—the 'Educated hog'—the 'Bearded woman'—the 'Zulu' and others." "This closed a very enjoyable evening's entertainment," reported the local paper, "and Concordians returned to their homes to retire and drift into dreamland, where their brains were filled with medley visions of Paul Revere and the Salvation army."[34]

"Traditions and Reminiscences" is, then, an inadequate guide to Gilded Age Concord. It tells us far more about what the community was like in the early republic than what it became a half-century later. Even so, it is notable that in his outlook on the late 1870s, Jarvis abandoned the social exclusiveness that had put off so many of his peers in youth. He was delighted that everybody in town, the gentleman and the workingman, the Yankee and the Irishman, attended parties at Town Hall. On such occasions, Concord was one family— exactly as he had wanted at the town's bicentennial in 1835. And unlike George William Curtis, he was confident that the Irish immi-

34. Concord's baseball team is the subject of an appreciative piece in the *Boston Record*, May 17, 1890; the report of the April 19, 1884, celebration comes from the local paper, but is not identified. Both are found in the Adams Tolman Newspaper Clippings, Special Collections, CFPL.

grants and their children could be assimilated in the pure culture of the native population. At a time of growing chauvinism among the descendants of Puritans and Minutemen, Jarvis remained a confident cosmopolitan, sure of the benefits in expanding one's social and intellectual horizons. It was, after all, only after he departed Concord and entered the wider world that he had won due recognition for his talents.

In Jarvis's view, the progress of fifty years had refined and strengthened all that was good in the older New England of his youth. No longer dominated by necessity nor forced to conform to inherited rules and involuntary associations, the people of Concord had redefined the community on new terms. The town was bound together by common symbols—notably, a civic identity as the birthplace of the Revolution—and by shared participation in progress. Thanks to these changes, the individual could realize, more fully than ever, the ideal of Unitarian moral philosophy: material and intellectual improvement, service to the community, pride in history. In this social consciousness, this awareness that communities are knit together by common manners and institutions, "Traditions and Reminiscences" expresses an enduring aspect of Yankee culture. Edward Jarvis has bequeathed us a significant document of New England regionalism.

At the end of his career, having achieved a reputation in the larger world, Jarvis returned in memory to Concord and reattached himself to the community where he was born and raised. Ironically, in the vicissitudes of time, he has been forgotten by all but a few medical historians and specialists in nineteenth-century intellectual history. He has become a merely local figure, an obscure Herodotus of the nineteenth century, absorbed into the collective life of the town, exactly as he is buried in Sleepy Hollow Cemetery a short distance away, in a common Jarvis family plot. But with the long-overdue publication of "Traditions and Reminiscences," he may finally obtain recognition as a leading intellectual of the generation and community that produced Ralph Waldo Emerson and Henry David Thoreau.

Cambridge, Massachusetts

One

Addenda to Lemuel Shattuck's
History of Concord, 1835

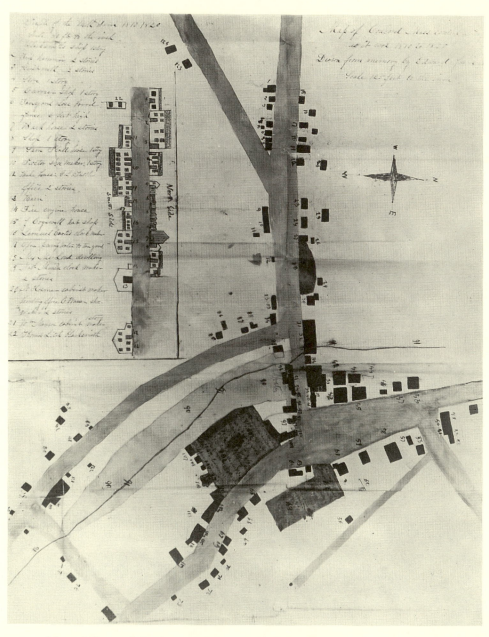

Map of Concord, "as it was 1810 to 1820, drawn from memory" by Edward Jarvis

Author's Preface

My father, the late Deacon Francis Jarvis, went to Concord when he was twenty-one years old, in 1789, with John Richardson, who bought and kept the old tavern now the Middlesex Hotel. My father had lived from his early boyhood in Watertown with Mr. Richardson and had learned of him the trade of a baker. But in Concord he aided him in the tavern for one year, doing all the miscellaneous work of clerk-book-keeper, barkeeper, etc.

In 1790 my father with Thomas Safford took the bake house which was in the building that was the Wright tavern in the Revolutionary War, opposite the Middlesex Hotel, adjoining the tavern. Soon Mr. Safford went to Lancaster, and my father carried on the business until 1824 and lived in the house until 1832. He then bought and removed to the farm, lately the property of Col. John Buttrick, and lived there until he died in 1840. The farm was occupied by my brother the late Capt. Francis Jarvis until his death in 1875. Since then it has been owned and occupied by his children, Joseph Derby and wife, and Cyrus H. Jarvis. From the early years of his residence in the town my father owned and cultivated lands sufficient for a small farm in the center of Concord until he went to the Buttrick farm.

My mother was Milicent Hosmer, daughter of James H[osmer], granddaughter of Stephen and great-granddaughter of Stephen, who were the descendants of James, one of the first settlers in Concord in 1635.

James Hosmer settled on the farm which Abel Hosmer now (1877) owns and cultivates near the Assabet River and [which is] opposite the site of the state prison. This farm has been in the family from 1635 and has always descended from father to son.

My mother's great-grandfather Stephen took a farm in Nine Acre Corner, near Haven Pond, and he and his son Stephen [and] his grandson James lived there three generations, and there my mother and all her brothers and sisters were born and lived until they were old enough to go into the world for life. This farm was then sold and passed into other hands. My mother was a bright, observing woman. She inherited a great interest in all Concord matters, and carefully noticed whatever was going on around her. She was full of the traditions of the past and was fond of telling of what she had heard and had seen of the people of the town—their habits and manners, sayings and doings.

My father was a man of quick and generous sympathies. He took [an] interest in all that was going on about him. He was a keen observer and saw all the local and contemporary movements and learned the traditions of the past. His business brought him into contact with a very large part of the people, and being very courteous and affable, he was early and extensively drawn into popular social confidence. He was fond of hearing of family, personal, and local history and thus gathered the traditions of the town for the generations that had passed. He was a man of great conversational power. He talked very much both with his family and with the people abroad. He was fond of talking of the history of the town and had abundant anecdotes of the people who had passed away and who were still living about us. He told so much of these people and these matters, both the past and the present, and he presented them with such graphic form to us, that it was afterward difficult for us the children, and is sometimes even now [difficult] for me, to discriminate between the events and persons that he described to us and those which we had seen ourselves.

So with my mother's and my father's early training we were led to take interest in all the past traditionary history of the town and the living scenes and movements that were about us. We noticed them with a lively intensity, and they were fixed in our minds almost as parts [of] our own being. We were made social in our feelings, conversations and habits. We lived not alone. The whole society, neighborhood, and town were almost a part of ourselves or at least intimately interwoven with the web of our existence. So we were trained from childhood to be observers, to let nothing within our sight go unnoticed. The public and the private affairs, the [fire] engine, the fire company, the infantry, the artillery and all military powers, the school, the stores, the shops, their men, and their [indecipherable] were all noticed and talked about and were to us the inseparable associates of our own being. And all

4

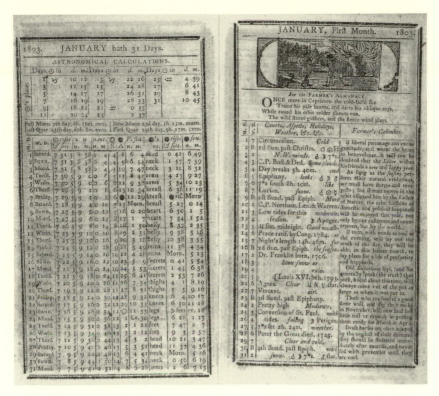

A page from *Farmer's Almanac*, 1803 (the year of Edward Jarvis's birth)

these impressions were fixed upon our minds and held freshly then through our lives, and even now they are my living companions.

I was born in 1803 and I lived at home until I was 16 years old, and went to the town school until 1819, when I went away. From that time until I graduated at Cambridge, I spent my vacation at home. After leaving college in 1826, I kept the town school one year, and then for one year I studied medicine in Concord with Dr. Bartlett. While finishing my professional preparation in Boston, I spent some time in Concord and was in frequent communication with its people. From September 1832 to March 1837 I practiced my profession in Concord. In nearly the whole of this period I was on the school committee and its secretary. I was superintendent of the Sunday school of Dr. Ripley's church, member of the [Social] club, [and] curator of the Lyceum.

After returning from Kentucky in 1842, I spent seven months in Concord, and since coming to Dorchester in March 1849, I have been much in Concord and in very constant communications with my

5

friends and the people in the town and retained an [indecipherable] interest in their doings.

With these opportunities of know[ledge] in the social, domestic and personal history of Concord, with these tastes for study of the minutiae of the past, and with these feelings of love and reverence for my native town, I have been long in [the] habit of revising Mr. Shattuck's excellent history and of writing notes of correction, emendation and addition on the margins of the pages and if need be on separate leaves or sheets which I have from time to time pasted into my copy of Mr. Shattuck's work.

In this way I have added these notes of more common matters which had escaped the printed history and endeavored thereby to give a more complete record of the life and manners of the people.

For many years this has been a very pleasant occupation and now, 1877, more pleasant than ever.

Court

The Supreme Court sat in March and the Court of Common Pleas in June and September in Concord. During the first third of this century and later, these courts drew great numbers [of] lawyer-jurymen, witnesses and others interested from all parts of the county. The three taverns were filled. Many of their table boarders were obliged to find lodgings in the neighborhood. Several families in the village and even as far as Deacon Hubbard and Capt. Humphrey Hunt took boarders on these occasions. Josiah Davis's house was a favorite home of the lawyers and the judges. The sheriffs mostly boarded with the sheriff, at least after Capt. Moore held that office.

There were no stages to or from Concord except on the single line from Boston to Groton and Keene, and these were only three times a week. Consequently people who came to Concord for court or other business came in their own or other private vehicles. These filled the tavern barn and sheds with horses and the yards with chaises, wagons etc., and also a good portion of the neighboring streets. The square in front of the Middlesex [Hotel] was usually covered in a large space between the house and the store opposite. Some of the former within easy reach also took horses to board for the week.

The trials in the courthouse attracted much attention. Besides those who had business there, many spectators came and watched the doings of the courts. Many citizens of the town and village [and] some farmers from the remote districts gave some of their time to this purpose. Some made it a part of their plan to devote a half day or more to the court at every session, and usually the large courtroom and its ample gallery and side seats for spectators were well filled, especially when any important trial, [such] as murder or other of public interest, was going on.

September Court

The Court of Common Pleas, albeit a court of the second grade, sat during the second week of September. It was the great day or week for the outside attendants. This, from time immemorial, was a great fair, an occasion for the assemblage of the gay, the idle, the fun-loving, the rowdies, and the people who for the time were willing to play the rowdy.

Along the whole length of the Common in front of the meetinghouse was a row of booths or board shanties erected for the sale of all sorts of drink—rum, gin, brandy etc., wine or its imitation, beer strong and weak called "small beer," flip,[1] toddy, and all sorts of compounds of stimulant and intoxicating liquors. Egg pop was the favorite.

They had also cakes, gingerbread, pies and some other eatables to tempt the palate and money from the people. Some of these booths were floored for dancing, and strolling (perhaps appointed) fiddlers were there to play. Those who danced were expected to pay the musician for his aid in each dance.

I found the one row of booths at my first consciousness in childhood. But this was a reduction, a decay of this method of dissipation. My brothers older than myself could remember two rows of these structures which were well supported by the former and larger numbers of the frolickers. Besides them, there were many other supplies for the appetite and indulgence—baker's carts, confections in carts and with portable tables of candy and peppermints, fruit sellers, with melons, peaches, pears, apples, pineapples, oranges; tables with pies, cakes etc., out of the booths.

There were also others with various sorts of merchandise—tin men etc., pedlars with everything that they supposed they could sell; men with horses to sell, to run, swap or in any way pass off for something of

1. Flip is spiced ale or cider, served hot.

more real value. There were sometimes races along the Lexington road.

There were great collections of people from towns all over the county and from other counties. The rioters or the riotous-disposed were sure to meet their fellows there. The booths kept open until late at night, and some until the run reopened, fiddling, dancing and merry making were heard plainly at my father's, which was within 10 or 15 yards of the booths. These gay and frolicksome people had nothing to do with the courts. They found their motive for coming and their fill of enjoyment in each other and in the scenes and events in and around the Common, and opportunities of indulgence.

This fair had its day and then its night came upon it. Popular taste gradually lost its interest in it. The drinking diminished, and the sellers found their profits going. Year by year fewer put up booths, until at length the town authorities finding public opinion unfavorable to their appearance ceased to grant any more licenses for this purpose. This class of people ceased to gather thus in the second week of the month of September, court was reduced to its classic purpose of administering the law, and the town was as quiet as the sessions in March and June.

In all my opportunity of observation of this gala week, I saw much fun, frolic, and the effect of drinking. There were noisy people, and now and then perhaps a dispute even a fight or quarrel, but I never knew of any serious fight nor a riot nor any disturbance that required the attention of the police, no transgression of the law except as below, an instance which, being in the course of virtue, it was universally admitted as pardonable or at least a sufferable wrong.

Huldah Williams

In the east quarter on the Lexington road between what was then Mr. Nathaniel French's (now Hon. E. W. Bull's) and Mr. Arvidson's (now Deacon Sampson Mason's) there was a small one-story house with only two small rooms. In this house lived Huldah Williams. I never knew whether she was married, single or widowed. I never heard her called Mrs. or Miss Williams but always Huldah Williams or more simply Huldah. She was a woman of bad reputation and probably of low character. She kept rum for sale to low people, and her house was the resort of men of low degree.

At one of the September Court periods she procured a harlot from

Boston or perhaps merely suffered one to come to her house to spend these holidays with her to tempt the wicked or entrap the unwary.

This was noised about the town and created great astonishment and indignation, and an immediate and stern resolve to remove this foul blot offered to the character of Concord. I do not know whether any warning or advice was given to Huldah to remove the woman back to her former place. But there was a general determination to remove her by force if this were needed to effect the purpose. There was a quiet subdued talk among the young men that they must do it and cleanse the town as early as possible. At evening I saw about the Common a gathering of these men—the respectable and high-minded of the town. They walked off on the Lexington road quietly, early in the evening. I followed them as far as Dr. Hunt's. I was too young to go farther from the house without leave but went home and to bed. Next day I heard all about it from boys older than myself who went with these self-constituted executors of the law of righteousness and saw the whole from beginning to end. This small multitude halted before the house of Huldah, some of them went in and told the woman the purpose of their visit and demanded that the offensive visitor go, at once, from Concord, never to return.

My informants, not being among the chiefs of the company, did not hear the conversation in the house. They only knew the results. The harlot was brought out by force. Others had a rail ready, which they found in a farm near by. She was placed on the middle of this extemporised vehicle, astride I was told; two or three men at each end carried the rail with its burden; one man walked at each side to support her in her position, and the company walked along before at the sides and behind. Thus they went eastward on the road until they passed the boundary into Lincoln. There they released her to go on foot. They charged her strictly to go back to her former home and never to cross the bounds of Concord again. There was much talk in town on the next day and afterward. Everyone rejoiced and honored the deed and the men who executed and removed this foul stain, so offensive to its moral sense, cast upon the town.

There were some threats of prosecution muttered by Huldah and her friends. Some feared that possibly the court, sheriff, or officers of the law might think it necessary to make public inquiry and perhaps punish their transgression of the rights of persons and the public peace. But nothing was done, and all the most fastidious as well as the careless of the proprieties of life felt sure that no court would entertain a complaint and no jury would convict of wrong against the peace the agents of this justification of the unblemished society of Concord.

I have no recollection of Huldah after this event. She disappeared before my general acquaintance with the people. Her name is not in the list of deaths. She removed elsewhere, and she is only known in Concord by her error and prominently by this defeated attempt to corrupt the people.

Joining the Church

It had been the custom, probably from time immemorial, for the candidates to first make application to the minister and obtain his concurrence. Next the minister announced or "propounded the desires of the candidate to join the church in full communion," to the whole congregation. The candidate then stood propounded for. At the end of this time when the morning service was ended or just before the last prayer, the candidate or candidates were called by the minister and rose from their respective pews and stood in the broad aisle about midway between the pulpit and the front door. Then the minister read aloud in very clear tones the whole covenant as on page 189–90. They bowed their assent and the minister then acknowledged their membership and they retired to their pews.

In the spring, May or June of 1823, several young persons, Hamett Moore, Mary Church, Eunice Church, Sarah E. Hurd, Edward Jarvis, Almira Hunt (and if others, the records will tell) desired to join the church. But they were diffident and felt unwilling to make so public a demonstration of their act and wished me to talk with Dr. Ripley.

I saw the Doctor at his house and stated our wants and our difficulties. He was very kind and sympathetic. I asked if we could not be admitted before the church alone, and not before the whole congregation.

He said he appreciated our feelings and wants and wished it were in his power to gratify us but this was the time-honored custom which both church and people followed and seemed to think needful, and left him no discretion. He advised that we join in the present manner, and then being in the body we could have an influence and perhaps a power to persuade the members to change the form.

I told him that these proposed candidates could hardly find courage to take this first step and probably would hold themselves back for an

Sketch of First Parish Church, Concord, 1841

indefinite period until they should gain more self-possession and firmness. We had several consultations in all of which the excellent Doctor manifested the utmost tenderness and sympathy. He wanted to remove the obstacle but did not see the way to do so. He consulted the Deacons and others, and at length they consented that the rule might be relaxed so far as to allow the candidates to stand in their pews and hear the covenant while yet the congregation was present. Dr. Ripley was much gratified with this accession of youth to the church and received them and others then and afterward with the most affectionate tenderness.

In my earliest day, Dr. Ripley was accustomed once a year to announce from the pulpit that he would meet the children at the school houses and catechize them there. He assigned the day for each district, one or more a week until all were catechised. No especial preparation was required, but he asked the questions in [indecipherable] catechism, and probably many were prepared by their parents in some degree.

Church Elements Bread and Wine, Remnants of

My father Deacon Jarvis had the care of the communion service, flagons, cups and plates and also provided the bread and wine from the beginning of his office to the latter years of his life or as long as he kept house and lived near the church.

It was the original custom to give the remnants of the wine and the bread to the minister and his family. But Dr. Ripley preferred Lisbon wine to Malaga, which was used in the communion service. Accordingly the residue of the church wine was sent back to the store (Deacon White's in my early day and Col. Shattuck's his successor afterward), and two quarts of Lisbon wine taken instead thereof for Dr. Ripley.

This thus was the business of one of my brothers or myself after breakfast Monday morning and before school time next following the communion to take the bag of the remaining long square pieces of bread to Dr. Ripley's, stopping at the store to exchange the Malaga for the Lisbon wine.

Deacons' Seats

In accordance with old customs the seats for the Deacons were adjoined to and in front of the pulpit in the church until the last alteration in 1840. The floor of this apartment and the seats were raised 8 or 9 inches above the rest of the house so that the occupants could see and be seen by all the congregation. The four deacons always sat there until the retirement of Deacons Parkman and White and by Deacons Jarvis and Hubbard until their death. Deacons Brown and Hosmer sat there on the forenoon of Communion day. The Deacons were always in their seats before Dr. Ripley arrived, and when he entered the house they all rose and bowed, stood until he passed them and ascended the pulpit steps; as he passed they reverentially bowed their heads, and the Doctor courteously bowed in return. This was a graceful and dignified ceremony.

Sunday School

There was no organized or parochial Sunday school until May or June 1827. Miss Phebe Wheeler and some others had individually had classes at their houses or elsewhere in May or June, 1827. Dr. Ripley proposed the establishment of one under the charge of the parish. For this purpose he invited such as he supposed would cooperate with him to meet at the primary schoolhouse, standing on the present site of Judge Brooks's house. At the meeting were Deacon Cyrus Hosmer, Lemuel Shattuck, Richard Hildreth, Edward Jarvis, Mary Church, Harriet Moore, Almira Hunt, Eunice Church, Melicent Hosmer and others interested in the work. They were all earnest and agreed to labor in the school. Mr. Shattuck was elected Superintendent. Edward Jarvis, scribe and librarian. The school began immediately, more teachers were wanted. I proposed to Dr. Ripley to enlist some other and younger ladies: Sarah E. Hurd, Susan, Ann and Martha Adams. The Doctor was highly gratified with their interest in the cause.

I was then teaching the town school, which was a great draft on my strength. I therefore was unwilling to engage in teaching on Sunday. Yet feeling great interest in the work, I offered to be librarian and was so chosen. Teaching a class would have occupied one hour each Sunday noon. The office of librarian occupied one to two hours each Sunday and moreover as there was no library it fell upon me to procure one, and as there was no money for the purchase of books it fell on me to beg the funds for this purpose.

With the desire to obtain the books best adapted to the capacities and wants of the children, every book was to be examined or its character shown by trustworthy evidence. This took up a large part of my hours out of school during the summer. Then the books were to be covered, catalogued and the name of the school written therein. This took still more time, and all my Saturday afternoons were devoted to this work. Yet this was to me a very pleasant and willing work, and my connection with the school [was] very happy. We had frequent teachers' meetings at which Dr. Ripley was always present and took great interest in all the proceedings. He was especially gratified that so many of those young people who had seemed to him to be mainly pleasant [and] fashionable came forward and entered the work with so much zeal and faithfulness.

Botany

When I was in college in the years 1824–26, and when I taught the town school in Concord, 1826–27, and while I was a medical student with Dr. Josiah Bartlett, and also when I was a practising physician in Concord in 1832–36, I devoted some of my time to the study of the botany of the town. I went into all parts of the town—the fields, the meadows and the forests—and gathered such of the plants as I could find. I kept these with others gathered in other places [and put them] into a herbarium which I preserved with great care until about the year 1846, when I gave it to the State at the request of the Board of Agriculture, who wished to have a complete collection of the plants of Massachusetts in the cabinet at the state house.

When the state established the Agricultural college at Amherst, this collection was transferred to its keeping.[2] In my studies I used the volume of Bigelow's *Plants of Boston and Vicinity,* and when I examined the plants and found the description in the book I marked it in the margin and generally wrote "Concord" in the same place and often the locality where the plant was found.[3]

I have copied these names on several sheets and pasted it in my volume of Bigelow and deposited the book in the Public Library, Concord. This list of the plants which I found in Concord embraces several hundred [species]—a considerable portion of the botany of the town. I have heard that Mr. Thoreau, who was a very careful observer, made a collection of the plants of Concord, but I have never seen it. If it exists it would be more complete than mine and very valuable.

2. A few specimens thought to be Jarvis's are still in the University of Massachusetts Herbarium.

3. Jarvis's entries in Bigelow's *Plants of Boston* have been transcribed, with updated synonymy.

Regarding the Mill Brook

By law, the proprietor of the mill on the dam was allowed to flow the pond indefinitely from the 12th September to the 12th of May. From May to September he was allowed to have but one flush daily at the outlet that then (1800–1825) ran under Deacon Jarvis's house and under the road through land belonging to the tavern, then under the jail and to the brook back of the schoolhouse.

Highways Repairs

The highway tax was separate from the other taxes. This was paid in labor. Those were paid in money. When the roads of any district were in need of repair, the surveyor called for as many shovellers and as many teams as he thought necessary. For many years as late as 1835 or later, the town took gravel for all the roads in the centre of the town, from the hill [in] back of the site of the Catholic Church or [at the] northerly continuation of the Burial Hill. A due proportion of the men were stationed with their shovels to fill the cars, others drove the teams, and a third party was placed on the roads to smooth the gravel and make the path easy for travelers.

Although this tax was honorably and fairly assessed on all according to their ability to pay, it was supposedly easier for the people to pay in labor. Yet this was a very wasteful way of expending force for the repair of the roads. For want of exactly proportionate distribution of men and teams, much time was lost. Teams were often kept waiting for shovellers and these for teams, and the levellers often stood idle with no gravel before them to spread. A man was allowed a dollar a day; a teamster, whether a man or boy, had the same. On one occasion a youthful teamster of 14, anxious to be considered a full driver and to earn his dollar for his father, presented his team to the hill as frequently as possible. There were more carts than could be constantly filled. The men, willing to gratify this ambitious youth, gave way to him, and they and their oxen stood idle. It was said that the boy carried twice as many loads as the men, and so it was generally the idly disposed and selfish [who] gladly let the more willing and faithful do the work.

Jail, Jail Limits, Liberty of the Yard

The old laws allowed creditors to send their non-paying debtors to jail to enforce payment. This savage law ameliorated itself so far as to

15

allow these debtors to go out of the prison into the yard on giving sureties that they would not go beyond these limits, and if they should thus transgress, the bondsman must pay the debt. In order to give these debtors some opportunity to earn their living, the courts were permitted to expand the ideal jail yard according to their discretion. In Concord these limits included all the square in front of the courthouse, all the road and street toward Lexington as far as Heywood St., all Heywood St. and Walden St. to the dam, all the dam, and all the buildings on the borders of these streets.

These debtors, called by the boys and others "jail birds," boarded with the jailor or [at] other houses and got such work as they could, wood sawing and gardening. Some were mechanics.[4] There were always a good number, six to twenty, more or less. Some were highly respectable, though unfortunate. Most of them were of small force and some [indecipherable] and intemperate. One, Mr. Benj. N. Haggar, originally a seaman's compass-maker, afterward a ship chandler in State St. Boston, failed and was brought to Concord Jail. He removed his family and lived in the house opposite Dr. Hunt's. He took a room for a shop in an old house that stood where now (1876) Mrs. Barber lives, and worked diligently at his old trade. Dr. Jarvis supplied him with capital, bought material for him, and carried his compasses to Boston in his chaise for sale. Thus Mr. Haggar supported himself and family very comfortably. He was a man of rare good sense and intelligence. He visited Deacon Jarvis [often] especially [on] summer evenings. I admired his pleasant conversation. After remaining ten years within the limits, he settled somehow with his creditors and then went to Baltimore.

[Schoolhouses and the Old Jail]

These three schoolhouses were all built in one year, of logs or timbers laid one upon another.[5] After the new jail was built in 1788, the old log or timber jail was used as a shop. From my earliest remembrance to perhaps 1815 or thereabouts, it was used as a hatter's shop. Ephraim Williams and Joseph Brown made hats in it in my early day.

---

4. "Mechanics" is Jarvis's collective term for nonfarmers (carpenters, masons, blacksmiths, etc.).

5. This section is inserted in Shattuck's *History* on p. 208, l. 6, after "grammar schoolhouse."

[Schoolhouse and a Vane]

Three primary schoolhouses were built in 1820.[6] One by the burial ground; one in East quarter opposite [the] house now (1870) of Mr. Emerson; one on land where Judge Brooks's house stands, opposite the house which Nathan Brooks occupied until his death. Dr. Heyward gave the bell weight as 125 lbs. The committee to build these four schoolhouses were Deacon Thomas Hubbard, Deacon Jarvis, and Josiah Davis. When they had about finished, Deacon Jarvis proposed a quill as appropriate for a vane on the grammar schoolhouse. Deacon Hubbard, who was an extreme and exclusive utilitarian though a very liberal and just man, said, "No, no vane; it is useless. I will do with the town as I do with my own affairs. I never expend money for any useless matter for myself, and I cannot consent to do so with the town's money." Deacon Jarvis took hold of the buttons on the back of Deacon Heyward's coat and asked what these buttons were for. Deacon Heyward laughed and said he had forgotten them and would not go without them and added, "I will consent to the vane."

Singing Schools

It was an old custom and a good one for the town to grant every two or three years a sum sufficient to pay for a singing school in the winter. Suitable teachers were employed, and all the young of both sexes were invited to attend and learn. The school was in the centre schoolhouse, and the room in the beginning was well filled or nearly filled.

The first step was to try the voice then to see if the pupil could discern a chord and a discord. If not, he was told that he had no ear for music and it would be useless for him or her to attempt to learn. This reduced the members somewhat. Afterward some fell away for various reasons, so that at the end of the school in the spring probably not more than half remained of those that entered at the beginning. Then all that were decreed sufficiently skillful in singing were asked to join the choir and sit in the singers' seats in the church. Spectators or listeners were courteously admitted to hear the singers at the school. Both old and young (even the extremely young) came to hear. As early as it was allowable for a child to be out evenings, I was permitted to go but with strict orders to go home in the middle of the evening, at recess.

6. Inserted at p. 208, l. 9, after the word "two."

While yet a boy, I went to learn. I remained through the winter and was taken into the singers' seats on Sunday. After a year's experience, finding my voice insufficient and my musical execution imperfect, I proposed to the leader that I should leave. He agreed with me, and I returned to the family pew below. In this way and for other reasons, others left from time to time, and in the course of two or three years the choir was reduced to small numbers. At the same time, another class of youth had grown up to the proper age and was ready to be instructed in the same way. This process of successive schools and supply of the choir [began] probably [in] the early life of the town and continued until nearly the middle of this century. It was a profitable custom, for thereby the popular taste for music was cultivated and many who could not make satisfactory singers nor be even admitted to the church choir yet became familiar with the rules and principles of music and [were] able to enjoy it in church and elsewhere.

Thanksgiving Day was the time of a musical festival. The choir met for several weeks and learned anthems for the occasion and people enjoyed this extraordinary and fitting display from the singers.

[Local Manufacturers]

David Loring made lead pipe at the site of Warner's pail factory farm [from] about 1830 to after 1847.[7] Nathanael Munroe made 8-day clocks on the dam. He had eight [hired] hands to aid him. He removed to Baltimore about 1818. Lemuel Curtis made time pieces, [and] wall clocks, on the dam. He moved to Burlington about 1820. Benj. R. Haggar made seaman's compasses in a building on the spot where Mrs. Barber now (1876) lives. He moved to Baltimore about 1818.

Peter Wheeler exported beef and pork, packed and salted, to the West Indies until his death in May 1813, aged 58. He lived in the house now occupied by Nathan Stow. Andrew Edwards made organs in a shop where Wm. Munroe afterwards made pencils. H. David Hubbard made pencils previously in an old shop on the north corner of Walden and Heywood streets next east of Mr. Vose's tan yard. Maj. James Barrett and Jonathan Hildreth made bellows for family use and sold them in Boston, 1822. Nathan Barrett carried on coopering and sent a large quantity of barrels to Boston and Brighton for the beef and pork packers. Stephen Wood had a tan yard on the mill dam. John Vose

---

7. These two paragraphs represent notes added to pp. 217–19.

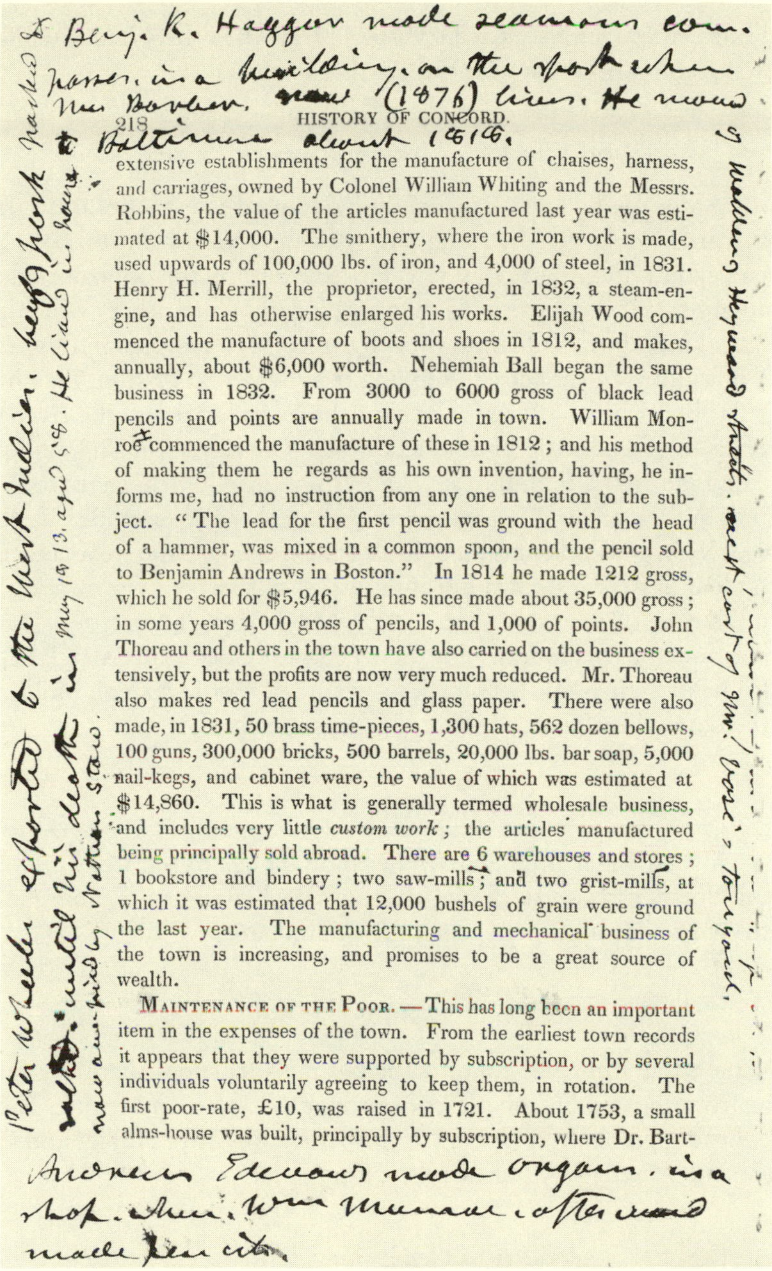

[handwritten top margin: Benj. K. Hagger made seamans com- pass in a building on the spot where Mr. Barker now (1876) lives. He moved to Baltimore about 1816.]

extensive establishments for the manufacture of chaises, harness, and carriages, owned by Colonel William Whiting and the Messrs. Robbins, the value of the articles manufactured last year was estimated at $14,000. The smithery, where the iron work is made, used upwards of 100,000 lbs. of iron, and 4,000 of steel, in 1831. Henry H. Merrill, the proprietor, erected, in 1832, a steam-engine, and has otherwise enlarged his works. Elijah Wood commenced the manufacture of boots and shoes in 1812, and makes, annually, about $6,000 worth. Nehemiah Ball began the same business in 1832. From 3000 to 6000 gross of black lead pencils and points are annually made in town. William Monroe commenced the manufacture of these in 1812; and his method of making them he regards as his own invention, having, he informs me, had no instruction from any one in relation to the subject. "The lead for the first pencil was ground with the head of a hammer, was mixed in a common spoon, and the pencil sold to Benjamin Andrews in Boston." In 1814 he made 1212 gross, which he sold for $5,946. He has since made about 35,000 gross; in some years 4,000 gross of pencils, and 1,000 of points. John Thoreau and others in the town have also carried on the business extensively, but the profits are now very much reduced. Mr. Thoreau also makes red lead pencils and glass paper. There were also made, in 1831, 50 brass time-pieces, 1,300 hats, 562 dozen bellows, 100 guns, 300,000 bricks, 500 barrels, 20,000 lbs. bar soap, 5,000 nail-kegs, and cabinet ware, the value of which was estimated at $14,860. This is what is generally termed wholesale business, and includes very little *custom work*; the articles manufactured being principally sold abroad. There are 6 warehouses and stores; 1 bookstore and bindery; two saw-mills; and two grist-mills, at which it was estimated that 12,000 bushels of grain were ground the last year. The manufacturing and mechanical business of the town is increasing, and promises to be a great source of wealth.

MAINTENANCE OF THE POOR. — This has long been an important item in the expenses of the town. From the earliest town records it appears that they were supported by subscription, or by several individuals voluntarily agreeing to keep them, in rotation. The first poor-rate, £10, was raised in 1721. About 1753, a small alms-house was built, principally by subscription, where Dr. Bart-

[handwritten left margin, vertical: Peter Wheeler exported to the West Indies, keys from wheels; until his death in May 1813, aged 56. He lived in house now owned by Nathan Stow.]

[handwritten right margin, vertical: Wm Heywood made (blacking?) sheets; next cont of Wm Bowe's Tanyard.]

[handwritten bottom margin: Andrews Edward made organs in a shop there. Wm Munroe afterward made pencils.]

Jarvis's addenda to a page of Shattuck's *History of Concord* had one on Walden St. near Heywood St. next to the pond. Stephen Barrett also on his farm near the Carlisle line.

Wood Sent to Boston by River and Canal

Mr. Amos Wood, who owned and occupied the house and farm (afterward owned by Mr. Dennis west of the river on the Stow road much beyond [the] house of Cyrus Hosmer and on the opposite side), dealt largely in wood from his own forests and from others which he bought. Finding the transportation by oxen very tedious and expensive, he conceived the idea of sending it by water to Boston. He built long flat boats of small draft and sent these loaded down the river to Billerica and then by the Middlesex canal to Charlestown. The shallow places, opposite Nathan Barrett's and I think in Billerica, gave trouble in times of low water. These were dredged and the river made thereby navigable. Mr. Wood continued this business two or three years I think but at length gave it up as unprofitable.

In the time of the war, 1812–1814, Mr. Nathan'l Munroe, clockmaker, added to his foundry for the wheels for clocks, also sleigh bells which he or rather Mr. Beckford, his founder, cast in a small building on the dam where now is [blank] harness shop.

Wire

Mr. Joshua Jones drew wire in his shop by use of the trip hammer wheel. Small rods were drawn through steel plates with holes successively smaller until he reached the desired size.

Nails

At the same time Mr. Jones made cut nails, cutting [them] by machine from the end of iron plates of proper thickness and width. Then these header pieces were put into a vice with a [indecipherable] and the upper end pounded by hand and a head made.

[Girls in Grammar School]

From time immemorial the town regulations admitted girls to the centre or grammar school from April 1st to Dec. 1st but excluded them during the other four months; then the large boys, sons of farmers and those who were apprentices or lived out, came in large numbers and filled the house.[8] In 1828, when I taught the school, finding the school small in November and apparently a smaller accession of boys to come in the winter, I proposed to the committee that the girls be allowed to attend the school at least as long as there should be room for them. The committee consented, and girls have not since been excluded.

Infantry and Artillery

These two companies had a generous rivalry toward each other. Each was desirous to enlist the young men who grew to the military age and status and those who came to the town from other places.

The interest in each company seemed to descend in families. The children followed the fathers and trained where they did. The infantry had more of the farmers' families and the old and early inhabitants. The artillery had more of the mechanics and the immigrants from other towns, and the residents of the central village. Yet almost all the families of Nine Acre Corner trained in the Artillery, and at our times all the commissioned officers were of the Wheeler family and the corner. All the nineteen captains of the Infantry [up] to 1835, the date of this history, except one certainly and perhaps two were born in Concord. Five of the twelve captains of the artillery were born elsewhere, and seven were born in Concord. The town held both of these companies in high respect and warm affection and wished prosperity for each. By nearly equal division of popular and personal favor and interest, both companies were kept almost constantly full. Both manifested satisfactory military discipline and gratified the pride and ambition of the town. May Training, the first Tuesday of May, which all the boys gladly remembered and joyfully anticipated, was a sort of holiday. The schools were dismissed by law of the town, and all men of due age 18 to 45 were compelled to appear in one or the other companies unless exempted by law of the state. No boy failed to remember the fall trainings (three in anticipation of winter), and their number were faithfully regarded. In order to have these parades as satisfactory as possible, it was the custom for both companies to meet, drill, [and] march for several evenings previous, to develop [and] train the new recruits and perfect the discipline of all. They had music—drum and fife, and one or more of each, and the bass drum after it was intro-

8. Inserted at p. 221, l. 27.

21

duced. This was considered an important accession to the martial music, and a wonder to the boys. I well remember the time when I first heard one. It was one May evening when Capt. Sanderson led the artillery. It was my early bed time. My brother Charles had gone to the chamber before me. As I followed, passing near the front door, I heard drums, and besides, the heavy booming sound, strange and beautiful to me. I could not resist going to the door to see if possible what the instrument was that made it. The music was at Capt. Sanderson's shop 20 rods distant. Barefooted and bareheaded I ran to it, and there I saw the bass drum. I stood close to it and heard its full sound. I wished that Charles could be there to see and hear it. But I was told that it would appear when the company should come out and [so] was satisfied with my discovery and hastened home and to bed. All of the companies had from that time or about that time bass drums.

Harrington's Drummers

Edward Harrington was an old drummer before my day. He had four sons, all drummers. Edward moved elsewhere and drummed. Jacob, a blacksmith, and Phineas, a stage driver, drummed for the artillery from my earliest consciousness for perhaps 20 years. Jonas, a blacksmith, did the same for many years for the infantry.

Troop Cavalry

Besides the infantry and artillery there was a part of a small company of cavalry which belonged also in part to other towns, and also a large company of militia. All obliged to do military duty, who did not belong to either of the three uniformed companies, were drawn into the militia. This company included many respectable men who, being strangers in town, did not wish to incur the expense of uniforms for their short residence; or who, having no interest in military matters, did their duty faithfully probably yet with the least possible effort or cost. Besides these, this company drew in the moral and social residuum of the town—those who would not be acceptable in the more favored companies, [and] some intemperate, some ill mannered or even vagabonds whom the law would not excuse but whom the better companies would not receive. Few of them added military power or grace in their public parades. Some of them were ungraceful, although most of this company would dress with propriety in their ordinary garments at trainings. Some wore their old working clothes, and some were as shabby in their appearance as they could make themselves.

At one of the preliminary trainings previous to muster, Capt. Joseph Barrett gave this company a severe reprimand on their unmilitary dress [and] their disreputable appearance and urged them to come on the musterfield clad decently if not soldierly.

Uniforms

The other companies have [always] manifested praiseworthy regard to their outward appearance. Although their uniform has been changed, yet it has always been appropriate and pleasant to the eye.

Infantry

In early years the Infantry wore short blue coats, faced and trimmed with buff or white, brass buttons, cut round on the breast, white vests, white cassimere pantaloons fitting close to the body and limbs and long black gaiters with a red tassel at top below the knee. The cap was of felt, closely fitting the head. It had a front piece of the same, covering all the forehead and rising about five inches to a point above the top of the crown in this shape 🛡. On the top was a crest running from front to back, and from this hung a broad layer of white horse hair that reached over the right side as low as the bottom of the cap. On the left was a cockade and a plume of black feather tipped with [blank].

Very early in my recollection these caps were changed, for leather caps of the helmet form and shape of the skull with a leather visor. The cap was painted black with a band two to three inches wide painted in stripes of red and yellow around the lower part, and [an] open-work crest of brass six inches wide ran over the crown from front to back. On the top of this was a tuft of red worsted going the whole length. At the side was a leather cockade, and behind this was fastened in a socket a high plume of black feathers tipped with red feathers at the top of the plume. About 1820 these were exchanged for very high and heavy felt-crowned, leather caps, stiff, uncomfortable, [and] unhealthy. They were at least eight or ten inches high with a long plume, about eighteen or twenty inches long for the soldiers, and twenty-four inches for the officers. The coats were changed for others somewhat longer and cut square on the breast, much stuffed to make an apparent full and round chest. The woolen pants were banded[?] by white linen and the gaiters left off. This change was made gradually through the years 1823 to 1825.

While I was in college (1822–25), in the September vacation, I volunteered with my classmate, George W. Hosmer, to train in the infantry. We had to borrow uniforms. It was easy to find old coats not in use but not the newer fashion.

Artillery Uniforms

There was a grace, a grandeur, and a dignity in this uniform. The cap was a chapeau bras, quite high [and] with a black plume tipped with scarlet and worn slightly angling or sidewise. The coats and pants were blue, the coat was long, reaching the hose, cut round or shad-bellied and faced all along the edges (in front and behind), and the meeting of the skirts behind, with scarlet. The pantaloons were trimmed in front, and down the seams on the legs, with scarlet. This gave the company a very imposing appearance, altho very unfitting for active duty in field or war.

The musicians of both of these companies wore scarlet coats, pantaloons, with feathers of the same color, from my first recollection to 1820–1824.

Uniforms of militia officers of that regiment and of the Regimental officers were long blue coats (faced and trimmed with buff cloth [and] gilt buttons), buff vests and small clothes or pantaloons, and long boots, chapeau-bras caps, and white plumes.

Recruiting Rendezvous—War of 1812–1814

The national government opened a rendezvous for recruits during the war with Great Britain in the unfinished house on Main St. in Concord afterward owned and occupied by Hon. Samuel Hoar. There was one commissioned officer and a sergeant or corporal. They soon enlisted a few who with drum and fife were frequently marched around the village for exercise and to attract attention and sympathy. These men were not the most valuable citizens. The war was very unpopular, and few would enlist from patriotism. Mostly they were men who could not otherwise find ready support and went into this new service from motives of necessity. I have no recollection of the whole number enlisted, but I used to see ten, twelve or fourteen reporting at a time, and they were sent off from time to time to join the army.

Company of Exempts, 1814

In the autumn of 1814, when the British Fleet lay off the harbor of Boston, the Infantry and Artillery of Concord were called to Boston to defend the town, with other troops. Also some were drafted from the militia company. In their absence, a company was organized in town of exempts, principally of those excused from age over 45 and others exempted for various reasons not referring to bodily disability. Some men over 60 and perhaps even over 70 enlisted. Certainly they were a very venerable and highly respectable company, apparently more fitted for the council chamber than the field or war. The officers were, I think, Col. Roger Brown, Captain; Maj. James Barrett, Lieutenant. I forget the ensign, but Mr. John Keyes was standard bearer. At least on the presentation of the flag there were two old drummers and Mr. Jonathan Wheelock, who had been drummer in the Revolutionary War. The other [was] perhaps Edward Harrington. If there were other musicians, I do not remember them.

The ladies bought a flag for the company. It was presented one lovely afternoon, in front of Gen. Hildreth's house, the county house opposite the courthouse, by Miss Mary Merrick, the most beautiful young lady in town, afterward wife of Nathan Brooks. A long table was placed in front of the door with platform from the house and all carpetted. Miss Merrick came forward, dressed in white, and presented the flag. Mr. Keyes received it with what seemed to me a very eloquent speech. The company paraded from time to time through the [indecipherable] and always attracted great attention.

Forts in Boston Harbor

In the autumn of 1814, when Boston Harbor was threatened by the British fleet, the public authorities asked for aid from the country to complete some of the forts. Then men went in large parties from various towns, with picks, shovels, bars and hoes, and rendered what aid they could in raising up embankments and doing what was needful on Fort Warner and Fort Stow under the guidance of appropriate national officers.

One such (and I think two or three such companies) went on different days from Concord. They started at 4 o'clock in [the] morning in wagons and such other vehicles, carrying their tools, provisions and whatever else was thought needful.

This was considered as a needless war sustained by the democrats and opposed by the federalists. But when danger threatened, all cheerfully united for the common defense both in the military companies and in these laboring expeditions to build the forts. To signify this union and harmony, the people of Concord and Lincoln who joined together in one company had a flag on which was inscribed "Concord, Union for the country's safety." I am not sure of the words except the first *Concord*, but this was the sentiment. This flag was placed with its staff in the midst of this company of co-workers.

Officers [and] spectators coming along, reading the motto and seeing the large number of shovellers, congratulated them on the patriotism and generosity of Concord in sending so many to help the country in time of need. This grieved and offended some of the Lincoln people, who took the flag down, refusing to work under a Concord flag.

Reading Room Club 1812–14

Some gentlemen—a dozen or twenty or more—formed a club in the time of the war with Great Britain and took papers from all parts of the country. Their room was in the north corner of Joshua Jones's house where the papers were deposited and read. The papers were spread on a long pine table which ran along the middle of this room. The papers were afterward distributed among the members. A file of the *National Intelligence* fell to Deacon Jarvis. He had it bound, and in 1875 I sent it to the Concord Library.

Debating Club

This was formed about 1820, possibly earlier. Certainly it was in full life and active when my brother Charles left college in 1821. It included all the active and educated men of middle age, and younger. They met weekly in the brick schoolhouse through the cool season and perhaps through the summer. A new president was elected each month; I think they took turns in this office. A question for debate was selected for each meeting; at the proceedings a part was assigned to take the affirmative and a part the negative. The discussions were (as is usual in such clubs) generally temperate and as able as the intelligence of the speakers would make them. But as they were required to take the side assigned whether true or not, they presented often times much sophistry. Sometimes there was sparring and unpleasant contradiction. I found the club in full energy when I left college in 1822. I joined it and so also did Richard Hildreth, who taught [at] the Academy. I was then elected secretary. When I left town in 1827, this club was in full operation, but in the next winter it gave way to the better organization of the Lyceum.

Lyceum

When the Lyceum was formed, the debating club ceased. This was an improvement on its predecessor. Dr. Ripley took great interest in it and so also did Dr. Lemuel Shattuck, Deacon Cyrus Damon and Deacon Nehemiah Ball. I think these were the most active and efficient members. Dr. Ripley, Mr. Hildreth and Ball and I believe Mr. Shattuck and many ministers and educated persons lectured gratuitously, except it was generally proposed to pay the lecturers' expenses and the stage fare of a Boston lecturer, and his board while in town. The meetings were in the hall over the Academy, and [the room was] generally full. I lectured twice or more in the spring of 1830. When I returned to Concord in the autumn of 1832, I found the Lyceum in a high state of prosperity. Lectures were easily obtained from Concord, the neighboring towns, Cambridge and Boston on the terms before mentioned. I was the curator for several years and had no difficulty in obtaining lecturers. And if any should fail to appear, we had the never-fail resource in Mr. Emerson, who had a supply of lectures which he always (with great courtesy) consented to deliver, and they were always acceptable. He required no previous invitation but was willing at the last moment when the stage came without the expected lecturer to come in and fill the vacancy.

[A New Fire Engine]

A small weak fire engine was owned by the town and kept in a small room or shed attached to the home of Deacon Jarvis next to the path leading from the Common to the dam.[9] This probably was one of the best of the time, but it was very ineffective and probably would not throw water into the third story of a house. It was pumped or played by brakes across the lever at the end of the machine. It worked easily and very rapidly like an ordinary pump. It was the custom for this company with the fire society (who came with their buckets) to react at

9. Inserted as an addendum to p. 229.

the town pump at sunset of the first Monday of each month from April to October or November. They filled the engine and then pumped it dry. Sometimes they dragged to the tavern or green store or Deacon Jarvis's house. Sometimes they dragged as far as Deacon White's store and there expended their force of the water. This meeting drew a small crowd of spectators, men and boys. Certainly there was one who from his earliest boyhood never forgot it and never was late. This old first company was organized under the law, and its members were exempt from military duty. My father Deacon Jarvis left the infantry and joined this engine company as much easier and more in accordance with his taste. He was for a while the captain of this engine company. The new engine was bought in Boston from the manufacturer, Mr. Hunnewell. When it arrived, it was received with great interest, but unfortunately it did not work as the old one did, easily and rapidly, perhaps eight or ten strokes a second like a pump handle. It worked hard and very slowly, one or two strokes per second. The people were disappointed, and some considered it a failure. But soon it was seen that it worked with great power and threw a large stream with great force, and the hard movement was necessary to produce this pressure on the water. And the pistons were large, holding much water and having the slow but very effective movement. It threw a stream almost to the belfry of the meetinghouse. Yet there was so much talk that it was thought expedient that Deacon Jarvis, one of the committee of purchase should visit Mr. Hunnewell. Mr. Hunnewell then came to Concord to examine the engine and put anything aright that he should find deficient. He examined it very carefully and explained it to the committee and selectmen and others that were present, and stated that all engines were now made in this way and worked in this manner. The committee and town officers and the engine men and others were satisfied—all but one man, who never gave up his doubts of the completeness and the efficiency of the machine.

Agricultural Society

Henry Moore, lawyer, afterward in Chicago, was the first proposer of the Society in 1834.[10] He was there through the summer and did great service in the work of the Society. The condition of membership was to contribute one dollar or one day's work in each year. They planted the trees on the Common and most of those on Main St.,

10. Inserted as an addendum to p. 231.

Monument [and] Walden Streets. I went with a hay-rigged wagon to Stow. I got the maples that now stand in front of the old meeting house.

[Representatives Treating the Town after an Election]

It was the custom for the representative after his election to treat the town with toddy and crackers.[11] I remember this of 1811. I think this was the last. Certainly my father did not treat in 1817. Toddy was his great aversion.

Dancing Schools

Dancing schools were opened and taught as often as scholars enough should be ready. This was about one in three years from 1808 to 1820 and later. It was a common wish of parents who could afford the cost to send each child over to learn this accomplishment in order that they should acquire some ease and grace of manner. Mr. Stimson[?] of Boston was the favorite teacher for many years. The excellent and trustworthy character of this teacher, his kind and graceful manner, his dignified and cheerful disposition and deportment, secured for him the confidence of the people, and they were unwilling to send their children to any teacher so long as he would come to Concord. Although sometimes other teachers offered themselves, they obtained no schools. My sister and two elder brothers attended Mr. Stimson's schools successively as they came to proper age. I did the same in the winter of 1819–20. About fifty [pupils] of my age or thereabout were in the school. This was at the hotel or stage tavern, the usual place for these schools. It was the custom to have a half-quarters ball at midwinter and a ball at the end called the exhibition ball. This was attended by the older youth and some of the middle aged.

There were balls every year—one, sometimes more. These were got up with great care and labor. The young and the cultured from other towns were invited. The dancing at these continued until late in the morning—three, four or even five o'clock. A sumptuous supper with meats, pies, cakes, coffee, tea etc. [was served] at midnight.

11. Inserted on p. 236. According to George Brooks's memorial essay in the Social Circle annals, Tilly Merrick was the first representative from Concord to decline to serve alcohol to the townspeople on the occasion of his election to the state house of representatives. Jarvis states Merrick was the *last* to serve alcohol. [See below, page 165.]

Private Dancing Parties

Occasionally there were dancing parties at private families' houses. They included the neighbors, friends, townspeople, and the usual visitors. A single violin furnished the music, for which each gentleman paid 25 cents.

The long kitchens of the old houses offered good dancing room. The entertainment was such as was usually offered at parties—pies, cakes, coffee and tea. The dancing was not continued late, seldom after midnight. These parties were simple in experience and in exhaustion [expenditure] of personal power. But the halls were sometimes as elaborate as the taste and means of the ladies or managers could make them, and very exhaustive to the frames of the company, who were very generally unfitted for exertion of body or mind on the next day.

Sleigh Rides

Sleigh riding parties were a very pleasant means of winter amusement. There were not then great sleighs that would hold a party, but most business families and farmers had single sleighs and horses. So each family went in their own sleigh. They gathered as many as possible. I remember in my early life there was a company that was said to include a hundred sleighs. They met at the tavern on the square and went in a line over the dam through Main Street to Littleton. There was a long file stretching as far as the eye could reach, and the many bells on every horse—one string and on some two strings more than a hundred strings in all—made a great and very exciting sound to the people and children. They went to some taverns in Littleton on the Common I think Kidder's[?], or his predecessor. They had then some entertainment, lunch or dinner, and returned in high glee. Littleton was the favorite terminus for these rides, yet they sometimes went elsewhere. These parties embraced all ages—young and old, the grave and the gay; all [were in] harmony and [there was] high enjoyment.

Fish Excursion to Squantum

Some years in the summer, parties were made up of a dozen, twenty or more, to go to Squantum in Dorchester, the southeast point of land on Boston Harbor about twenty five miles from Concord. They started from home very early intending to reach their destination by seven, eight, or nine o'clock. There was a place of entertainment and a supply of fishing boats, and all sorts of fishing apparatus; the fishing grounds within easy reach were spread all about, eastward and southward. These parties went out fishing for a few hours and caught what they could. Meanwhile the hotel and tavern-keepers prepared a dinner of fried fish, chowder etc., which the [fishermen] ate with great exhilaration on their return from the water. After this they went home and reached Concord usually late in the evening. Mr. Nathaneal Munroe was the most interested and active in getting up these excursions, and after he left the town I heard of them no more.

Walks

In my young day, 1815 to 1830, walking was a very common exercise and enjoyment for the young men and women of the village. In summer afternoons walking parties to Haven Hill and also to Walden Pond were very frequent.

Skating

The brook running through the village and under the mill dam was constant-flowed, and the pond [was] full especially during winter. This afforded excellent skating, which was earnestly improved especially by the boys. The river was full and flowed over the meadows, which also presented wide and extensive opportunities for skating. Females were not known to use skates until 1821 or '22, when Miss Bradford (sister to Mrs. [Josiah] Bartlett) came to town and could skate. This was a wonder to the people and even admiration. But none followed her example for nearly thirty years, when it became a fashion in Concord and elsewhere for girls to skate.

Spirits and Wines Sold in Concord, 1828–1833

In the year 1834 (I think in January and February) Dr. Josiah Bartlett and I (both then practicing physicians in Concord) proposed to ascertain the quantity and the cost of spirits and wines sold in the town in the years 1828 and 1833 at the stores and the taverns.[12]

In 1878 Mr. George Hildreth kept the store on the Lowell Road

12. Chapter IX below contains extensive findings from Jarvis's inquiries.

about a mile northwest of the village, Col. Shattuck at the north west end of the square near the courthouse, Messrs. Burr and Prichard the Green Store standing where the Catholic church now is, Mr. Charles B. Davis in a store on the square next the south corner of the burying hill. Messrs. Moses Davis and Cyrus Davis had kept in the two buildings at the east end of the Common, but I do not now know whether they still kept their stores in 1828. Certainly they closed their store soon thereafter if not before. Mr. Phineas How [often spelled without the *e* in Concord] kept store which stood where now is the front yard of Judge Brooks. Mr. Josiah Davis kept store that stood where now is the barn of Mrs. Calvin Damon. In 1833, Messrs. Burr and Prichard had given up business and Mr. J. P. Haywood took their place. Mr. Josiah Davis had ceased to do business and his store remained closed. All the other remained in their stores as in 1828, and all except Mr. Charles Davis sold spirits and wines both in 1828 and 1833. Mr. William Shepherd kept the upper tavern opposite the site of the library. His was the genteel tavern when the stages from Boston stopped for breakfast. Mr. Heartwell Bigelow's tavern stood next the burial ground where now stands the home of Mr. Reuben Rice. This was a tavern for teams and for travellers who asked for a coarser fare and at less cost. It was also the principal resort of those townspeople who only wanted to drink. Mr. Thomas Wesson kept the Middlesex Hotel, which might be considered more a town tavern than any other. There the selectmen, assessors, committees, etc. of the town met, if in any public house. Each of these kept for a long time both before and after 1828 and 1833. They each in his several way kept good and respectable houses, certainly so far as board and lodging were concerned. We, Dr. Bartlett and I, called on all of these keepers of stores and taverns and stated our object. They all received us courteously and professed a willingness to give us all the information that we desired. All of them except Mr. Prichard gave their statements in writing. Mr. Prichard gave me a verbal statement of the sales in 1828 five years before the inquiry. Apparently most of these consulted their books, but some seem to have given estimates of sales or purchases and costs. These reports were left in my possession and carefully filed away. I find them now, 1877, and here, Dorchester, Mass., among my papers. As they are an important element in the social history of Concord, they should be deposited and preserved in their original condition in the public library, and ever open for perpetual consultation by those who in any time or age hereafter may wish to know of the manners and morals of the people

Middlesex Hotel, Concord Center

in middle of the first half of the 19th century. I therefore herewith sewed them in [in] connection with those sheets.

Second Centennial Celebration

It was proposed [by Jarvis] to the social club in the winter, 1834, to consider this matter and ask the town to celebrate this occasion. After much discussion it was so voted and a committee appointed to lay the matter before the town. An article for this purpose was put into the warrant for March town meeting. The town referred it to a committee

33

to consider and report at the next meeting. They reported a recommendation of the celebration. The town accepted the report, voted to celebrate 12 Sept. 1835, and granted a sum to pay the expenses. The town elected a large committee to carry this vote into execution. This committee had [met] early and held frequent subsequent meetings during the intervening season. They divided themselves into subcommittees for the several elements and parts of the celebration. They first determined to have an oration, but they had unnecessarily much difficulty in obtaining an orator. Among the committee and in the town there were very different ideas of the object and character of the celebration. Some wished it to be a domestic, a Concord, celebration, at which all the citizens of all the town should be gathered and besides these all those then living in other places who had emigrated from Concord and also as many of the children and children's children who could be drawn into this occasion. They wished the sympathy of other towns especially those of the neighborhood and would invite all these to this love feast. They would have an oration, singing and religious exercise in the meetinghouse and a dinner in a tent large enough to accommodate great multitudes and so simple and plain that none should be kept away on account of the cost. They would have toasts in reference to the town and its history and speeches from Concord men or those of Concord blood. They would not exclude others who would sympathise with them and represent their feelings and principles. In their opinion this should be a new cement of all Concord life wherever found and however remotely descended.

Others desired this to be a grand celebration to draw men of high degree from other towns and sites, and [to] give Concord a name and fame abroad. They wanted an orator of the greatest eloquence and renown whose speech should impress the world and carry the name of Concord with it. They wanted a magnificent dinner that would speak well for the town and speeches from noted men whose words would give honor and dignity to the occasion in other lands and in after times.

The last prevailed, and it was agreed to invite Mr. Webster to be the orator. He declined. Then they asked Mr. Everett to be their speaker on the occasion. But he also declined. Then Mr. Choate was thought of. I do not now remember whether he was invited and could not be obtained, certainly he was not the orator. After much doubt and anxiety as [to] distinguished men whom they could not invite, the committee came to the very man whom they should have first asked and who would better represent the hearts and history of Concord and

Ralph Waldo Emerson (1803—1882)

be more an honor to the people and their principles. They asked Mr. Ralph Waldo Emerson.

Mr. Emerson was the favorite choice of the first party and the necessary choice of the ambitious party. Their choice was completely justified by Mr. Emerson's orations, beautiful, strong, loving, impressive, and now forty years have strengthened our conviction of the wisdom of this election.

The dinner tent was in the field where now (1875) stands the dwelling of Judge Brooks. Mr. Shepherd, the excellent keeper of the hotel, was professionally ambitious and unwilling to set out a cheap dinner to which the multitude should come. He would get one that would be honorable to his hotel and to the town. The majority and the leading influences in the committee agreed with him and accepted his proposition to have a dinner at the cost of a $1.50 for each person. There was not then nor has there since been any doubt that Mr. Shepherd's dinner was worth that sum or that as a matter of entertainment it was an honor to his skill and good taste and honorable dealing with customs. But although about 400 ate at this table and enjoyed the intellectual feast that followed, there were yet very many to whom the payment of the price of $1.50 was a burden and others to whom it was an impossibility and these were kept away, who otherwise might have joined in the festivity and contributed by their presence to swell the gathering of Concord and her children and children's children at their family homes.

Nevertheless, on the principle assumed, the dinner and the company was all that was expected or even desired. There were the elite of the town, and many of Concord, some from abroad. There was the Governor and Judges, Members of Congress, men of distinction in other states, and Philip [indecipherable], alderman of New York.

Speeches learnéd, eloquent, interesting, and instructive were made mostly by these strangers. Mr. Keyes, Dr. Ripley and Mr. Emerson were the only men of Concord, or of Concord origin or blood, that spoke. Rufus Hosmer, Rev. George W. Hosmer, Judge Minot of Haverhill, Mr. Hoar, Ephraim Buttrick, Rev. Samuel Ripley and others of Concord or Concord descent did not speak and pour forth their Concord love or their heart's affection for Concord present and past.

It was an intellectual feast of high and honorable order, satisfactory to the ambitious. Yet almost all the speeches had no special reference to Concord or to her two hundred years of experience. They related to matters more general than local. Most of them would have been as appropriate and acceptable at any other festival in any other place and at any other time as at the second centennial anniversary of Concord.

Mr. Emerson's oration was all that the Concord heart and intellect could desire. It was historical as to the town, it was loving as to its people, [and] reverent as to the generations that had lived there from the beginning. It was a valuable contribution to the earlier and later history of the people, especially of this spot and generically of all the towns of Massachusetts. It showed the principles of character of the first settlers and the intervening generations down to 1835 who have each fulfilled their destiny and prepared the way for the development and the life of those that successively followed them. The oration was delivered in Mr. Emerson's most impressive and winning manner and held the undivided attention of the audience for more than an hour and a half.

The committee of arrangements in their endeavor to provide for the best representation of the sentiments of the town found other difficulties besides those relating to the orator and the dinner.

The collation in the courthouse for the ladies of Concord and others from abroad seemed the most desirable means of entertaining them, while the men ate and heard speeches in the tent. Almost universally the families contributed materials for this feast, and there was an abundance both substantial and elegant, freely given. Yet there was an element of discontent and jealousy, bitter and active among some, and this was found and encouraged by some who assured to be the especial friends of the poor and the humble. It was represented that this feast was for the aristocracy, the cultivated, the favored, to which the less-favored might be admitted to look on and admire and perhaps to receive some of the bounties as gifts from the superiors to the inferiors, but they were not to be admitted into the families and equal companionship of the projectors and lady mistresses of the elegant feast.

They remembered and bought up the scene on the Common when Lafayette was entertained in 1825 and said that this, like that, was for the glorification of the rich and [that it was] framed [planned] with the necessary consequence of the mortification of the mass of the people. Means were taken and influences used to persuade people not to accept this hospitality as alluded to in the article opposite then printed in the Concord paper.[13]

13. A letter dated Sept. 12, 1835, signed, "The wife of a Middlesex Farmer," describes the events of the centennial celebration: "I noticed those who in independence might leisurely recline on a hair-cloth sofa with a volume of the *Iliad*, or ride in a splendid carriage to

The ladies wished some one to attend at the coffee urns and fill the cups for the company. For this purpose they engaged a young woman who was employed by Mr. Foster, the hatter, to bind his hats. They offered her a large and satisfactory compensation for her services, and she gladly consented. She was handsome, had graceful manners and self-possession, and would fill this position with dignity and grace and be a very pleasant help to the festival. But after this was all arranged, it was represented to her that this was a menial service, a humiliation that she ought not to submit to. So she withdrew from her contract and refused to appear in the office of coffee distributor for the ladies. Finding these influences so working against them and fearing the same would prevent anyone who could be hired for pay from doing this work, the committee determined to do it themselves. Mrs. Keyes and Mrs. Jarvis offered their services, and they poured out the coffee for the assembled multitude of ladies.

The military escort was not more easily managed. The committee wanted both the artillery and the infantry to lead the procession. They were of Concord and a part and parcel of the town and could not be dispensed with. A difficulty arose. Which company should take the lead? By all military etiquette in all parades, artillery takes the right and, when marching, goes in front. Should they not do so now in the procession? On the contrary, artillery do not do escort duty. That is assigned to lighter armed soldiers, [i.e.] the infantry. Should not this last company take precedence in the procession? The officers of each company urged their claim to take precedence but very courteously left it for the committee to decide. The committee assuring that escorting is the exclusive duty of the infantry, [decided] *that* company should now perform that office. The artillery should be considered as invited guests and mount immediately after the infantry. This decision satisfied both parties, and there was complete harmony thereafter between them. The singers proposed an anthem which however excellent would exclude some of the part-songs, odes or hymns pertinent to the occasion. This was therefore rejected, and Mr. Elijah Wood the head of the music concurred in this view of the matter.

When the committee had finished their work and paid all the bills

---

variegate the scene; here were those, who in the humbler walks of life ply their needles or tend their dairies for a livelihood—all, all seemed happy without any inequality or distinction. . . . Most of us have the *means* of educating our children, as well as those who count their thousands; let us do it, and ever impress on their minds that true greatness and superiority consists more in wisdom and merit than in splendid equipages and fine houses."

for expenses incurred under their direction, they found that they had exceeded the town's appropriation by about one hundred dollars. At first view, seeing that all this money had been expended in carrying out the purposes of the town, it would seem that this excess should be reported to the town and an additional appropriation asked for the payment. But the committee remembered the dissatisfaction that had been manifested by some and the undercurrent of censure that had been stirred by the leading malcontents and thought it more wise to ask no more grant of the town and avoid any opportunity of public complaint or unkind taunting at the gathering of the people. They therefore unanimously agreed to pay this deficiency out of their own private funds, each paying an equal proportion of the whole.

Reception of Lafayette, 1825

The Marquis de Lafayette in his tour through the United States in 1825 passed through the town. The people of Concord sent a committee to invite him to stop, rest and lunch with them. He was glad to do so, but the plan of his movements allowed only an hour or two for Concord. [Since] he would not be there at breakfast, dinner, or supper, he would only partake of a collation. This was fixed to be on the Common in front of the meetinghouse. The ladies provided an ample feast of cakes, confectionery, coffee, tea and everything desirable to the palate and pleasant to the eye. A bower or open tent with only a roof or covering to keep off the sun was built and the table spread beneath. The ladies had the matter in charge and several at the table. An ample space was kept open by a cordon of rope around the bower, and guards of soldiers marked the boundary line and kept this space clear from all but the officials of the town and the occasion—the selectmen, the committees of reception and of arrangements, the ladies who had the charge and responsibility of the collation and a few invited guests and a few who were asked to aid in serving the food to the company. I was then a junior in college and was among those asked to render their aid to the managers. In this space around the table, the Marquis and his company and sister and some strangers from abroad, the officers of the government who escorted Lafayette on his journey, were received. Here the town committee of reception were stationed, and here the speeches of welcome and Lafayette's answer were made. It was intended to have this space around the table sufficiently large to give all these guests, and their entertainers, and the helpers freedom of motion, but not so large as to keep all others at such a distance as would prevent their easily seeing the General and the strangers, and hearing the speeches. There was a great collection of people from all parts of the town and some from other towns. All classes left their business, their work on their farms and in their shops, and came with their wives and sons and daughters to see and hear the nation's guest. There was universal gladness, welcome, enthusiasm, and all wished to get as near as possible to the strangers. The crowd around the space and the bower was dense and pressed open the rope and required the incessant vigilance and decisive firmness on the part of the guards stationed on all sides to prevent the concentrating movement from breaking the line and filling the open space. There was consequently some complaint, even scolding and probably angry words, between the people without and the guards that kept them there. Some looked with eagerness to the privileged people within and even jealously wondered why those favored (or cultivated or more fashionable) ladies of the village and those men (the older and the younger more used to society) were admitted within that charmed and charming court [and permitted] to come in near contact and opportunity of speaking to or being spoken to by the great French hero of our revolution, while they ([just] as faultless and respectable) were shut out from these opportunities and privileges. They were not as well dressed not as educated in society nor as free and easy in manner and speech as these within, but their fathers had served the country, some had fought with Lafayette in the battles of the revolution, and they were as grateful for his services. They loved his memory, were as anxious to speak their gratitude as those before them who seemed to have no restraint on their movements [or on] their intercourse with the visitors. Thus among some of the people there assembled, a deep feeling of disappointment arose; in some there was engendered a deeper feeling of jealousy and anger which was not easily subdued. It did not go down with the sun. It was not left behind when they returned to their homes.

The feeling of disappointment was strong in many. It amounted to anger in some, and the last did not let it rest. They fanned it until it was kindled into a flame, and they imparted their earnestness to others. They talked of the aristocracy and their haughty treatment of the common people, the wives and daughters of the farmers and mechanics. It is rare that any single event in the town has so agitated society and produced so much jealousy between the classes or rather on the side of the aggrieved toward the offenders. These last were unconscious of any intention of even slight cost [to] their fellow citizens, and they were pained that any should be suspected. But they could only say that the arrangements were such as seemed most convenient and even necessary for the reception of Lafayette, and the others would have done the same. Among the discontented there were some cunning, some crafty demagogues who were willing to aid in the social alienation to gratify their selfish purposes. So the jealousy was kept alive in various degrees by conversation [and] by articles in the paper, disturbing the harmony of the town, impeding or preventing some plans in which it was hoped that all would unite and cooperate. It reappeared at various times, even for years, down as late as 1835, when the ladies of the town at the centennial got up the collation at the courthouse and asked all to join in this love feast of hospitality but found the old feud revived and that some not only looked with jealousy on the project and would lend no sympathy nor aid but even strove to prevent others from aiding or even attending this festival. Articles were printed in the paper with this intent as shown in the account of the doings of the centennial. Nevertheless, the great majority of the people reflected with satisfaction on the manner of receiving the European visitor. They regretted that any offense was given even unintentionally to their friends, brethren, and sisters in the town, but still they could not see any better way of accomplishing their hospitable purpose.

Others at length, some after many years of unkind alienation, became reconciled to the better view and let their feeling of jealousy die out and their natural love and confidence take their place. Besides this hospitality and speech in the bower, there was a military parade in honor of the military hero. The infantry and artillery were called on and gladly responded. The militia company also volunteered, somewhat to the disappointment of the better disciplined and more showy soldiery. But these plain soldiers were warriors as well and as much as those who were uniformed. They were as well dressed as the army of the revolution who fought under the distinguished and noble general. So they claimed to be admitted to the escort of the occasion and the parade on the Common before the eyes of European military experience. There was then all the show of martial power the town could offer. The general spoke kindly and respectfully of and to them. All marched well and carried their armour well. None found fault with even the militia in their many colored coats. In this matter all were in harmony then and thereafter.

Two

Traditions and Reminiscences
of Concord, Massachusetts,
or,
A Contribution to the Social
and Domestic History of the Town,
1779 to 1878

To my Life long friend, Rev. George W. Hosmer, D.D.,
whose love for, and interest in, Concord,
the place of our birth, like my own, have never faltered,
this book is affectionately dedicated.

EDWARD JARVIS

How dear to my heart are the scenes of my childhood
  Whose fond recollection presents to my view
The orchard, the meadow, the deep tangled wildwood
  And every loved spot that my infancy knew.

WORDSWORTH

Edward Jarvis

AUTHOR'S PREFACE

For reasons given in the preface to my manuscript notes, in my copy of Mr. Shattuck's printed *History of Concord*, I have written this book. My original intention was merely to add such traditions as I had heard concerning the early times of the town, and my own recollections of the events that had occurred within my own observations, to the pages of Mr. Shattuck's volume. I began by writing notes, comments and additions to such of his pages as seemed to require them. At first, I wrote these on the margin of the printed pages, and when there was insufficient room for these, I wrote on separate sheets which I pasted in. In some cases there were several sheets thus added.

When I had gone through the book, there were other topics that seemed to require separate and longer treatment. I intended then to write these out and to bind them, in the printed volume, at its end. I did this to some extent by pasting a few of such accounts in that book. But the work grew upon me so rapidly, and I found that I had much more to say than I had supposed. I wrote on, chapter after chapter, when soon it was manifest that my collection of written sheets was too large to be bound with the printed volume. Then it was determined to bind the volumes separately. There is much in the notes and additions to the printed volume that should be in this. But those were written mostly in connection with Mr. Shattuck's paragraphs and would not be separated without lessening their significance nor without more labor of reconstruction and rewriting than I have strength to do. They all however form one work, and should be treated only as such.

This is not a complete history of Concord, even for the century which it goes over. It was not intended to describe all the elements and interests of the town, but only such as had come within my observation or had interested my mind and heart.

These pages have been copied from my original manuscripts by my wife, Mrs. Almira Jarvis, my sister Mrs. Lydia G. Jarvis, my niece, Miss Mary H. Davis, and in very small part by myself.

Writing this book has been a pleasant pastime to me for the last three years. But I regret that my health will not allow me to revise it as I wish. As it is, it is my wish to deposit it in the Public Library of Concord, for anyone to examine, read, or quote from it as he may desire. I reserve to myself however the right to withdraw it if, at any time, I may think proper to do so.

Edward Jarvis

Dorchester, Mass.
July 1880

CHAPTER I

Early poverty. Privations. Economy. Pecuniary straits. Scarcity of money.
Cooperation. Minister's wood. Apple bees. Quiltings. Huskings. Raisings.
Breaking roads after snow storm.

The first settlers in Concord and their successors for many years carried but little property with them. They obtained their lands for cultivation at small cost and beyond this had little left. With most of them, their lands, their few cattle and implements, and also some means of sustenance for the year while their first crop was growing, were their whole fortunes.

Fish in the rivers, brooks, and ponds, and some game in the forest supplied them with some food, but for the rest they had to depend on what they could raise from their farms. Their land was originally wild, uncultivated, unbroken and mostly covered with forest. They could clear, break up, and cultivate but a small proportion in any year, and consequently their crops were small. It was necessary to raise grain, vegetables, roots, etc., sufficient for the food of the family and, besides the natural pasturage, hay and other materials for the support of their horses, cattle, swine, sheep and fowls.

The cattle did their farm work, supplied them with meat, milk, butter, and cheese; their sheep supplied wool for clothing; the fowls their eggs, and they, with the swine, at last supplied them with meat for their tables.

They raised flax, with which they made linen for clothing, bedding and other household purposes. With [a] mixture of linen and wool they made what was called linsey-woolsey cloth, much worn by women and by men in winter. More than this, the farmer needed other materials and the aid of other persons in the cultivation of the land and support of the family. The carpenters and masons were needed to build and repair his house and barns; the blacksmith, to shoe his horses and keep his tools in repair. Shoes and some clothing which could not be made at home and also some other materials of life were also needed.

As the products of the farm were the only resources, it was necessary to raise sufficient from the farm not only for the sustenance of the family and animals, but also to be given in exchange for these aids and materials from others. Moreover there were the taxes to be paid for the making and repair of roads, for schools and support of religion, the expense of which must come out of the produce of the farms. To accomplish all this with their narrow means, the farmers were compelled to work with extreme diligence, to live with the straightest economy and undergo many privations of comforts. Gradually their cultivated lands increased, their method of culture improved, and they raised larger crops; [they] had more for their own consumption and more to sell, or to give in exchange for other men's labors, or their merchandise. Nevertheless they had no market beyond themselves. There were no larger centers of population which were in need of the farmer's supplies. Boston, Charlestown, [and] Cambridge were then agricultural towns like Concord, and raised their own food. Moreover, there were no roads over which loads of hay, grain, etc. could be transported. The farmers then could only sell their surplus produce— grain, hay, vegetables, milk, butter, cheese, fowls, eggs, veal, beef, mutton or pork (when they killed animals)—to the professional men, mechanics, traders and others, who had no means of producing them. Gradually these non-producing consumers increased in the village; the roads were opened to other towns, and improved; and in course of time Boston grew to be a market for country produce, and Concord farmers began to send their surplus productions there.

Nevertheless, during the first one hundred and fifty years, from the settlement of the town, the people were compelled to practice the most rigid economy and undergo many privations. Yet as the circumstances of the successive generations improved, they bore their hardships cheerfully and with thankfulness that they could live with more comfort than their fathers.

Revolutionary War

This condition of narrow circumstances and hard struggle of life continued until the Revolutionary War, when they [were] increased by

48

the necessities of that period. All the interests of the people were concentrated in that struggle for independence. There was no surplus money to pay the taxes and support the army. All that could be given was done by more rigid economy at home and by great privations. The people underwent these cheerfully, they ate poor food, wore less comfortable clothing, in order to save for the soldiers who suffered intensely—but their friends at home suffered with them. Even after the war, the national distress prevailed, and severe domestic economy was necessary and practised.

In [the] progress of time, even in the later years of the century, agriculture still further improved, better crops were raised, and farmers had more to spare besides feeding their families and cattle. Roads were improved. The village of Concord had more people, mechanics, traders, and others who needed the farmer's supplies. Boston became a large town of 20,000 or more people, all of whom depended on the country for their sustenance and offered a market for the farmer's produce. They sent much hay to the village, taverns, etc., and to Boston. This however impoverished the farm. Wood became a very important matter for the market. Much of the remaining forest land was cleared and the wood carried "below," as Boston, Cambridge, and Charlestown were called, and some made a business of buying wood standing in the forest, cutting it and taking it to the market. This was a sure but laborious method of earning money. Teams of four oxen and one horse could draw two cords of wood; it usually took near twenty-four hours—that is a day and part of a night—to go and return, and the driver walked by the side of his team, at their very slow pace. This was [a] very laborious even exhaustive means of earning money, yet it has brought much to Concord.

Pecuniary Straits

Concord had the common experience of every new society. In all these is inevitably a want of money or circulating medium, and all complain of hard times with good reason. Much of their trade is then done in barter or on credit. This was very prevalent in the last century and in the first quarter of the present, in Concord and other parts of the state. A large portion of the people had accounts at the stores, which were frequently allowed to run to the end of the year. The mechanics were subject to the same custom of giving credit for much of their work and manufacture and get[ting] their pay at the year's end or even allow[ing] a further delay. The farmer could not find a ready sale for

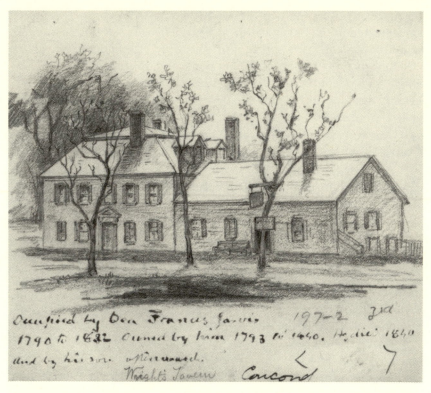

Sketch of Wright's Tavern, Concord, occupied by Deacon Francis Jarvis, 1790–1832

his surplus crop and often paid with it for his store supplies and mechanic's labor. Many were living in anticipation of their income— the farmer actually consuming the value of his crop while it was growing, and others in the prospect of earning and paying at future time. Physicians settled once a year with their families and then collected what they could of their charges. Employers, farmers, mechanics etc. were accustomed to pay their workmen, laborers, journeymen etc., not monthly or weekly, by giving them small sums from time to time as were needed, and then at the end of the time or year settl[ing] and pay[ing] the deficiency if they could. Ministers paid some of their bills in orders on the town treasury for the salary, which they had already earned which the town treasurer had not been able to pay. So the whole people in greater or less degree were embarrassed by the want of ready means of payment in themselves or in those for whom they had worked, or to whom they had sold goods, merchandise, or the products of their land. The poor especially suffered from the scarcity of money. They needed, but frequently could not obtain, the reward for their labors. Very small sums were of course given to them, and they were obliged to resort to any honest means to supply their necessities. They borrowed when and where they could.

My father at his place of business always had money and needed it only when he made his monthly remittance to merchants of whom he bought in Boston. He was very kindhearted and glad to aid people in their distress. They came to him and borrowed very small amounts— 10 cents—nine pence—shilling—quarter of a dollar. A half-dollar borrower was a large customer. I do not remember that my father ever refused any one. Yet I have no doubt there were unworthy applicants. They almost all paid according to their promises. There was one man of very minute exactness in all things. He came frequently, usually for 25 cents, to be "paid next week." This he never failed to do—always Saturday night at nine o'clock. There was another borrower, to whom my father always lent, but with less heart. He was a journeyman tanner and a large customer. He asked for five dollars. He was a usurer. He was not poor. He did not want the money for himself but to lend to the poor, of whom he exacted an exorbitant interest—as 10 or 20 cents for a week's loan of a dollar; and even higher rates did he sometimes charge for his money. He was very cautious in looking for security and rarely lost. He paid my father no interest, nor did any of these borrowers. The man afterward did a large business in this way, and at the middle age of life he had acquired forty thousand dollars. He left Concord in his early manhood but still continued this system of brokerage with similar profits, and even larger, as his capital increased.

There were so many of these customers of my father that he kept an amount book exclusively for them. This was labeled *Petty Cash Book*. It is now probably among my father's account books in the attic of my late brother, Capt. [Francis] Jarvis's house, now the property of his children. I do not know when my father began this business, but I found it in operation at my earliest observations, and he continued it as long as he lived in the village until 1832. His borrowers rarely failed to pay, yet I have no doubt that he sometimes lost his petty loan and that some failed in promptness who paid at a later day. I never knew him to dun any of these debtors. Certainly he never sent any of his boys to do so. He always excused them by saying they were very poor.

Cooperation

In early times in sparse population, the people had less means of affecting their purpose within themselves. But this in some degree, perhaps in a great degree, was compensated by the ready mutual sympathy and friendly cooperation. So we read of various ways of neighbors and friends joining their forces to help a weaker one to do his work. These were what were called *bees,* in which the friends combined to help one out of straits, as when one with limited help in his family was sick at the time his cornfield should be hoed, his neighbors would gather and hoe it for him.

Minister's Wood Bee

The town formerly owned a wood lot from which the minister obtained his fuel. This became his right from his settlement and continued as long as he held his ministerial connection with the town. I think the minister was to take the responsibility of transporting this wood from the forest to his house. Often the people combined gratuitously and helped to do this work or a part of it, as the minister perhaps had neither man nor team to do this work. This was found to be a wasteful way of supplying the wood. The miscellaneous collection of men cut the trees injudiciously. Sometimes they destroyed such trees as were more valuable for timber and often [cut] young trees that should be left to grow longer, [and] they injured others by their careless driving.

The town then made a new contract with the minister: he consenting to surrender his right to cut wood on the town lot, and they agreeing to deliver him a certain specific quantity, sufficient for his wants, annually. This cooperation ceased from this time, and wood on the lot grew so abundantly that the town supplied all the minister's wants and sold, in [a] course of years, sufficient to create a ministerial fund which, with accumulated interest, amounted in 1826 to over $11,000.

For other purposes when the work could be concentrated in time or space, this kind of cooperation of friends has been in occasional practice and sometimes with much social enjoyment. *Apple Bees* were among them. When a housekeeper wished to prepare a large quantity of apples for the year's stock of applesauce, or for drying, she (either for convenience or pleasure) sometimes invited her friends to come to her house to help do this work. If in the afternoon, usually only the female friends were invited; if the bee was to be in the evening, the husbands and brothers also came. Each took a pan of apples in her lap and cut the skin clean from end to end, quartered and cored them and threw them into the general depository. Skillful workers would so cut the skin in one circular ribbon whole from end to end of the apple. Then as a part of the fun, a person would take this long skin and swing it round his or her head three times and let it fall on the floor, where it would lie in an irregular shape. Then the frolicsome people would endeavor to find in it some resemblance to a letter in the alphabet, which would be the initial of the name of the future husband or wife. The playful boys and girls told fortunes from the number and arrangement of the seeds in apples. The youths would ask the girls or a girl would ask a youth to name his or her apple. The name secretly selected and applied to the uncut apple was usually someone who was supposed to be agreeable to the holder of the apple. When it was opened, the seeds were counted and some fancied interpretation given to show the probable future relations of the holder of the apple and the person named. This afforded much amusement to the parties. Sometimes the boys and girls snapped seeds at each other and in many sorts of ways made the time very joyous to themselves and also profitable to the giver of the bee. If the assemblage was in the afternoon, the ladies had tea and a pleasant supper. When the bees were in the evening there was some less elaborate entertainment at the end, after which the party broke up and went to their several homes. Those occasions had gone out or nearly gone out of use even in my early day. But traditions of the elders were handed down to the children of my time.

Quiltings

This was another form of cooperation that happened more frequently than the apple parings and continued in practice for a long time. Many families had *quilting frames* for their own and for the neighbors' use. These were simply four separate strips of smooth pine boards about twelve feet long and three inches wide, with many holes through their whole length. In one edge a strip of listing or other strong cloth was fixed by tacks. When used, these boards or frames were fastened together at the ends with a nail put into holes already there, making a square frame, with the listing, all on the inside, to which the quilt was secured. This frame was placed on the tops of chairs. The quilters sat on all sides and sewed as far as they could reach. When this was done, so much as was sewed was detached from the rails at the corners and these were rolled inward, and again fastened as before. This brought to the edges more of the blank quilt, which was then served, and the rolling process was repeated, until the whole was finished.

The bed quilt was made of two pieces of calico, either whole or of pieces sewed together called patchwork, of the size of the quilt [with] a thin layer of cotton wasting between. This was what was quilted together in straight or angular lines—any figure that the owner chose, "herringbone," "shell," etc., etc.

When quiltings were in the long afternoon, at dark a nice supper was eaten and sometimes they stayed for the evening, when the gentlemen would be invited to come. This was made a pleasant gathering. Bed quiltings were used by all families more or less. The white bed spreads now so common were rarely seen, but now bed quilts are getting out of general use.

Huskings

Some families, in former times, were accustomed to get all their corn into the barns, then invite their friends and neighbors to come and husk in the evening. Usually the invitations were general, and all were expected. But young men and boys were the most ready to accept and to enjoy the gathering and work. There was often much hilarity and frolicking among the young. They threw corn about and made some waste. After the husking was over, the farmer gave his company a plain entertainment of pumpkin or apple pie, or crackers and cheese, and water or cider. Sometimes when the farmer in the morning came to see the result of his enterprise, he found the corn scattered, the good and the bad mixed; some was broken, some trampled on and trod in the dirt, and some among the husks. In my boyhood, sixty years ago, I went to two huskings. I think they seldom if ever occur now, for the farmers considered it bad management and could do the work themselves with their ordinary and paid cooperators.

Raisings

In former times, when the primitive forests were yet standing, the trees were large and the timber heavy, then people built their houses,

54

barns etc. with very large beams. A house near me in Dorchester was built in the 18th century. The lower beams are twelve inches by twelve. The carpenters made the frames and got the separate parts ready to be put together and raised to the form of the intended building. But the timbers were so heavy that his ordinary force could not lift them to their high places and put them in their appropriate positions. Hence more help was needed, and the neighbors were invited to come and aid in the great work, and a general invitation was given out for all that would, to come to the raising. The appeal was cordially met. Many went to the place mostly to work, but some to look on, and some, especially boys, from love of being where a gathering was to be found. With more zeal than discretion and much shouting, the timbers were raised and put in their appointed places, and the frame presented the future form and size of the building. After the work was done, the host entertained the cooperators and the multitude with crackers and cheese, with water or toddy-rum and water sweetened. Most drank the stronger drink but generally very moderately. A few drank more.

I have been to only one raising as a worker. That was Cyrus Hubbard's house in 1817, sixty-one years ago. I was then fourteen years old, and was busy handing the pins to the men, who drove them into their appropriate places. This cooperation justified me and some other boys in eating of the bread and cheese, which we did with a relish. This was just at night [sunset] and we were soon to go to our homes to eat a warm and much more inviting supper, yet there was a charm in even eating crackers and cheese out of doors and with a cheerful multitude.

This method of mutual help has been long discontinued. Smaller and lighter timbers are used. Builders concluded that it was easier and cheaper and much more satisfactory to raise their frames with the help of a few men hired for the occasion. Those with ropes and pulleys easily raised the building without accident.

Snow Path Roads

Formerly, when a snow storm was so great as to block the roads and require any extra effort to open a sleigh or sled path, it was the custom for the farmers to take their oxen and sleds which were turned upside down or with ploughs on each side, and force their way from their houses to the center of the town. The most distant started first and was joined by those next in order of his progress. Usually they put their teams together and the sleds of the other behind, so that on some of the roads, where many farmers lived, the team of gathered oxen became quite a long procession before they reached their journey's end; and the accumulated sleds ploughed an open and somewhat smooth path as they moved along. They had shovels to dig open the drifts which the oxen could not wade through. These working processions all came to the centre by every road, from every quarter, and this opened the paths to all the parts of the town. It was a pleasant and exciting sight to look upon so many large teams gathering in the square. It was a delight to the boys, if not in school, especially if they could get onto any of the sleds and have a ride. The men then went into the taverns where they found warm and hospitable fires and were usually treated with hot flip, whether at the cost of the landlords, who doubtless felt very grateful, or of the town, for this was a public benefit, I cannot say; but I have no doubt that both were willing to make this little compensation to the generous farmers and their men who had thus cleared the highways. This custom, like the others before mentioned, went several years ago, into disuse. By general consent the people concluded that it was an expensive way of breaking out the roads; much more was expended, often more than was needed, and sometimes the work was imperfectly done; and it was not considered right to throw the burden on the farmers alone of keeping the roads open in winter, but the whole town should pay the cost. Other plans have been adopted with less cost on the whole and [which are] more satisfactory. The town recognizes its obligation to make the roads passable and easy and safe in winter as well as in summer.

Local agents are employed who can readily see the difficulties and at once give just the remedy needed [to] make the winter travel easy and comfortable in every part of the highways.

The people of Concord are no less kind, sympathetic, and generous than their fathers, but they are stronger in leading and in heart. They are more self-sustaining, and it is better that each should do his own work, with his own hands or by such aid as he can compensate in the ordinary way. Those burdens that in past years required the cooperation of friends and neighbors are now but ordinary affairs and are met by the ordinary means and their own exertions. The wasted work is now as well and completely done as ever, and people both individually and sociably are as happy and more prosperous and are loving, generous and ready to aid in distress, poverty and sickness, whenever they shall present themselves in any family or neighborhood.

CHAPTER II

Domestic Life 1775 to 1825

Food. Meats. Salted beef and pork. Fresh meats. Farmers killed their own beef. Fish. Fresh. Salt. Vegetables. Pickles. Applesauce. Dumplings. Bread. Johnny cakes. Cooking apparatus. Open fires. Kettles. Bake kettles in kitchen. Roasting jack. Tin bakers. Cooking stoves. Ovens. Drink at table. Cider. Pea soup. Tea. Coffee.

Food

In the last century and earlier, the people were compelled to live as economically as possible, and eat such food at times as would now be considered as intolerable. We learn from tradition, not by experience or observation, of some singular articles of diet. Mr. Webster speaks of a family in the upper part of New Hampshire who, 70 years ago, were eating soft grass fried in lard and nothing else for their food. I have known a very poor Irish family make a complete dinner of cabbage for all. Some of our own Concord families have dined and supped on baked pumpkin and milk. In the time of the Revolutionary War, this economy was made more necessary, as the absence of many of the farmers and their sons greatly lessened the produce of the farms, and much of the grains and roots that were raised was sent to the army when within reach or sold to pay the public taxes.

At my earliest period of observation and through my boyhood, milk was very much used in families that had it, often for all the members, for occasional dinner and other meals, and generally for the children at morning and night.

In my father's house the children always had bread and milk for breakfast and frequently for supper. This was varied frequently with hasty pudding of corn meal, which the boys enjoyed. This usually served for two meals when first cooked, and after being cooled and consolidated, it was cut into small cubes about half an inch square and then boiled in milk. This was very pleasant to us. In summer when whortleberries or blueberries were ripe, we had these in our milk with the bread, and in the autumn baked sweet apples were used in the same way. Baked or roasted potatoes with salt or butter were not unfrequently eaten as the sole element of a meal. Brown bread sliced and toasted with molasses, and sometimes cider, very much weakened with water sweetened with molasses, was warmed with brown bread cut into small pieces. This served occasionally as an acceptable dinner or other meal for the children and even adults of careful families.

Meats

The butcher's cart was not then a daily visitor at the houses of most people, especially those that were out[side] the larger villages. Fresh meat, to these families, was not a daily or even a general indulgence. Salt meats were the main dependence of a large part of the people, especially the farmers.

It was the custom of my father and of most farmers to kill a cow or ox every winter for domestic use. They sold some of the meat to neighbors to be repaid in money or in meats, when these neighbors should kill a cow or ox and have a surplus. They saved as much as they could for steaks and roasting pieces. They put such as they could not eat before spoiling into barrels or boxes filled with snow and ice, and by constantly replenishing the snow and ice, these meats were kept fresh until spring. But they became very dry, hard, and tough and unpleasant at last, to eat. The rest of the meat was salted for preservation. Thus the family was provided with corned beef, which was their ever-present reliance for the year. This beef by long contact with the brine became hard, and often green within. Nevertheless we all ate of it frequently and freely.

Every farmer kept one or more hogs, and most mechanics and even some laborers also kept these. They were a necessary part of the domestic economy, to consume the waste of the house and to provide food for the family in the winter especially and, to less extent, through the rest of the year. People killed their hogs in November or December.

The spareribs and steaks were consumed while fresh. Much was made into sausages, which served the family through the greater part and some through the whole of the winter. The legs were smoked into bacon for use during the rest of the year. Col. Jonas P. Buttrick had a smokehouse to which many sent their hams and legs to be smoked. The sides and other parts were salted down for preservation. The farmer, who had several hogs more than he should need for family use, usually sold the surplus, dead or alive, to the butcher or other who wanted it for sale or use. No thrifty farmer or other housekeeper would feel that he had been faithful to his family unless he had his barrel, or barrels, or tubs of salt beef and salt pork, according to the number of eaters in his household.

Boiled Dish

Boiled dish, as it was usually termed, was the most common dinner in these families. Salt beef and salt pork were put into one pot. Some at times had only the pork. But in either case, the beef and the pork, or the pork alone, were put into one pot with such vegetables as they wanted, except the onions, which were boiled separately. Turnips, cabbage, beets, carrots were all boiled together and in some poor or rude families were all served up, on one great platter, in the centre of the table. In most families, as in ours, there was a platter for the meats and for each of the kinds of vegetables. The remnants of the meat were often eaten cold, but more frequently minced with potatoes, alone generally, yet sometimes with the other vegetables all chopped fine and warmed together. I once met this at dinner with onions mixed, and the workmen ate it with an apparent relish as if they were used to and enjoyed it. It was very offensive to me, but I was a boy, too timid to complain or refuse to eat it in a strange house. Probably salt meats constituted more than two-thirds of the animal food of a large part of the families.

Calves

Farmers and others who kept cows had calves in the spring or summer. These were usually killed for family use. Yet, as it was impossible for one household to eat an entire calf while it was fresh, they sold some, and frequently they merely exchanged with each other to be repaid in kind when the purchaser should kill his calf.

Mutton

Those who kept sheep killed them on the lands from time to time, for food, as they were wanted. The butcher also offered mutton for sale, but this meat was not so common as others before mentioned.

Poultry

On Thanksgiving Day almost every family had a turkey for dinner. But very few had it at any other time. Most farmers and many others kept hens and ate them from time to time. I remember the Thanksgiving appointed by the President in the peace of 1815. It was in April, out of the season of turkey or poultry. My father bought a leg of veal for the dinner. We, the children, were very much disappointed that we had not turkey. We were all Federalists and had a great dislike for the war and no respect for the President's Thanksgiving as such, yet we were very willing to eat turkey even on that occasion.

Soups

Soups, generally beef soup, were very frequent. Beef, sometime pork, potatoes, and other vegetables were all stewed together. Besides these materials, often little cakes of dough made of flour unleavened were put into the mixture and boiled all together; the cakes of dough sometimes fermented and became porous and light, but more commonly they remained compact and solid and were very heavy in the stomach of the eater. Soups were not then as now a mere preliminary to the more solid dinner of meats, etc., but they constituted the whole of the meal except the pudding, and with some without this exception.

Fish

Salt fish boiled was the constant Saturday dinner in my father's house and many others. Generally salt pork was cut into very small cakes and fried, and the fat with the solid bits used as gravy on the fish, but some made a gravy of butter and flour with milk or water. This was put on the fish and potato, on the plates of the eaters. Beets boiled were usually eaten with this meal. Afterward, the fish was chopped fine with potato, and moistened with the fat or the drawn butter and warmed for supper or breakfast. We always had this Sunday morning. *Fresh fish* from the sea was rarely brought as far as Concord. But when it came, it was fried and considered a great luxury, and eaten with great eagerness. Some small fishes were caught in the river and pond. These hardly supplied a meal a year to most families, yet there was now and then a thriftless family who preferred this method of living and depended in great measure on the food which the river offered them as fishers or the fields and forests to them as hunters.

Baked Beans

Baked beans were much eaten. In many families they were the noonday dinner, for the convenience of the women who were then occupied with the weekly washing and did not wish to give their labor or room at the fire to the preparation of food. Beans were always baked, with a piece of pork in their midst, in a large pot which held enough for one dinner and some subsequent meal. They were a general favorite as well as a cheap and nutritious food.

Gardening and Garden Vegetables

Gardening, 60 to 100 years ago, was in far inferior condition to that of the present time. Farmers generally, however good and successful in the cultivation of their fields, were not good gardeners. They seemed to think it a misuse of their time and strength to work in such small space as a garden and raise such small matters as garden sauce, when great fields of corn, rye, hay and potatoes needed and paid them well for their labor; consequently they had small and poor gardens and their families a comparatively meagre supply of garden sauce.

Mechanics

Mechanics in the village who had no great fields to look after and were glad of the opportunity to get exercise in the open air generally had good gardens. Nevertheless, all in various degrees were accustomed to have on their tables at dinner some or all of the fruits of their gardens in the summer. At my mother's we had, in their season, greens, at first dandelions, afterwards young beets or cabbage sprouts, lettuce, summer squash, green peas, string and shelled beans, cucumbers, beets, carrots, parsnips, green corn, new potatoes and cabbage. We, the boys, were fond of getting ears of green corn and roasting them ourselves, for luncheon or other than meal times.

Tomatoes

These were a late introduction. They were never raised in my father's garden, nor eaten in his house. The first I ever saw were in 1845, a great rarity and eaten in very few families. None of the farmers raised them then. Now they are among the most common articles of diet.

Pickles

Families preserved, for pickling in vinegar, cucumbers, green peppers and also frequently beans in the pod; and sometimes bearberries, green grapes, small muskmelons or cantaloupes were added. The last were cut open, the seeds etc., scraped out, and the cavity filled with spices—cinnamon, allspice, mustard seeds. These [fruits] were put in brine and then in vinegar, where they were kept in good order through the winter and spring and even the following summer. Pickles were considered a very pleasant accompaniment of dinner, and some ate them with other meals. Thrifty families put up in the fall sufficient for the coming year a quantity according to their number and taste, perhaps a whole or half barrelful.

Applesauce

Applesauce was made in farmers' families and others in the autumn, sufficient for the year—a tub, a half or whole barrel, according to their number and taste. It was made with cider boiled down to double its natural strength, and apples stewed—after being pared, cored, and quartered—in this strong liquor. It could be kept good through the year and was generally used at dinner and often at the morning and evening meal.

Puddings

Puddings were almost if not quite universal in all but the poorest families. Those made of Indian [corn] meal were most eaten. These were generally boiled in a conical earthen pan made for the purpose with a cloth tied over the top. Often suet puddings with bits of the untried fat of beef, mixed in the whole mass, were made for the dinner. When cooked and warm, the suet was soft and pleasant to the palate, but when cold, these were consolidated like butter. Molasses only was used on the suet puddings, but on others butter was added, to make them palatable. With beans usually an Indian pudding was also baked. Other puddings were of bread, either the original slices cut from the loaf or the fragments of slices cut for other purposes or partly eaten.

Dumplings

These were very common and great favorites. The dough was flattened and made [into] a large circle. The apple was cut and piled in the centre and then the edges doubled up so as to meet and cover the apple, which was thus entirely enclosed. This then was again enclosed in a cloth, wrapped all around it, and the sides brought together and held together with a string and thus boiled in a large pot. These were often very heavy and compact, yet acceptable. Sweet sauce was eaten with them. I have no recollection of berry dumplings in my early day, though [they are] common at the present time; yet whortleberries were often mixed in the bread pudding. Boiled rice was often used, and also baked in puddings. Tapioca and Sago were not then used in my experience. Puddings were then eaten before meat at dinner.

Pies

Every family at Thanksgiving provided themselves with a large quantity of pies of apple, pumpkin and minced. Some had pies at various times through the year. Besides these three kinds, they [the families] made them of berries in their season and of custards. We began Thanksgiving with three kinds of pie at breakfast, and at dinner we had turkey, plum pudding and the pies as before. In my experience pies were not eaten at dinner, except at Thanksgiving and only at supper.

Bread

Nearly the whole of the bread in farmers' (and other working) families was brown made of Indian corn and rye meal. Very little wheat flour or white bread was used. Very few families bought flour except in small quantities, generally 7 or 14 lbs. at a time. This was for

Kitchen, The Old Manse, Concord. *Courtesy* Trustees of Reservations, Beverly, Massachusetts

pies, cakes and for company. This was bought at the stores and the bake house. Most of the baker's bread was crackers bought by families for company and especial occasions.

Johnny Cakes

Johnny cakes of Indian meal baked on a platter or in a shallow tin pan before the fire were very common and acceptable. They were eaten with butter, hot, and were very good cold. Sometimes they were split open and dipped in drawn butter as toast. These were also made of rye meal, and then split open and spread plentifully with butter. Besides these, *pancakes*, or soft batter generally of rye meal and dropped a spoonful at a time into boiling fat and there kept until fried, were very frequent. They were mostly light and porous, but too frequently solid and heavy. These were for ordinary food but there was a nicer kind of fried matter or *doughnut*. These were of flour, sweetened and made delicate. The dough [was] rolled out in sheets and cut in various shapes

64

and fried. They were very palatable and made for company. They could be kept many days or perhaps weeks.

Cooking Apparatus

In my mother's kitchen was a large fireplace, four feet wide at the back, so that wood of that length could be burned (yet the pieces of wood were only two feet long), a pair of large iron andirons, a crane about four feet long, and half a dozen hooks, with a trammel or abiding hook with holes in the upper or fixed half and a tooth on the lower or sliding branch, to be inserted into the eyes or holes of the upper [half]. Thus the trammel could be extended to suit the necessity of the case, even to double its closed length. There was one great and one small brass kettle, holding about 10 and 5 gallons, used principally for washing and other occasions where much warm water was wanted; a great iron pot holding about 8 gallons and another of half the size used for cooking; a dish kettle, iron, broad and open at the top; a tea kettle of iron and one of copper; a brass skillet on high legs holding two or three quarts; two iron skillets holding a quart and a pint; a large and a small spider; a tin and a copper coffee pot; a gridiron; a dripping pan 15 by 8 inches, 2 inches deep; there was a bake kettle or iron vessel about 12 inches in diameter and 5 inches deep, with a large iron bail and an iron cover made with iron sides so as to form a pan 2 or 2½ inches deep. This bake kettle was hung on one of the hooks on the crane over the fire. Dough was put into it, the cover put on and filled with burning coals. Thus the heat of the fire below and of the coals above easily and effectually baked the bread.

My mother had no tin kitchen for roasting meat, but she did all this kind of cooking on a spit 4 or 5 feet long, before the fire. A hook bent both top and bottom was hung by the upper corner to one of the andirons. One end of the spit was placed in and rolled in the curve of the hook. At the other end of the fireplace a *jack* was fixed to the wall at its upper part. This jack was of clock work, made to run by a weight when wound up. A band was over one of its wheels, which was grooved. The wheel on the end of the spit was placed in the other lower end of this band. The wheel on the end of the spit was about six inches in diameter and grooved on its edge for the band. When they roasted, they wound up the jack and set it agoing. It carried the spit round slowly and regularly until the meat was cooked. The dripping pan was placed under the meat and caught all the gravy and fat that dripped.

Sometimes meat was roasted in a cruder way. It was suspended before the fire by a string attached to the mantle or the front part of the chimney. The cook watched and turned it as occasion required. But it was often roasted unevenly, too much in some parts and too little in others.

The *tin kitchen* or roaster was later very common in families. This was a tin, in form almost cylindrical, two feet more or less long and one and a half feet high, open on one side, with a lid at the top fixed by hinges. There were holes in the middle of each end for a spit, and a circle or ring (three or four inches in diameter) of small holes around one of the ends, or [on the] spit, to hold a point in the spit, which was occasionally moved from one to the next, to regulate the roasting. The other end of the spit came through the other end of the kitchen. The bottom of the kitchen received the drippings from the meat.

Tin Bakers

Among the improvements of their time was the *Tin Baker*, a box open in front. This was for baking bread, cakes, etc. and was, like the tin kitchen, placed before a hot fire. In both the tin kitchen and the baker, the direct rays of the heat from the fire struck upon the matter within, the reflection from the tin also aiding the cooking.

Cooking Stoves

Until about 1815, families universally cooked their food by an open fire place. When the cooking stoves first began to appear, they were clumsy, yet highly praised and urged upon the people. A few took them, and some went back to the open fireplace.

Ovens

No kitchen was complete without its oven. This was built of brick, by the side of the fireplace, about three, four or five feet deep, according to the number in the family, and about two feet wide. It had a separate flue for the escape of the smoke. This went upward and outward, along the side of that from the fireplace, yet it sometimes opened directly into the fireplace flue and its smoke went up and out in that.

This oven was used to bake the bread, cake, pies, pudding, beans, and sometimes the meats. It was a necessary means of this [form of] cookery until the cooking stove, with its oven, superseded it. Even long after the introduction of the stove, some housekeepers still preferred the brick oven to that of iron, especially for bread baking. Nevertheless these stoves were improved from time to time by the many inventions that were sought out and added. They gradually gained in favor and at length overcame all opposition after a struggle of twenty, twenty-five, or more years, and then gained complete possession of all the kitchen.

Drink at Table

I regret that I have neither record nor tradition of the *drinks* that were used in families at meals, 150 and more years ago. So far as we can learn, cider was used at dinner in the last century by farmers who had it or could provide it. It was put on the table in mugs large or small, out of which all drank, as tumblers were not then in common use. But probably a large part of the families drank water, and the children and men in all other families did the same. In my father's cellar the cider always turned very sour and hard; yet it was on the table at noon. None of our own family touched it, yet the workmen drank it in various degrees.

I remember in my boyhood, a neighbor—who had been respectable but who had become very intemperate—used to call at our back door and ask one of the family to give him "just a drop of your good cider." His drop meant a half mug or a pint. This we always gave him; he drank it all, courteously thanked us and said it was good.

Cider went out of general use in the second quarter of this century, and tea very generally took its place at dinner. Now two-thirds of [all] American families in Concord have it at noon, and cider is almost never offered at the table.

Drink at Breakfast and Supper

Neither *tea* nor *coffee* were in general use 150 years ago. Mrs. Derby, now 85 years old, whose parents died 54 years ago, tells me that she had heard in her youth that in her father's and grandfather's family, pea soup and bean soup were drunk with the morning and evening meals. Some used tea of common herbs, some root or other beer instead. Many drank water, and some drank milk with their food at these times. Yet *tea* was in use at her home even in her early day, the latter part of the 18th century.

The fact that the British government laid a duty on it before the Revolutionary War, in expectation of obtaining a revenue worth the trouble and the chance of a quarrel with the colonies, indicates that considerable quantities were used here. The resolution of the people (that they would use no tea as long as duty was imposed, showing thereby that they were willing to endure privation on the cargo, probably a small one, sent to Boston and destroyed in the harbor) indicates that it was in somewhat general use among the people of New England as early as 1770–1775. But from my earliest day (1808) tea was universally used at supper and generally at breakfast. There were two kinds used, black or souchong was almost universal in all families, green tea was kept in most families for company and special occasions. There was a cheaper and commoner kind, Bohea, that poorer families sometimes drank; and gun powder tea [green tea, each leaf of which is rolled into a pellet] was the rarest luxury for the wealthiest.

Coffee

Coffee was not much drunk in the last century. In 1700, 100 tons were used in Great Britain. A century later, 500 tons were used; and in 1850, 17,000 tons were there consumed. The use of coffee has increased probably at a more rapid rate in the United States than in Great Britain.

At my earliest recollection we had coffee for breakfast in our family [on] Sunday mornings. After some years, from the increasing cheapness of the material or the improvement of my father's circumstances, we had it Sundays and Thursdays, and on the rest of the days we had tea. Occasionally we had chocolate, or [cocoa] shells, but these were as costly as coffee. After a few years more, I heard my father say that he thought that now coffee was as cheap as tea. This delighted all of us, for we were very fond of this drink, and learning that my father had not told my mother, we did so; but my father kept nothing from my mother, and soon thereafter we had coffee daily for breakfast.

Substitutes for coffee

During the war of 1812–1814, coffee became very costly and people used many substitutes for it. Rye, burned and ground, was the principal one. Rye coffee thus prepared was put up in pound packages and sold at the stores at enormous profit to the traders. Brown bread burnt and pounded, and wheat or flour crusts were used for this purpose, but these, though good economy, were never acceptable and we were glad to get back to the real coffee.

CHAPTER III

Heating. Fuel. Cooking. Fireplace. Fires. Matches. Tinder box. Preserving fire through the night. Borrowing fire. Friction matches. Lighting. Candles. Dipping candles. Mould candles. Candlesticks. Snuffers. Lamps. Oil. Whale sperm. Burning fluid. Coal oil. Kerosene. Comparative lighting power and cost of present and former time. Lanterns. Domestic help. Clothing. Domestic cloth. Gentlemen's dress. Breeches. Hats. Felts. Fur. Women's dress. Bags. Dr. Ripley's flannels. Overcoats. Thin clothes. Cloaks. Women's clothes. Gowns. Linsey-woolsey. Calico. Outside coverings. Foot clothing. Barefoot boys. Boots. Traveling shoemakers. Economy in women's dress.

Heating Fuel

Every complete farm had its wood lot sufficiently large to furnish, by its constant growth in wood, enough for the family use through the year. Open fireplaces and wood fires were universal in the first quarter of this century. Stoves were in shops and schoolhouses, but not in kitchens or rooms of dwellings.

Open Fireplaces

In the neighboring cities, to some extent in Concord, and probably elsewhere in the country, some foreign bituminous coal was used in parlors and in stores and also by blacksmiths. Cooking was done at the open fireplace and with wood. The fireplaces in kitchens and ordinary rooms were supplied with andirons of iron, but of brass in the parlors by such as could afford them. The most careful, when they had opportunity, put, in the fireplace on the hearth back of the andirons, a large log of green wood or another log or large stick of wood on the andirons in front. This was called the forestick and the other the back log. Then the fire was made between these two larger logs or pieces of wood of smaller and more readily combustible pieces and then the fire was replenished and kept all day. At night the coals were all carefully placed on this back log and the whole covered with ashes. By this means, there was no danger from fire's communicating to wood of the room, and the fire was preserved through the night; in the morning, on moving the ashes, a bed of live coals was found. With those the new fire was easily begun for the day.

Matches

There were no friction matches in those days, only the flint and steels, tinder box, and sulphur matches. Families kept these. Gun flints were generally used, and an old file or any other piece of steel tinder was made by burning cotton or linen rags to a charcoal, and extinguishing the flame before this coal was converted into ashes. This was kept in a tin box made for this purpose. It was so light and combustible that a spark from the flint and steel would kindle it. The matches were of domestic manufacture. They were simply small strips of very dry pine wood, 4, 5, or 6 inches long, with one end coated with sulphur [made] by dipping it in when the sulphur was melted. This end being applied to the burning tinder, the sulphur took fire and kindled the wood and thus the fire was begun.

Keeping the Fire Over Night

This was a troublesome process, for the heat of the burning tinder was very slight, and it required, sometimes, much patience to kindle the sulphur with it. Most families intended to preserve burning coals through the night, yet sometimes these failed, through necessity or carelessness, and some had neither living coals in the morning nor any means of kindling a fire. They were compelled to send to a neighbor to beg a coal or a brand, and when those neighbors were distant, it was with very great difficulty that the fire could be carried in open air. I remember, in my early childhood, a neighbor's family not unfrequently found themselves in the morning without fire and means of creating one. They sent to my mother for coals or brands, and sometimes more than once, in the same morning, for the same carelessness that failed to preserve the fire through the night failed also to keep it alive, while it was carried across the wide street. Now *friction matches* are in every house and shop and such privations as these never happen.

Lighting

There are traditions of the economies, the privations, and the inventions for lighting rooms in the evenings. I have not personally known, yet I have heard, of cases where individuals or families read by the light of pine knots burning in the fireplace, yet I have no doubt that at evening when the men had nothing to do but talk and the women were employed in knitting which could be done mechanically, some families were satisfied with such means of lighting.

My earliest observation found candles the common means of lighting. The candles were universally made of tallow and in a large part of the families made by themselves at home. Those who killed any cattle for food saved the tallow, others bought it of the butchers for this purpose. This was effected by the women of the household. The untried tallow or fat in the cellular membrane was cut into pieces and all matter [put] in a large kettle—in our family the brass kettle used on washing days and holding about 20 gallons. It was about 20 inches in diameter. The wicking was of soft, loose, cotton yarn made for this purpose. As many of these pieces as would be sufficient were cut into pieces a little more than twice the length of the proposed candles. These were doubled and very slightly twisted, leaving a loop at the end. Slight rods about a foot long were run through these loops and the wicks spread along the rods about 2 inches apart, extending a little less than the width of the kettle in which the tallow was melted. Then an extemporary frame was constructed on which to hang these rods after the wicks had been dipped in the tallow. The operator, sitting between the kettle and this frame, continued dipping the wicks into the tallow and putting the rods on the frame to cool till the candles were of the right size, adding coating after coating of the tallow as fast as the tallow cooled and hardened. These candles were for common use of the family and answered all the ordinary purposes of the household business.

Another and nicer kind was made in moulds or cubes. Of these two

72

or more or even eight were attached to one frame. The moulds were of the size and length required, tapering at the lower end. The wicks were placed in these tubes, which were then filled with the melted tallow, the wick in the centre of each one. A little hole in the bottom or pointed end of the tube enabled the wick to just fit in, while it was kept up at the top by a rod, thus the wick was in the centre. Then after being filled [the candles] were set aside to harden. The moulds after the tallow had hardened, were dipped into warm water. This slightly warmed the surface and then the candles [were] drawn out easily. These candles were handsomer and used on extra occasions only.

Candlesticks

These were merely to hold the candles. Those in common every day use were made of iron, of different shapes, with a socket the size of the candle in which the candle was put, having a piston by which the candle could be pushed up when nearly burned out. The nicer candlesticks were made of brass, sometimes of black tin, and the nicest of all were silver or tin plate with silver. There were, in some houses, candelabras or branching candlesticks, with a socket in each for a candle. These were fixed on the wall or stood on the mantle piece [or] sometimes suspended from the ceiling. In shops I have seen wooden blocks with a hole bored in the center, to receive the candle. These were rare and dangerous, as the block might burn. These candles gave but a meagre light, and I cannot now conceive that people could read by them.

Snuffers

Candles implied the necessity of snuffers, as the tallow burned and left the wick above. This checked combustion and made the flame dull, and diminished the light. It was needful then to cut off this charred part. For this purpose snuffers were used, which opened like scissors and thus cut off into a box at the end, the charred part. Then the candle burned brightly again. Snuffers were in every house where candles were used. For ordinary use these were made of iron, but the better ones were of steel and [were] kept carefully polished. Some used scissors, but they dropped the charred wick on the floors. I have seen men in shops snuff the candle with their fingers, but this was at the risk of burning their skins.

Oil Lamps

As far back as I can remember, in 1808 and afterwards, oil was coming into use in lamps. It was somewhat more expensive than tallow, and those who were supplied with tallow from their own beasts still used candles. *Whale oil* was used. This was coarse and gave an imperfect, dull light. The lamps were small and generally with only one wick. Afterwards those with two wicks were substituted. Lamps were generally of tin, japanned, which stood on pedestals more or less high but some had no pedestal, merely the lamp an egg-shaped cup with a projection at the bottom. Black tin was used at a later date and also glass.

While I was in college, 1822–1826, I used two such lamps, each having two wicks. These four wicks only gave sufficient light for my study. Larger lamps, Astral, Solar, etc., were made in later years for parlors, larger rooms and on tables. Those had a better draft, burned more brilliantly and gave a much better light. Sperm oil was a richer source of light and was used by all who could afford it, a few years later than whale. Later, about 1830–1840, lard oil was used and was a good substitute for the fish oils and [was] more economical.

Burning Fluids

There were many kind of burning fluids invented for lighting. Most of them had alcohol as a large ingredient and were very combustible. These were much praised by the manufacturers and sellers. They gave a brilliant light and were much used, yet they were liable to explosion. They took fire readily. Many accidents occurred—the glass lamps falling and breaking, the fluid taking fire, endangering the house, also the clothes of the women on their person. The vapor of this fluid, when exposed to the air, spread rapidly and would take fire, if in contact with a blaze. Some lives were lost in consequence. Nevertheless these fluids had an extensive use, until the coal oils took their places and the place of all other means of lighting in the country, excepting gas.

Coal Oil; Kerosene

About 1840–1850, Mr. Samuel Downes, a large refiner of whale oils, was convinced that ordinary coal oil could be purified and converted into a convenient and safe oil for ordinary lighting. After much investigation and many experiments by Mr. Merrill, his chemist, they succeeded in eliminating its dangerous and offensive elements and obtained the very safe and brilliantly burning *Kerosene oil*. This is not only the cheapest means of lighting that has ever been known, but it gives a larger light than any material except gas, which can be used only in cities. Gas is very much more expensive than kerosene. Downes's kerosene is pure and safe, is sold by the barrel now, 1878, (1877 for 12 cts.) for 15 cents a gal., and at retail for 20 or 26 cents a gallon. A gallon of this oil will burn in an ordinary lamp 142–150 hours. A gallon of whale oil, costing 60 cts., will burn in an ordinary lamp with two wicks 31–33 hours. A gallon of sperm oil, costing 120 cts., will burn 30–31 hours. A pound of tallow candles, costing formerly 20 and now 14 cts., will burn 48 hours and give only about 1/15 or 1/20 as much light as the kerosene. The light given by kerosene, in [an] ordinary hand lamp is 12–14 times as great as that of a sperm two-wicked lamp. So it seems that the poorest of our people now enjoy 45–60 times as much light as the richest of our father and grandfathers [at] about the same cost. Kerosene oil gives a softer light, which wearies the eyes less than any other, and people are more comfortable as well as richer by this great and new blessing.

Lanterns

Until about 1830, the[re were] tin lanterns. They were mere cylinders, pierced with numberless holes about a quarter of an inch long. The light of the candle shone feebly through, but the wind could not penetrate, as the holes were punched from within outward. From 1830, we had glass lanterns, globular, conical, cylindrical and other forms made to hold small oil lamps, now improved for kerosene oil.

Domestic Help

Formerly the aides in the household work were not servants but help cooperators. These were often daughters of comfortable families where there were more daughters than were needed at home, or distant relatives. These found pleasure in working for good families where they were treated as members of the family, ate at the table with the parents and children, and sat with them in the sitting room. My mother always had a cousin or niece or other family connection. They had their wages, and one who lived with us 26 years left, when she died, a good little fortune for one in her position.

Some families more ambitious of style hired such as they could find generally among the poor. They were kept in the kitchen. Later, the American girls were unwilling to live in kitchens and have the positions of servants or even of domestic help. They went to factories where they found sufficient employment and a larger reward. And thus Irish and other foreign servants began, and now they occupy nearly all the kitchens.

Clothing

There were no factories in this country at the beginning of this century. Our cotton cloths were imported from the East Indies, from Great Britain and France. Our woolens, of the best kinds, were made in English and other European factories. Our best linens also came from Europe, but a great part of the woolen and linen cloths were made of household manufacture in the manifold families of the country. Every farmer's family and many mechanics and others had their spinning wheels—the larger for wool and the smaller for flax. These people had woolen yarn spun every year to be woven either in the house or neighborhood for the cloth for the common wear of the men and boys, [and] also [for] flannels without nap. Some of this flannel with the yarn colored [was used] for common winter dresses for the girls. The cloth for men and boys was sent to a mill and colored, dressed, and fulled for use. If the cloth was to be gray, the darker part was colored in the wool and mixed in carding. These cloths were coarse but strong and looked sufficiently well for every day wear for farmers and mechanics. Gentlemen and others for their best suits bought foreign cloths, generally English. Our grandfathers and grandmothers dressed more ambitiously than their children. They wore variously colored coats, blue, olive, brown, green. At the time I entered college, the government had established a uniform of grey (black with one-sixteenth part white) for all the students' coats and pants. No others were allowed to be worn in Cambridge. The object of this was to prevent extravagance in the more fashionable students who were in the habit of having several suits of various colors. This was particularly the case when my brother was in College, 1817–1821.

My father . . . had, in my early boyhood, a green coat, [although] generally he wore black throughout. Looking at the portraits in Me-

ordinary working man

Costume of working man, taken from "Costumes of the Revolutionary Period: Sketches by Marian Blackall Miller," 1925

morial Hall of Harvard College, one is convinced that the boasted simplicity of the fathers was a myth. They were fond of gay attire. Breeches [and] small clothes had gone out of general use when I was first able to observe. None were worn in Concord for ordinary business life, except by Dr. Ripley, who wore them through his life until his death in 1841. Dr. Heywood also wore them until he was 50, when he married and assumed pantaloons. I remember seeing my father dressed in black breeches in a Masonic procession. Younger men then sometimes wore them at balls. President Kirkland and Prof. Henry Ware sen[ior] always wore them as long as I was in college.

Dress, in all ways, was much thought of by young men. In college, 1817–1821, my brother Charles had a new hat every six months. I had the same in my day, 1822–1826. The stove-pipe, cylindrical, fur hats were always worn—stiff, heavy, uncomfortable and sometimes painful to the head. Men who could afford it felt proud of their ten-dollar beavers made of fur throughout. Others were napped, but the body of felt was covered with fur. Boys in the country wore wool hats which were also cylindrical, very stiff, hard and uncomfortable. One singular use the boys sometimes made of this headcovering—the hat had in it much glue, which by exposure to the rain and air lost its strength, then the top fell in and formed a dish or saucer. We found this convenient for a drinking cup. [Since] it would hold water, we poured into it and drank from the edge. Sometimes these wool hats, from long use and exposure, assumed a conical shape—the top projecting above the sides or cylindrical front.

Boys' Clothing

Boy's clothing was the simplest possible. The suit was [a] cotton jacket and trousers, both fitting the form like natural skin. The jacket was first put on and encased the chest, then the trousers. The legs were buttoned all round to the bottom of the upper garment. In this suit no cloth was lost in ornament, only sufficient was put in to cover the boy's body.

Women Tailors

Mrs. Sanderson, the excellent wife of Henry Sanderson, saddler and harness maker and Capt. of the Artillery, living in a house that stood north of the Court House, was the tailoress for boys and others who wished to save expense in their clothing. When our mothers sent us to her with the cloth for any garment, we were always instructed to tell her to "cut them to grow." That is, we were growing larger every year and our garments would last two years, so they must be made too large for the first year and would get to be too small for the second. I well remember my mortification, in the last year, when my coat or jacket could not be made to reach my hands, nor my trousers reach my ankles. I thought all the boys in the school were looking at me and spying their deficiencies. In those days, boys, as soon as they could, emerged from the earlier and closer garments and wore short coats

78

that reached as low as the hips. Workmen and many others about their business wore the same, but men in more genteel occupations and all for their Sunday and visiting suits had long coats with skirts reaching nearly, or quite, to the bend of the knee. In the law of Harvard College in 1822 regulating the dress of students, the coats were required to reach to the bend of the knee. But fashions varied and sometimes required the skirt to be shorter. This happened in our college life, and the students' coats followed the fashion rather than the law. One of my classmates, tall and long-legged, had this shortness in his coat, which was very noticeable. The President, who was a pleasant wit, as well as faithful administrator of the law, called him up, and asked him "where is the bend of the knee." He made no answer but renewed the skirts.

Dr. Ripley's coat, the fashion of which he retained until his death in 1841, came down to the calf of his leg. This represented the [length] of garments in the latter part of the last century, which the excellent Doctor liked and preserved. This coat was cut round or circular, from the collar in front, to the end of the skirt behind. This was the fashion in the time of the Revolutionary War. The parts met in front only at a small line, leaving the front of the chest and, except at this point of meeting, the whole of the abdomen, uncovered by the coat. But the *waistcoat,* properly so named, compensated for this deficiency. It covered the whole trunk, from neck to thighs, and was truly warmer. It was cut open in front below to give free play to the thigh in its movement. This also the Doctor retained to his death. Indeed, he told me in his later years that he had never worn a small waistcoat, nor a pair of pantaloons, nor a straight or small coat. These, with his long black stockings and shoes (in summer) and long boots (in winter) and his low broad-brimmed hat and white neckcloth, buckled behind, constituted his dress, during the whole of my observation.

The skirts of men's dress coats in the last century were very broad and spreading, almost covering the hip and thighs. In the early part of this century they were made narrow—merely strips covering the back of the thigh; sometimes they came almost to a point at the bottom.

Frock Coats

Frock coats were rare, but deemed a great elegance. Socks such as now are almost universally worn by workmen and very generally by others were not known until about 1840. As undergarments, frocks and waistcoats and drawers of wool, cotton, or silk were not worn, certainly [not] by young men, even in the first quarter of this century. Not even old men had them before 1800. No such inner garments were used by the college students in my day, but soon thereafter, they came into use. Men before then had only the coats and pantaloons, such as we should now call thin, for their winter protection.

Surtouts

Surtouts an outdoor garment for winter cut in [the] form of a frock coat except longer, open behind, were generally worn. Yet great coats, more in the form of a wrapper, whole behind, have always been more or less worn, and for the last 30 years, to the entire exclusion of the surtout. These garments 15 to 20 years ago—1840–1860 even earlier and later—were made singularly short, coming only to the hips and leaving the entire locomotive apparatus unprotected in the coldest weather. This fashion has changed and now men protect their whole frames.

Cloths

The cloths of former times were much thinner, and the garments, especially the great coats, gave less protection from the cold and winds. Homespun cloths were loose and pervious to the air in comparison with the broadcloths and the cassimeres which were woven and fulled closer and more compactly. [They were] less penetrable by the winds without and [more conservative of] the heat within. Great coats and surtouts of homespun were worn by many, and [those] of common broadcloths by all others. These garments were made of one thickness of even this thin cloth. They were not lined nor wadded as they now are. Thicker cloths such as one now used for outer garments were sometimes, though rarely, used. I only remember two instances as early as in the War of 1812. My father had a drab greatcoat of this (called then) West of England cloth. This was an extra garment made large enough to be worn over another outside garment. All the family used it on occasions of great exposure. When I first began practice in my profession, my father, fearing my suffering from winter riding, got me a surtout of Petersham English cloth of the common quality. Now cloths of this thickness are common, and not only all outside garments but most of the body coats for winter, and pantaloons, and even some waistcoats are made of it; and more than this, the inner and body coats are also lined and wadded. I think that the great coat which I now wear with its thicker cloth, lining, and wadding weighs full twice as much as that which I wore in College, 55 years ago.

Cloaks

As long ago as my memory extends, Dr. Ripley wore a black cloak. When my brother was in college (1817–1821) [and] during my college life five years later, cloaks of Scotch plaid were universally worn by students and in the country by a few persons. The outer part was thin, without nap, loose, pervious to the wind and [a] good conductor of heat. They were lined with flannel, which was not thick, and both together afforded but a light protection from the cold of winter, and yet this was all the outer garment that most of the college students had. Some ministers and other professionals, even others who wanted a second outer garment, had cloaks of broadcloth (black or blue) lined with flannel. These were much warmer than those of the college students. In 1838 when he was 70 years old, my father had one which he gave me at his death in 1840. I have it now (1878) in the exact form that he had selected: black, thick, broadcloth, very warm and comfortable in extreme cold weather over my heavy great coat.

Summer Clothes

My father had a piece of cotton cloth made nearly every year. This was woven, twilled and was strong. It was sent to the clothier, where it was dyed with fustic, which gave it a brown or coffee color, and was corded and had a nap. This was called fustion. We all had suits of this in the spring cut by Mrs. Sanderson. These suits were reserved for Sundays and other important occasions the first summer and worn as everyday clothes in the second year. Some boys had their suits of blue and white check or striped cotton. This was sold at the stores and was a little higher in the scale of fashion than fustian, and the children of the most genteel families wore it.

Nankeen

Nankeen cloth, blue and yellow, and sometimes bombaset was worn as dress pantaloons. When I was 16 and first went away from home, I had for my Sunday summer wear a pair of bombaset pantaloons and a blue nankeen spencer [short jacket without skirts] which then satisfied my highest ambition in this line of life. During my college days, *lasting,* a stiff, smooth, woolen material, was much worn for Sunday pants [and] by students, at all times, in the warm season. Vests, in my early day, were of cotton called marseilles—white, buff, or brown, spotted, figured or striped. When I was just a grown boy, I had one for Sundays with which I was very happy. These were for summer, woolen [was] for winter.

Women's Clothes

In earlier times, women seem to have undergone more privations and suffered more discomforts from insufficient clothing than men. Their outer protections were very meagre. Like their brethren they were not provided with flannels, waistcoats, or frocks for the chest and trunk, still less with drawers for the rest of the form. The last were not known until the first quarter of this century. They were therefore very much exposed in the winter. Their skirts were light and narrow and often short. The winds easily reached and chilled their unprotected surface.

Gowns

Gown was the term in common use for the outside house garment. The materials for the common, every day gowns of the woman in the country were generally of domestic manufacture, made in some of the country houses. If none of the family could weave, some one was hired to do it, [and] also the spinning.

Linsey-woolsey

Linsey-woolsey cloths of combined wool and linen or flax were made for winter gowns and underskirts. This also served for outer garments of some women. Ginghams, checked or striped, blue and white and other colors were woven and much used for common wear. Calicos were worn for better dressing. In my day, ginghams of factory origin were also worn. The calico became common as early as 1820, when ladies wore them for house garments, after their morning work.

Costume of country maid, taken from "Costumes of the Revolutionary Period: Sketches by Marian Blackall Miller," 1925

Outside Garments, Shawls, Coats

Our mothers must have suffered much when abroad in winter. They had but slender and feeble protection against the colder storms and winds. Some had cloaks, some shawls, but these were thin and light. A friend who was [the] daughter of a prosperous family of Boston told me that in 1794, when she was sixteen years old, she went with her father in an open sleigh from Boston, Mass., to Amherst, New Hampshire, and she had only a shawl over her house clothing. They had nothing in the sleigh to protect them, no buffalo robe nor bear skin, nor even a blanket. They sat on the bare wooden seat and in the unobstructed open air. Her father had been an Army officer through the Revolutionary War. He had been much exposed to cold and hardships in service and though not better protected on this account suffered less than his daughter.

Foot Clothing

In my early life, nearly all boys—all sons of farmers, mechanics, and other laboring people—went barefoot in summer. I think more than three-quarters of the boys under 12 years wore no shoes nor stockings at school or about their ordinary work or play in the warm season. This was no hardship, but rather a pleasure. We were always impatient in May for our Mother's permission to leave these garments off, and unwilling to wait until she thought it prudent to expose our health thus to the cold. When we first began, the feet were a little tender, but they soon acquired a hardness and did not suffer from the rude contact with the sharp stones and wet earth. We enjoyed the freedom and regretted the approach of cold in September, when we must put shoes on our feet. All mechanics, farmers, and other working men and their sons wore cowhide shoes for every day life, and calfskin on Sunday and other important occasions. For more effectual protection of the ankles and legs, they had leggings knit of woolen yarn like stockings with the lower part made to cover the upper part of the foot, with a strap to go under the foot and hold the leggings in place. These were drawn over the shoe and reached up the leg, generally to the knee, where they were bound by a garter. They were good protection against dry snow and the cold air, but not against water.

Boots

Boots were not used except as a part of dress. For gentlemen and all genteel purposes they were long, almost reaching to the knee with a tassel of silk hanging in front. With breeches they were an elegant part of the costume in the winter; pantaloons (when they came into use) were worn under the boots. But in the time of Napoleon's wars, a shorter kind, or half boot, came into universal use. They were called

"Wellington boots" because they were said to be invented by Lord Wellington for his army, as more convenient and healthy than either long boots or shoes. When my father had a cow or calf killed for family use, he sent the skins to the tanner and these supplied the leather for our shoes. This was a frequent and I think common custom with such as had these means of providing meats for their food.

There were, in these days, *traveling shoemakers* who carried their benches and tools from house to house where they were employed as long as was needful to make up the shoes for the year for the whole family, and [to] repair such as needed it. Mr. Taylor was this traveling mechanic of Concord in my day. He came to my father's in the late autumn, and as I remember he worked there a week or more at each visit. Thus he found employment, always boarding for the time with his employers.

In all working families the distinction between the Sunday and every day garments was carefully preserved, from their beginning to the end. We had our thick, stout, cowhide shoes to work in, and to go to school in, and our calfskin shoes to wear to meeting, and their different uses were kept up. In earlier times the straightened circumstances compelled a straightened economy in these matters.

Women's Foot Clothing

I have heard my mother and others tell of their experience in this matter. They, like other girls of comfortable families, had good white stockings and calf skin shoes for best wear. My mother was daughter of Nathan Hosmer and granddaughter of Stephen Hosmer, good farmers in Nine Acre Corner. Their only means of conveyance was the saddle horse. On Sunday the whole family went to meeting. The father or grandfather rode in the saddle, the mother on a pillion behind him, and one of the younger children before him. The others walked. The girls wore their every day stockings and shoes and carried their Sunday foot clothing in their hands until they came to a field just out of the village. Here they got over the wall into the field and changed their foot garments, put their coarser shoes and stockings into a hole in the wall and wore their nicer ones to meeting, and returning after meeting stopped and again exchanged them. This was a common practice in those days for people living so far from town.

CHAPTER IV

Furniture. Improvements. Hereditary. Pewter plates. Chairs. Kitchen. Parlor.
Chamber. Arm chairs. Easy chair. Settles. Mahogany chairs. Cane seats.
Beds. Bedsteads. Feather beds. Straw mattresses. Bedding. Quilts. Tables:
kitchen, parlor, centre, candle stands. Table furniture. Dressers. Beaufet.
Fireplace. Shovel. Tongs. Bellows. Carpets. Wall paper. Pianofortes.

Furniture

In this matter, the skills of inventors and the cultivation of taste have, in all ages, found a pleasant field for operation in the homes of the people and have almost constantly made improvements. The furniture of the 19th century differs very materially from that of the 17th. The furniture of the third quarter of the present century differs widely from the first quarter, in all classes of society. From generation to generation the children endeavor to improve on their fathers, and they succeed in their attempts to make the dwellings more comfortable. A lady of a prosperous family in Massachusetts went to Kentucky in 1818 and was absent without any return over twenty years. Then, when she visited her home, she said that in that period, the furniture and the style of domestic life had entirely changed. Much of the furniture became heirlooms, passing from father to son, or more commonly from mother to daughter, and constituted a part of the means of housekeeping for the new generation. The rest and in the greater part, the new family made up by new purchases.

My mother's . . . father and mother both died when she was only ten years old. She then remained in the old native home with her grand-

86

parents. The furniture of the family went, on the death of this elder generation, to her older brother and sister. Nothing ancestral came to her that I can remember except two large pewter platters and half a dozen pewter plates, which used to stand on the dressers, as bright as the material would allow. The platters were occasionally used to hold cold meats and vegetables which were put away. The smaller plates served to bake fired cakes on, and these were their only uses in my mother's family.

My parents were married in 1793. My father had been successful in his business and bought the house very near to and north of the meetinghouses, where they lived until my mother died in 1826, and until my father moved to the Col. Buttrick farm, north of the river, in 1832. They began life in a simple way, and so continued until the final breaking up thirty-nine years thereafter. They had simple but generous tastes, and for their purposes and ideas of domestic comfort and style of life, they had, with careful economy, sufficient means. Accordingly their house was furnished, as to the kind and quantities of the several articles, much in the style of young mechanics and farmers in their days. As they were but two, with the addition of an apprentice and a journeyman, they needed comparatively little, but as the family grew in numbers, and my father in pecuniary ability, other conveniences or necessaries were added from time to time until the whole house was furnished as those of the elder and prosperous farmers, with such as the world offered for sale at the shops or demanded to be in reputable, working-families' houses.

Chairs

The chairs of the kitchen had four perpendicular posts, which formed the four legs below. The back legs rose high enough to support the back. There were 4 or 5 flat strips behind, two or more inches wide, bending backward in their middle and fixed into the posts at each end. These constituted the back against which the sitter leaned. These frames were coarsely made of oak, maple, ash, or other hard and strong wood often unpainted and generally unvarnished. Their seats or bottoms were usually woven of flags, which were very destructible under wear and pressure and needed frequent repair or entire replacement.[1] There were men skilled in such work, who easily restored the

1. Ed.: Flag in this context is almost certainly not iris but cattails (*Typha latifolia*).

failing bottoms to primitive order. But apparently these were more, perhaps much more, expensive seats than those of wood. Some of these perpendicularly framed chairs had seats of split wood or basket work. These, though sufficiently strong and durable, were rough and destructive to the garments of the sitters.

Parlor and Chamber Chairs

Other better and more costly chairs were in the sitting rooms, parlors, and chambers. These usually had wooden seats made of plank, round or roundish, somewhat hollowed for ease of sitting. They were of hard wood, of the nicer kinds, maple, birch, etc. The legs and the other parts were turned, sometimes elegantly. The legs were inserted into the bottom of the seat; they were sufficiently strong, but not so large as those of the kitchen chairs, and generally inclining outward, so as to give the chair a wider base on the floor than the seat. These legs were held in their direction and prevented from spreading by cross rounds or rods fixed at each end into one of the legs in front and back and at the sides. The back was composed of two posts, one on each back corner, of nearly the size of the legs; at the top, one or more [crosspieces] connected these main pillars, and several smaller rods passed from the seat behind up to these crosspieces. The whole leaned somewhat backward. These chairs were painted of various colors and varnished and sometimes striped with other colors. There were many kinds of these wooden chairs, as to the back especially, the rounds and their means of support. In some the side pillars of the back were of one piece of wood, bent in and out at the top, and the ends inserted into the seat at the back corners. The intermediate rods ran from the back of the seat to the arch above. In these and the other chairs, these upright rods were two, or two and a half, inches apart, and then they gave a comfortable support to the back of the sitter.

Arm Chair

In these the upper part was continued around [from] the sides, in a semicircle, to the front, which alone was left open to the sitter. This [upper part], as high as the shoulders or higher at the back only, at the sides reached only to the elbow, with a cover for the rounds there, on which the sitter's arm would rest. The arm chairs for the kitchen and for rougher use were similar in coarse and strong architecture to the smaller chairs in that department. They had four very stout legs, one and a half, sometimes two, inches in diameter. The rear parts went up high enough for the back and the front, as high as the elbow, eight or ten inches above the seat. Their bottoms were usually of flags, sometimes of basket work, rarely of wood. Some people rocked in these, throwing themselves forward on the front legs and backward on the rear legs, coming down on either with a great jar or noise.

Arm chairs for parlors and other use were but extensions of these smaller chairs, made for similar purposes. They had the high back of rods and pillars running from the seat below to the cross top or arch above, and the arms of the sides of similar means. These were of manifold form and combinations: some were deep and some very narrow in the seat, which was generally of wood. We had two arm chairs for the parlor, like those before described, very strong, not deep nor easy. They were like many in the houses of the people of the time. The chair arms were one and a half or two inches wide for the arms and elbows to rest upon. These were very strong. The legs below were held firmly in their position by rods—before, behind, and at the sides—the ends of which were inserted into the [legs]. The back parts were connected together by cross pieces of thin, flat boards, bent backward, to give a comfortable support to the human frame. Thus these chairs were very strong and could bear very hard usage. All the comfortable stuffed easy chairs, with or without rockers, are of comparatively late introduction.

Sofa

This also is of modern creation. It was hardly known in Concord in the first years of this century, and very few were there even as late as 1825. Now very few comfortable families are without one, and some have more.

Easy Chair

There is one other chair worth mentioning. By a singular perversion of language it is called [an] easy chair. Intended for the rich and feeble, or the next resting place after the bed, it was large, strong, awkward, [and] built of heavy materials firm enough to bear the jolt of travel over rough roads. It was erect behind and at the sides, with arms for the elbows. The sides and back and seat [were] all at right angles. It was stuffed and lined, but the cushioning was very hard, and with all efforts it was impossible for the well and the strong to find an easy position in it. My father had one of these chairs. It is now in the family of my nephew, and from the little use it can be put to, it is likely to last ages. In the first century, settles were very common in the farmer's kitchen. These were plain board seats, 6 feet long, with back also of boards, as high as one's head. These were placed on one side of the large fireplace. The kitchens were large and somewhat loose. The outer door opened directly to the air. There was very great pressure of air or even wind toward the great fire, so this high back of the settle was needed to protect the people, when sitting there, from the cold. Indeed the whole means of resting the weary body is very greatly in advance of such as were enjoyed by our fathers and by their contemporaries. These settles had almost disappeared at my earliest observation. There were then a very few in the oldest families, and no new ones were made. They were uncomfortable to the sitter on account of their perpendicular backs and narrow seats. They were very heavy and in the way, but they served a good purpose in the days of poverty, and then disappeared.

A few of the old families, not the farmers of Concord but the more ambitious, had mahogany chairs with seats cushioned and covered with leather which were fastened to the frame or to the seat of the chair, with brass tacks all around. Some of these have come down to us as relics of older time. They were very elaborately made, with some carvings and much cabinet work in the border. They had cross bars between the legs in front and back and at both sides, to give them firmness. The modern mahogany chairs, with no cross bars between the legs, depend entirely on the perfectness of the joiner's work for their support. These were not then known. I rarely saw them before I left college, in 1826. Now these are in every modern family, both mechanics' and farmers'. *Cane seat chairs* are also a comparatively late improvement. We had them on our marriage in 1834, and they were then in many houses, and now they are universal. They were much easier than the wooden or the flag or basket-seated chairs. They gave a better support to the frame.

Beds

In earliest times the bed supports were of the rudest structure such as the means of the people would permit; as soon as possible they began to make frames rude indeed but strong enough to support the sleeper. Those of the period, within my earliest observation, were usually of oak, or any other hard wood. Those for ordinary family use were low, with posts about 2 feet high; the rails were of the same material. The posts were generally painted, often plain; the rails [were] of the natural wood color. These were pierced with holes about 6 or 7 inches apart, and cords through these holes ran across the frame from side to side and from end to end. Thus they formed a network for the bed to be on. It was needful that these ropes be drawn as tightly as possible, to give a firm and unyielding support to the bed. For this purpose it was necessary to have a *bed-winch* and pin by which the cords could be drawn closely and fastened. These instruments were in every neighborhood. My mother had them and frequently lent them to the people about her.

For the best or guest chamber, those who could afford it had a bedstead of mahogany with posts 6 or 7 feet high and on the top of these a frame for the support of curtains. Some of these frames were flat or horizontal; more generally [they were] arched, the centre reaching nearly to the ceiling. Later what were called French beds with posts 3 or 4 feet high were introduced. These were not of oak, but of maple, birch or other fine wood, sometimes of mahogany. Those who could, used them in all their chambers. My brother (1817–1822) and I (1822–1826) had the older form of bedsteads in college, and ours were in general character [similar] to those of other students in Cambridge at the time. More recently sacking bottoms [have been] introduced. A piece of sacking 3 or 4 inches wide was fastened to the inner, upper edge of the rails at the ends and on one side. There were eyelet holes on the inner edge of this. The main sacking was nearly large enough to fill the space between these lines of sacking attached to the rails. This was attached to one of the side rails and reached within 5 or 6 inches of the sacking attached to the ends and the other side rail. This had, on its three free edges, eyelet holes corresponding to those in the strips on the rails. Then the side and end strips and the main centre were laced by cords and drawn as nearly together as possible. This gave a firm foundation for the bed and the sleepers. In some beds narrow strips of thin boards were laid 4 or 5 inches apart. These were thin, somewhat elastic, and strong enough to support the weight of two persons. The beds, universally for rich and for poor, for family and company, consisted of one sack filled with hay or straw, generally the latter. This was at the bottom. A feather bed was at the top and nearest to the sleeper. In the summer, generally people reversed this order, and put the feather bed at bottom, and the straw bed at top. This was cooler and more comfortable. The straw and the feathers were enclosed in simple sacks, and needed much care to keep them equally distributed, so as to make a level bed for the lodger. This was disturbed by his inevitable movements in the night, and was daily readjusted by the chambermaid. To remedy this and give a permanent condition of these beds, mattresses were made [with] threads or cords running through from the opposite surfaces [which] held the contents in their place and thus they were kept even and smooth, undisturbed by the motions of the lodger. These mattresses were filled with many kinds of material: straw, husks, and other vegetable matter, and [were] used both for underbeds and for the upper bed, in near contact with the body of the sleeper. These were very useful and made in large quantities at shops and factories. Nevertheless the great body of the farmers, mechanics, and other country families clung to the primitive beds of straw and feathers. *Hair mattresses* are a comparatively modern invention. I first saw one in college, in some of the officers' rooms; they have gradually crept into use among people who care more for health and comfort, I think. They are very generally used among such now. I doubt not most such families in the village have them. Except when abroad, I have not slept in any other for perhaps 40 years. Spring beds or mattresses resting on springs of coiled wire are now much used by those who can afford them. They add to the comfort when well made, but otherwise they are painful to the sleepers.

Bedding

In early times the sheets were of linen, of domestic manufacture. Women spun the flax and wove it, or caused it to be woven on domestic looms, into cloth for sheeting, pillow cases, towels and for underclothing, both for men and women. Young women before marriage thus prepared themselves with their proper outfit in this way for housekeeping. American cotton was not known then, and India cotton was expensive. Later cotton bedding came into almost universal use. Blankets were all spun and woven at home. Besides these, *bed quilts* were in general, perhaps universal, use. These were of double thickness, the inner, a lining made of some old blankets worn nearly out; the outer cover was usually of patch work, [i.e.] old garments cut up and made into square or fancy shapes of many colors and sewed together. Between these two was a thin layer of wadding of wool, and the whole quilted throughout. This was a very heavy and not a very warm covering for the bed. This kind of quilt has gone almost out of use. Few or none have been made within the present generation and are to be found only in the older families. Their place is taken by a kind made of cotton or silk covering, wadded with cotton. These are much lighter covers and more comfortable. A pleasant fashion of the quilt was formerly in use. This was called the *album quilt*. When a young woman was about to be married, her female friends sometimes combined to make such a bed covering. Each one contributed a square, circle, or other form of calico, muslin, or silk, with a small piece of white cloth sewed on it, and on this was written the giver's name. These were all sewed together and formed the outer covering, and this with the lining and the wadding between was quilted in such manner as was thought proper. This then was used on the bed in the guest chamber or elsewhere as a life-long memorial of the affection and sympathy of the friends of the housekeeper when she began her new responsibility. There were other kinds of bed coverings made at home, in checks, or plaids, in white and blue or yellow, as our mother happened to have of the yard for the weaver. Subsequently quilts or coverings were made at factories and sold at stores, and generally [were] improvements on their predecessors.

Tables

Every kitchen had, as now it has, its washing table of pine, made generally by a carpenter. This was strong and capable of bearing much heavy pressure and shaking. On this, the bread was made and moulded, the meat cut and the vegetables prepared. There was also usually a larger table made of pine or some firm and harder wood. This was for the purpose of eating and was [put to] various uses according to the exigencies of the family. Nearly all farmers' and mechanics' families ate, 30 years ago, in the kitchen; and those of any class who did not eat there, ate in their sitting room or parlor. I do not remember a room devoted exclusively to eating in any house in Concord, in my early days, and even among the most ambitious there were very few dining rooms in the town. The dining table was constantly in the ordinary living room usually standing against the wall. But in some it was kept in another room in the entry and carried in at meal times. Besides this, the family that ate in sitting rooms or parlor [was] provided with a crumb cloth, to be spread on the floor under the table to catch the crumbs that might fall and thus prevent the soiling of the carpet. This cloth was of woolen, bocking,[2] or of some cotton or linen material. After eating, the table was cleared and removed, and the crumb cloth taken up and shaken out of doors and folded and laid away. In the parlor was usually a dining table of mahogany, which was 4 feet square, with two leaves, 15 inches wide, on the sides [which were] attached to a central part 18 inches wide. When in use the table was placed in the middle of the room and the leaves raised. One leg on each side, attached by a moveable arm to the centre, was turned out and gave a firm support to this leaf, and then the full 4 feet square of surface was made for the table furniture [dishes] and the food. After the meal was over and the table cleared, the moveable legs [were] returned to their places under the middle part, the leaves dropped, and the table reduced to a surface of four by one and a half feet. Then if there was a larger family or company than could sit round this table, it was necessary to put another by its side, for there were no extension tables, in those times, in Concord.

The card table was in a large part of the parlor. This as it stood by the wall usually under the looking glass, was about 3 or 3½ ft. long and 1½ feet wide, with four legs at the corners. The front corners were rounded. This table was double, of two leaves held together by hinges at the back side, and when taken away from the wall and one of the legs turned out, the upper half or leaf was turned over upon this leg, and the two leaves formed a square table with four rounded corners. This was of mahogany nicely finished and used (as its name indicates) for card playing when this amusement was much more common than it is now. This is an old piece of furniture and found only in old families. Probably none have been made for fifty years. I never see them in the modern families.

Centre Tables

Centre tables were circular or roundish with no leaves to turn up and down, [just] one unbroken surface. These stand in the middle of the room for books, working, reading, writing, etc. We had one at our marriage in 1834; most new housekeepers had them, and now they, or tables for similar purposes, are universal in sitting rooms or parlors of families that can afford them. They are of very many forms, with drawers, writing tables to be drawn out and other conveniences. Some

2. Ed.: Heavy cloth for use on floors, made in Bocking, England.

had circular tables in earlier times that were made to turn up on a hinge to the vertical position when not in use. There were other smaller tables for the chamber and bedsides as now.

Candle Stands

These, in almost every house in former times, were made of [a] single board, square or circular, about 12 to 15 inches in breadth or diameter. This little table rested on a single pedestal 1½ or 2 inches in diameter, and this rested on a tripod of three legs [with] feet branching outward. Those for the kitchen were of cherry tree or some other cheap wood, but the parlor stands were usually mahogany or cherry.

Table Furniture

Coarse, strong delftware (usually white, sometimes blue or other color and white) was in use in all farmers' families, also in mechanics' in Concord in the last century, and as far as I had an opportunity of seeing, this was the common table furniture—but nicer china was used for company. This was very delicate and was kept in the parlor closet or buffet. Both sets included all needful for dinner and supper and tea—coffee and tea pots, sugar bowl, cream pitcher and all the dishes for meats and vegetables, cake and puddings. (But farther back, before this, delft and crockery were for dinner, pewter plates and platters were used, and still farther remote, wooden plates were used for common purposes.) The knives and forks also were of two kinds: the coarse and strong for daily use, and the more delicate for extra occasions. Both were of steel. Silver and plated knives and forks were not known 50 or 60 years ago, except for a few. Iron spoons were used in the kitchen. In early times most families (and in later periods many poor families) used pewter and iron spoons, large and small, for all purposes in cooking and at table. Silver spoons, large and small, were universal, the size and quantity differing according to means and fashion. Glassware tumblers were not universal. In the time of cider drinking, the cider or water was put on the table in a mug, or, earlier, in a tankard of black tin or very rarely of silver. Each one drank from the mug or tankard. Dr. Alden of Randolph now (1878) 90 years old, tells me that when he was in Harvard College (1804–1808) the students drank in this way at table. Comfortable families had decanters for spirits in their closets and on their sideboards, from which they served their company in tumblers or wine glasses. Castors[3] were not common in working families as old as my father's. We had a pepper box, a mustard pot and a vinegar cruet, a little glass bottle, holding about ⅜ of a pint. We never had catsup or oil or red pepper and had no vessel to hold them.

Dresser

Connected with [i.e., to hold] the table furniture, there was in most kitchens, certainly in the old houses, a set of shelves (on one side of the room and attached to it) called the dresser. This was, in my father's house, about 6 feet long and running up to the ceiling. Under these shelves was often a closet with two doors for pots and kettles, pans, etc. This was about 18 inches deep and 2½ feet high. Over this were the shelves, the lower one of the same depth of the closets, but the other shelves were about 8 inches wide and 12 inches apart. On these shelves the table furniture was placed when not in use. In the parlor was a small closet, about 3 feet long, running across one corner of the room, closed below. In the upper part were several shelves running from side to side. Sometimes this open part had glazed doors. Here was kept the silver and glass and the chinaware used for company. In this closet was kept the cake box, green tea, loaf sugar and the nicer kinds of stores.

Shovel and Tongs

The parlor usually had [a] handsome shovel and tongs, sometimes of steel, but usually of brass, kept very bright, as also the andirons of the same material, to correspond. The kitchen andirons and shovel and tongs were of iron, coarser and heavier. In some kitchens was a large iron shovel about 4 feet long with the blade about 8 inches square. This was especially used for the brick oven. Every kitchen had an oven, in which bread, pies and cake were baked.

Bellows

This article was necessary, and found in both parlor and kitchen, to blow up the coals in making the fire burn. It was made of two pieces of

3. Ed.: Cruets, or small pitchers, with their own rack.

Large parlor, The Old Manse, Concord. *Courtesy* Trustees of Reservations, Beverly, Massachusetts

board, the same size and shape, with folded leather between, to lift and close, which forced out the air through a nozzle of iron or brass. These were coarser or nicer, for parlor or kitchen, more or less ornamented, the leather tacked on with brass nails for the best ones, and iron nails for the common.

Carpets

Our forefathers were not able to cover their floors with carpets, as do their children and grandchildren of the present time. I remember that which was in my mother's parlor, in my boyhood. It was called a rag carpet, made of old woolen cloth, cut in very narrow strips, half an inch wide. These were sewn together and made into long strings, and woven as the filling. The warp was of threads of flax or cotton or wool, usually some of each. This filling was of different colors. Wool took a better dye than cotton or flax. These carpets were very durable and looked quite well. A few are now still in existence. My mother made one within my recollection. She prepared the materials and sent them to Mrs. Nehemiah Hunt on Punkatasket [*sic*] Hill, to be woven. This was a common kind of carpet, for most farmers' and mechanics' families. They were of various colors, some striped and some in checks. English carpets, woven in factories, came later, and were in families of the more wealthy and ambitious. Now there is hardly a house without carpets on all or nearly all the rooms. Many years ago, the kitchens and perhaps sitting rooms were sanded over, after being scoured with sand and water. The sand, when the floor was dry, was scattered all over the floor and the next day was carefully and lightly swept in herringbone shape, thus looking quite pretty.

Wall Paper

As far back as I can remember, the parlors and sitting rooms and guest chambers of most houses had paper on the walls. Some of these papers were very rich and heavy. Some were landscapes. Generally they were very plain and cheap.

Pianoforte

I think there were not more than three of these in town, at my early day. But they have now become very common. [See Appendix I.]

Pictures

The houses of our forefathers, even down to the first quarter of this century, were bare of pictures. In my father's house, there was not one upon the walls. Some old families had their coats of arms framed and glazed. Maj. Barrett had such, so also had Mrs. Reuben Hunt. These seem to have come down from their fathers. Probably other families had such. But these are all that I now remember. Dr. Ripley had some engravings of scripture scenes and of distinguished ministers or writers. I remember in one house a picture of Gen. Washington, with the 13 states characteristically represented (as Mass[achusetts] with an Indian and tomahawk, etc.,) surrounding him. This hung on the wall with wooden frames. Col. Hurd brought home from China some Chinese paintings which for many years adorned the walls of his father, Dr. Hurd's, parlor. I believe these [paintings] (sold at auction after Dr. Hurd's death) are still in Concord. In my senior year in College, I bought three engravings for 90 cents and pinned them to the paper on the wall of my room. Very few in college had pictures. In this matter there has been greater change than in other things. Pictures were formerly rare and expensive, few were printed and few for sale, and at a higher price than people thought they could afford. None [were] for sale at any store in Concord; [there were] few or no stores exclusively for these in Boston. Consequently few of any class and almost none of the farmers and mechanics had them in their houses. Now this is all changed. Pictures, engravings of nicer kind (steel and copper), lithographs, photographs and chromos have multiplied in marvelous degree and are for sale in many stores exclusively in the cities and at the book store in Concord at prices that put them within the reach of all. The Irish laborers adorn their walls with religious pictures, and all, in every degree of prosperity, indulge in them. Probably every farm house and mechanic's dwelling has them of some sort, and some have many to adorn every room. In my brother's house, where my father had none, there are from 4 to 18 in each of the rooms: parlor, sitting room, dining room, chambers, etc. [4] Of course the[y] are of various grades of excellence.

4. In October 1874, I counted the pictures in my nephew's (formerly my father's and lately my brother's) house. There were 78 on the walls.

C H A P T E R V

Personal influences of leading citizens' manners in early times. Want of mutual personal regard. Practical jokes. Hardy. Thomas Heald. Cruel jokes made and tolerated. Disrespect to the poor, the peculiar and unfortunate. Change of manners in this century. Elements of high character among the early inhabitants. Desire for education. Effect of college life of sons on homes. Concord youth in college. Concord college graduates. Clarification as to occupation. Youths in college. Pres. Eliot's opinion. College graduates living in Concord, 1878.

Morals and Manners of Concord

The people of Concord have justly had the reputation of superior culture and manners for several generations and especially for the last fifty years. Their constant grammar school has given a higher tone to education, which has been followed in some degree by the districts. The long and very efficient ministry of the excellent Dr. Ripley, the personal influence of Mr. Hoar and some other lawyers, and of Dr. Bartlett and Mr. Emerson (the more cultivated society of the village) have all had their weight in elevating the tone of manners and character of the whole people.

Whatever may be the moral and intellectual condition of the towns at the present time, 1878, it has been a matter of culture and growth from ruder states in preceding generations. Concord has had its due relation to the rest of the country, in the progress of civilization. It has passed through its coarser and less refined stages and manifested among its people some of the spirit that held and governed the people of other parts of the country. Among the characteristics of a ruder generation or people is a want of respect and tender regard for each other and each other's comfort and happiness. No inconsiderable portion of their enjoyment is in their verbal or practical jokes at others' expense. Saying or doing things that cause mortification or pain, "poking fun at each other," was the frequent amusement of many. This is seen in the books of anecdotes of the past century, in a large part of which something was said to cause a laugh at someone's expense and a corresponding mortification in the object. The wits took pride in their power to raise the laugh, and others—hearers and lookers-on—countenanced them by a laughing approval. This was not malice, not a desire to inflict pain, but it was wantonness, a willingness to let pain follow their keen and hard language.

In the same spirit were the practical jokes of the ruder generations. These were common within the reach of my traditionary information in the last of the early years of the present century. I heard much of these in my early youth, most of them had happened in the years gone by, but they were then fresh in the memory of my elder informants.

Practical Unkind Jokes

In the early part of this century and before, Mr. Ebenezer Hardy was a farmer in the East Quarter, 1 mile from the village. He was an irritable man of violent temper and much disliked, yet otherwise a respectable man. One night after dark, he called at Dr. Hurd's and tied his saddle horse to the post. There was a journeyman hatter of good standing among his class, but wanton and fond of playing tricks on others. He took a rope about 30–60 feet long, tied one end to Mr. Hardy's horse's fetlock, the other to the post.

Mr. Hardy mounted his horse, and with his usual impatience, struck him with his whip. The animal started on the canter, and when he reached the end of the rope he fell, and both animal and rider were somewhat injured. The hatter was so pleased with that feat that he boasted of it. He was arrested and tried and sentenced to jail for one month. He went cheerfully to his prison and expiated his crime, considering that he had done a noble deed and was the hero of the occasion and a martyr to his daring. He was not mortified nor depressed bur rather exhilarated and boastful. His friends seemed to so view his case. They visited and cheered him in prison. He had company at his window or the wicket of his door. They carried him many sorts of indulgences—pies, cakes, and things pleasant. He was the pet of his class and seemed to be upon exhibition for *his* world's gaze and admiration. So he and they seemed to think. When his sentence expired, his associates escorted him to his house, where he was kindly and affectingly received, as well as at his shop by his fellow workmen. He lost no caste. He was held in the same esteem as before. He did not feel punished, and the moral sense of the community at large, if it did not oppose his act, at least did not effectively condemn it.

Similar outrages were not unfrequent. The rowdy spirit of the wanton and reckless led them to much secret mischief—oversetting small out-buildings in the night, etc. These were mostly before my day, yet I remember when two of the old sleds which stood behind the meeting-house, down the slope of the Common near the pond, were tipped over into the water in the night.

In various other ways the class of rowdy young men manifested their disposition to create discomfort. They were inclined to drink and have their sprees, but these were not limited to mere indulgence of their appetite. Abel Davis kept an indifferent tavern on the Carlisle road where the late Abel and Thomas Davis, his sons, lived and died. This was much the haunt of drinking men from Concord and Acton. Thomas Heald was then, 70 to 80 or more years ago, a lawyer in Concord. He lived in the house where Deacon Tolman and his son necessarily have lived for more than 60 years. He was fond of rioting sprees and was (according to tradition) a frequent leader in such ways. He and his companions went frequently to Mr. Davis' tavern and were in [the] habit of endeavoring to give him trouble. His supplies were uncertain, and they would discover what he was out of and then ask for that and urge him to send to town to get it. But when they could see the messenger returning with the deficient article, they would plead great haste and the impossibility of waiting for the matter and leave the tavern. They prowled about the house [even] into the kitchen, pried into the works going on there, looked into the pots over the fire, and sometimes put things into them. It was said that they once put a kitten into a boiling pot. They told of these tricks themselves and even boasted of their feats of this nature as if they were praiseworthy acts.

The moral sense of the community did not approve nor did it effectively condemn them, and some [who] would not engage in nor give any encouragement to them would yet consider these tales as proper means of entertaining their friends or others.

In my early life I many times heard of a witticism of Mr. Heald. He and his associates were having a spree at the Middlesex (this tavern was then kept by Maj. Paine) in a room by themselves. They called several times for more liquor and were quite noisy. Maj. Paine the host went to their rooms and reproved them for their needless uproar. They promised better manners and asked for a new supply of drink, which was sent by Phin[eas] Harrington, then a little waiter in the tavern. They laughed at the little boy and abused him so that he cried and went to the major and told him of their ill treatment. Maj. P. was indignant and went to the room and spoke to them very severely in condemnation of their bad conduct. The party heard him with apparent indifference. They did not seem to feel any compunction for their conduct when the major said such treatment of a little boy was not to be borne in the house, however much their riot and noise were to be tolerated. To all this Mr. Heald answered with the utmost coolness, "Put him in the bill." To this the company roared in laughter. They seemed to think this outweighed all their rowdiness and unkindness to the boy. And the story was told freely abroad. The witticism was put forth as full compensation for all the vulgarity and cruelty of the occasion.

These things occurred before my age of observation. I knew of them from tradition. But they represent the unruly spirit of a class in the town and probably in the state before the end of the last century and beginning of this. They passed away, and their sad history was not repeated. Nevertheless the towns and the world were not completely and at once relieved of this sort of wantonness. I remember two young men, kindhearted, gentlemanly in a general way, who walking one night after ten o'clock came to the house of Mr. Kettel, an old baker, 75–80 years old. He baked a little bread which he sold at his house. It was late. The family were all in bed. It was a frosty evening in November. They knocked at the door. Mr. Kettel got up [and] came to his chamber window. They said they were foot-travellers and very hungry and wished for food. He came down in his night dress, brought a basket with cakes and biscuit to the door. They examined all his offered eatables, found fault with each, and the price, and after keeping him shivering with the cold, they bought one cent's worth and went home, which was within a half mile of Mr. K's. They told of this feat as a good and very proper joke and entertained their friends with their descrip-

48 Walden Street, Concord

tion of Mr. K's uncomfortable position almost naked and cold. These men were not malicious. They did not intend to be cruel. But they were wanton and found plenty of sympathy among their associates.

And still the desire to make fun of others—the weak, the odd, the unfortunate—was common; to create a laugh at their expense seemed to gratify the bold and the sharp and to find encouraging approval in others that saw and heard.

Ben Stearns was a stage owner, bold and unrefined. In my early boyhood I saw him on horseback in the angle of the meeting of Walden and Main Streets. There was a small collection around him, and in their midst was a poor, thin, intemperate, timid fellow, Luther Osborne. Stearns was taunting, abusing, insulting him, and he had not power or courage to resist. The spectators were enjoying the scene. They laughed at Stearns's jokes, approved his insolence, and he, the hero of the occasion, found his encouragement in their sympathy.

Yet Stearns did not intend to be cruel. He too was wanton, and the people that gathered about him were also wanton and careless in their sympathies.

Disrespect for the Poor and Unfortunate

It was common for some boys and even rude men to throw ridicule, even insults, on certain men for their foibles, their misfortunes or their faults. Mr. John Stone was a glazier, simple, honest, but not dignified and very quick in movement. He walked with a jerk. He was called *Hop Stone* and jeered on account of this peculiarity. Brister Freeman was a passionate negro, profane and suspicious. He was said to have once stolen a haddock and was therefore tormented and hooted by boys. Then he would swear and storm. This gathered boys and men about him who insulted and violated him to greater passion. This want of respect for humanity and disregard of men's feelings was extended to many of these classes of the weak, and the higher cultured had not power or did not see their way to overcome it. They did not approve nor encourage these waywardnesses, but they endured and even found amusement in relating them to their families and neighbors. It must not be supposed that these were indications of the whole moral being and manners of the people. Besides and contemporaneous with these, there was abundant kindness and pleasant feeling and bearing probably in a higher degree than in the average of the towns of New England.

These manifestations of the lower, moral element passed away with the early years of this century, and the frolics of this coarser sort ceased. This lowest stratum of society ceased to exist as such, while the upper advanced its greater culture. Nevertheless the fun of the ruder continued in less painful way[s] and then found pleasure in the laugh at each other, yet with gentler means than in the generation that had passed away.

The presence of families of high culture, the refinement of their social influence, the sympathy of the favored classes with the other— all these wrought a good work in the town, and Concord gradually became what it now is, one of the most cultivated towns in New England. Another characteristic is the harmony of all classes, the people of the village with the farmers in the outer districts, the highly educated with the less disciplined and learned.

Social parties are held at the town hall to which all the people are invited to come—they, their wives and their children. There they assemble in their best attire, all equal, all agreeable, and all in pleasant feelings toward each other. All are requested to bring some food for the occasion as far as perfectly convenient, but all are asked to partake as far as their appetite may allow them.

These gatherings of the people (generally, almost universally, meeting in the best sympathies and confidence) increase the mellowness and the polish of the people and make their mutual appreciation more and more easy and happy.

Elements of Character in Early Ages

The first settlers of Concord and their children through successive generations had among them the elements of high character. There were among them men of great intelligence and moral worth and even of educational ambition for their children. They early provided school for all, and when they had fifty families they conformed to the law and opened a grammar school where boys and girls could be taught the higher branches of knowledge and opportunity offered for preparation for entering college.

One of the first manifestations of this character was the desire of some families to send their sons to Harvard College. Within these years after the first adventurers had arrived in Concord and built their cabins in the sand bank under the hill in 1638, their minister, Rev. Peter Bulkeley, sent his son to the college at Cambridge, and in the next year, 1639, his associate, Rev. John Jones, sent also a son to the college. Mr. Bulkeley afterward sent two other sons. This was a great beginning which was followed by others of their people, and their example has been followed in all the generations through the two hundred and forty years to the present time, 1878. During this period, one hundred and three of the sons of Concord have received a college education.

Concord College Graduates

Mr. Shattuck, in his *History*, page 240, has given the names and some amount of the origin and life of the Concord graduates from 1652 to the time of his writing, 1835. I have completed the list to the present time. [See Appendix II.]

Effect of Life in College on the Family and Friends at Home

The good influence of college education is not confined to the immediate recipient. The life and experience of the student in college are carried to his home in his corner of residence by himself in his visits and his vacations. The family became familiar with the conditions and the associations and interested in the advantages, the elevated purposes of the institution of learning. And thus they, in some degree, share in the development of their son and brother. These sentiments, ideas, and feelings are diffused from house to house in the neighborhood. College is no longer a stranger to these people of the country, nor is its influence lost upon them. The presence of our youth in that desirable place opens the way for others. Public education and professional life seem to be as valuable for the brother of the college student and to the sons of others families as to him who is already in the process of attainment and to them, they seem to be as near and as attainable as to him. The neighbors and their sons see that their friend has found the way and overcome the difficulties of labor, preparation and the cost; they can do these as easily and gain the prize of educated and elevated life as well as he. Here they are inspired with the same desire and animated with the same hope and take the same steps. So the mere fact of going to college tends to create its own repetition, and the more a town send its sons, the more it is inclined to send them and to find the courage and the means to bear the labor and the cost. Not only is the influence of the college felt in the character of the people at home, but the power of this domestic character is manifested in the students from the town in the college.

Rev. Dr. Peabody, Professor of Morals and Pastor of Harvard College, assures me that the Concord boys and young men that have been in the college have held a high rank as gentlemen and generally as scholars. He had not seen but one failure in moral character. He felt, whenever one came from Concord, the college had a youth of high aim and true purpose of life.

CHAPTER VI

Relation of parents and children in olden times. Old notions of school discipline which precedes teaching rude boys. Masters from Harv[ard] College. Mr. Paige. Severe punishments. Approval by the people. Cruelty and offensiveness of punishments. Coarseness of some masters. Discipline ameliorated. Bodily punishment needless. Lax discipline of some masters. Uproarious boys. Love. Self-respect takes place of flogging. Teaching. Reading books. Writing. Books. Ruler. Plummet. Pens. Arithmetic. Manuscript. Adams's Arithmetic. Algebra. Geography. Grammar. Composition. Declamation. Latin and Greek. Manners. Dancing. Bowing in and out. District School. Schoolhouses. Seats. Desks. Heating. Ventilation.

Schools of Concord

From the beginning Concord had a high reputation for its schools, and this reputation is well founded on the character and management of the institutions. As soon as the early settlers had built their cabins for shelter, they built a larger one for public worship, and next followed the school cabin where the children could be taught to read and write. The early law of the Province required every town of fifty families to maintain a grammar school. As soon as the town had that number of families, it complied with the law and opened a perpetual school, in which any or all children could be taught reading, writing, arithmetic, grammar and the Latin and Greek languages. This school has continued, in various forms, up to the present time and, with its

School at Nine Acre Corner, Concord

coadjutors in the several districts, has wrought a good work for the civilization and culture of the people.

The schools were necessarily modified by the opinions of the times. In the earlier and ruder ages the relations between the governors and the governed were in a great measure those of power on one side and submission on the other. The rulers must have sufficient force and authority to compel obedience, and the ruled had only their choice to obey the law or suffer its penalties. This also entered into the family government. Parents governed by authority rather than sympathy or affection. It was common in England within a hundred years to call their father not "Parents" or "Father" but "Governor." A friend of mine who was born in the latter part of the last century used to tell me that his father was kind and supplied all his wants yet gave him no sympathy and familiarity, and he always looked up to him with simply distant respect and fear.

The schools came under this category. The prevailing idea seemed to have been prominently that the [students] had to be governed. This condition seemed to take precedence over the idea of teaching, for without good government all attempts at teaching would be unavailing. Hence the head of the school was always called School *Master*, or one who governed the pupils, and even now this term is retained although its signification is very much softened and expanded.

In the purpose then of exercising his proper authority when he began school, every master armed himself with a *ferule*. This was an instrument of mahogany, walnut, oak, maple or thin strong wood, eighteen to twenty-four inches long, one and a half to two inches wide, [and] three-eighths to four-eighths inches thick. For each of my four winter schools and my town school in Concord, I provided myself with this instrument of discipline.

The ferule was used by striking the boy on the palm of the hand, which, like the Turkish bastinade on the sole of the feet, inflicts very great suffering. There were other means of punishment resorted to by various masters to which I will refer hereafter. When the master came into the school daily, he took out and laid upon his desk such books and other matters as he wanted, including the ferule, which was plainly, conspicuously on the desk in sight of the scholars.

This show and exercise of authority by means of force when occasion required created among the scholars a general sentiment rather of fear than of love, and among those not amicable or easily disciplined there was often a spirit of antagonism towards the master. In some schools there were large and rude boys who were impatient under the authority of the master and were restive under the discipline which was imposed upon them. This amounted sometimes to open quarrels with the larger scholars who thought themselves too near manhood to be punished and [who] resisted with violence the attempts of the master thus to control them.

In earlier times of this (and in the last) century, there were traditions of masters being turned out of the schoolhouse by combinations of the larger and insubordinate boys. I never heard of such an instance in Concord; nevertheless feruling, and flogging, and other means of punishment which we should now call cruel, were resorted to as means of government during all my experience as a scholar.

For more than a century, the masters of the Common School were graduates just from college, mostly from Cambridge, who taught school not as a permanent profession but to get money to carry out their purposes of professional study. Most of the these taught one year; only a very few taught two or three years.

My earliest recollection was of Elijah F. Paige, who graduated at Cambridge in 1810 and came immediately to the Concord school. He taught one year. I was then seven years old and went to his school all that year. He was a man of great force of character and an excellent scholar and teacher. He was a magnetizer and inspired the school with a love of study and they made great progress under his care, but his great reputation was as a disciplinarian, which was justly founded, for he punished very frequently and severely. He seemed to be very hard on the dull scholars and the bad boys, and his management did not improve them. He was very tall—six feet and several inches high. His desk was on the platform two steps (about sixteen inches) above the main floor, but he had another desk made and placed on the top of this desk, at which he could stand and write. The top of this must have been six feet or more from the floor. There was a large boy, whose name I have now forgotten, who lived with Dr. Hurd. He was willful, disobedient, and it seemed to me the object of Mr. Paige's especial desire to flog him into good behavior. I have seen Mr. Paige take this boy, take off his coat, then tie him by his hands to the top of the desk with a rope so high that his feet could not touch the floor. Then with rods which he had sent for, to be cut from the willow trees back of the schoolhouse on the borders of the brook, he flogged him with many blows while thus suspended. I have seen him take William Mann, who was not a good boy and whom the master endeavored to convert by similar ungentle means, sit him down on the dirty floor in the presence of all the scholars, make him draw his knees up to his breast and his heels to his hips and bend his head down to his knees and thus reduce him to as compact a mass as possible, then in this condition he took a very long cord and wound it around him in every direction, so that he was hardly more than a ball that might be rolled over, helpless and [with his] limbs immobile.

Nevertheless, Mr. Paige was very popular and acceptable to the town authorities and people, and when he left I recollect no one whose departure was more regretted than his. Next followed Mr. Simeon Putnam. His advent was preceded by great alarm among the boys. He was a man of very highly cultivated musical taste and an accomplished singer, and [he] led the music in church during his residence in Concord. Before he came, it was rumored among the boys that he had such a delicate love for music and sound that he could tell exactly in which seat any whisper was made in any part of the schoolhouse, whether he was looking that way or not. Nevertheless he came. He was strict indeed but not severe. He taught a good school but had not the power either for good or evil of his predecessor.

Mr. John Brown, a native of Concord, taught in 1813 and 1814. He was not a man of personal dignity and failed to interest the school as some of his predecessors had. From my early recollection till the last of my school days in 1820, the discipline of the school grew more mild and effective. The gentler and more affectionate treatment of the scholars had a better influence over them and won them more to a cooperation in the purposes of the school than the severity previously practised. Nevertheless some of the earlier severity was practised—feruling and flogging—and sometimes the erring boy was compelled to go to the willows and cut the rod for his own punishment. Boys were sometimes very willful [and] some tried to appear as heroes before the whole school. I remember one such boy, handy, tough, good natured, with a large love of approbation. He was a frequent trespasser and the object of the master's apparent dislike. One day the master feruled him with very great severity. The boy bore it unflinchingly and with quietness. When the master had finished, the boy looked him in the face with most insolent composure [and] said in a tone which he meant to have all the school hear, "Thank you sir, I feel much refreshed." He felt himself the hero of the occasion; he rejoiced in his conspicuousness and the praises the boys gave him afterwards. Certainly in this case the master was not the victor.

Besides the feruling and flogging, there were many other means of corporeal punishment practiced by the masters in the schools. Sometime a boy was required to stand on the floor and hold out [one arm] horizontally, at extreme length, with a heavy book in his hand, and if from weariness the arm should fall from its horizontal position, the master with a blow of his ferule would remind him of his delinquency. Sometimes the boys were taken by the collar and shaken about the floor with great violence. Sometimes the master would box the ears a hard blow. Another form—boys were required to stand on the platform of the master's desk and bow the head under the desk and hold it there, with his legs from the hip to the foot erect. This was a very painful position, but the boys were required to continue it as long as they could possibly bear it. The bottom of the desk was twenty-four inches from the floor. The average height of the boy's hip joint from the sole of the foot was, of those 9 years old, 27 inches.

10 y. old	28.54 inches
11 y. old	30.00 inches
12 y. old	31.36 inches
13 y. old	32.64 inches
14 y. old	33.82 inches

Measurement of Boys in Inches[1]

Age	Sole to Hipjoint	Bottom of Spine to Top of Head	Bottom of Spine to First Vertebra
9	27.00	24.41	17.05
10	28.58	25.24	17.68
11	30.00	26.02	18.31
12	31.38	26.77	18.85
13	32.64	27.52	19.45
14	33.82	28.27	20.00

When a boy stands with his legs erect and bows his body to a right angle with them, the top of his horizontal back and head is 2 to 2½ inches higher than his hip joint. Then the *horizontal* or upper surface of the back and head would for the ages 9, 10, 11, 12, 13, 14 be from the floor 5, 6, 8, 9, 10, or 11 inches higher than the under surface of the desk, and he must bend his head and neck so many inches below his hip joint and the horizontal line in order to fit them under the desk. This was a distressing position and very hard to be retained. In another form of punishment the boys were ordered to sit on the floor, under the master's desk, which was two feet high. The distance from the bottom of the spine or the seat of the boy on the floor was, in inches:

Age	Neck	Top of Head
9	17.11	24.41
10	17.68	25.26
11	18.31	26.02
12	18.86	26.77
13	19.45	27.52
14	20.00	28.27

None of these could sit erect. He must bend the head down from one-half inch to four and a quarter inches.

Some of the Masters, one certainly, was coarse and far from neat and even vulgar in some of his habits. He had occasion to relieve himself of the saliva of his mouth and the mucus of his nostrils and he had no spittoon and he neglected the use of his pocket handkerchief, so the floor was made the substitute for both. I well remember a circumstance illustrating the class of punishment last described and this unfortunate habit of the Master. John Horn, a boy from Canada about 14 years old, was sent to Concord to enjoy the benefit of this school.

1. This is taken from Quetélet's *Tables de mortalite* [Bruxelles, 1872]. The measurement is of Belgian children and probably represents ours.

He ordinarily behaved well, but for some transgression he was ordered to sit under the desk. But the Master could neither persuade nor compel him to do so, and after a long and ineffectual struggle with the boy he concluded to appeal to the school committee to aid him in overcoming this resistance to his orders. The committee came, there were three of them, Dr. Ripley, Dr. Heywood and the third I have forgotten. The boy was called out before them and the Master gave the account of the whole matter. The committee seemed satisfied that the Master was right and the boy wrong. They told the boy that he must obey the Master's orders, for the rules of the school must be enforced. The boy said that he would not sit under the desk. The committee asked him why he refused! He answered, "I will not sit down in that *spit* and *snot* which is all over the floor under the desk." I have no positive recollection of the result. My impression is that the committee seemed to think that the boy was right, but the authorities always sustained the government of the school.

These severe punishments were supposed to be in obedience to the Law of Solomon[2] and were in accordance with the general spirit of the times. There was occasional complaint from parents of the severe punishment of their sons but the community generally imputed this to the parental partiality and sustained the master. Nevertheless, with the progress of the age, the ideas of the government at home and at school were gradually ameliorated. Punishment became more and more mild and less frequent.

I taught this school in 1826–7. I was not quite ready to discard corporeal punishments, and yet I made some use of these means of government. I corrected with a ferule, yet mildly, for I was not then perfectly satisfied with the principle that the infliction of pain upon the human body was a proper way of gaining love and respect from the scholars, or creating in him a willingness to obey the law. I well remember the case of one boy who was willful and unyielding. It seemed my duty to compel him to conform his habits to the requirements of the school, but all in vain. It had no good effect but rather the contrary on his feelings and conduct. Another boy of 14, ordinarily of unquestionable propriety of life, once with several smaller boys transgressed a rule which was necessary for the administration of the school. Doubtless he did this from forgetfulness. I did not want to

2. "He that spareth the rod hateth his son. He that loveth him chastiseth him betimes" Prov. 13th 24th.

punish him, but as it seemed necessary for the good of the school that I should punish the others, I could find no way of escaping punishing him with the rest, but he bore the infliction with such mild and dignified submission as if he concurred in the propriety of it that I was glad when it was over. He is now a respectable citizen of Concord, and I never see him without sorrow for the pain I inflicted. And looking back from my later point of view upon this part of my administration, I recollect no instance in which with my later sentiments I might not have produced a better influence on the boy's mind and character without resorting to the infliction of bodily pain.

And now looking over the whole, I think the good order of the school was not in proportion to the multiplicity of the number and severity of the punishments. But where physical force was used the least, where tact took the place of force, where the Masters appealed to the self-respect of the scholars rather than their fears, when the scholars were treated with the most courtesy and affection as was the case when Mr. Samuel Barrett taught the school in 1818–19, there was the best order, the greatest propriety of conduct, and the best development of character.

Some masters seemed to have the power to win and persuade all the scholars to cooperate in all their purposes from the love of order and study as did Mr. Barrett. Some others, unfortunately, and I may say, unconsciously, by their want of tact and incapacity to appeal to the right motives of action, seem to provoke the scholars to opposition and contempt of authority and to wantonness of behavior. Under one master, I now recollect, the school was a frequent scene of disorder, almost of uproar. Boys, apparently accidentally but probably intentionally, would let their slates and rulers drop on the floor, and this was repeated by others sometimes in rapid succession. The lids of the boxes [desks], two in a seat, were made of such imperfect carpentry that when partly raised they would rub against each other with a harsh grating sound. At such boxes one [boy] would often raise his lid, when the other was shutting his down and thus [there would be] produced this loud and unpleasant noise. The boys in shutting their lids down were not careful to do this lightly, but on the contrary were careful to do it with a force that produced a sound that might be heard all over the room. Excepting the back row, the seats were fixed to the desk behind them. As these were not firmly fixed to the floor, the boy sitting in front could easily, through carelessness or wantonness, press or strike against the desk behind him and shake it so as to disturb the one who was writing on it. Then the one attempting to write would cry out, "He is joggling, sir." This was frequently heard in the school. Added to these means of confusion, some of the boys would have a persistent cough. The epidemic was contagious—it seemed as if almost every boy was seized with an irrepressible coughing. I remember seeing the Master and how distressed he looked, unable to discriminate between the cough of disease and the cough of intention, or between the unavoidable noise of accident and that of design. He saw no way to overcome the uproar except by punishment and being unable to discern between the innocent and guilty sometimes chastised the one who should have gone free. This, reacting on the boys, increased the irritation and the willingness (even desire) to join in the disturbance [at] the next opportunity.

Sometimes the boy, missing his ruler, would complain aloud to the Master, "Some one has got my ruler," whereupon the master would call aloud to the whole school, "The one who has got this boy's ruler must bring it to the desk." Then the boys all over the room would hold up their rulers and cry out, "Is this it, is this it?"

I was ordinarily a well-behaved boy, but I had a better reputation than I deserved. Mr. Jones had built a triphammer at his mill on the dam, and I had imitated it with my little water wheel in my father's garden. There was an occasion to gratify my mechanical taste which I perhaps could not, certainly I did not, forego. I took a strip of shingle an inch and a half wide, and about twelve inches long and with a nail through a hole about two inches from one end, fixed it to the inner wall in the farther side of my box about half way from top to bottom but so loosely that either end would move. I then fixed a string to the short end of the shaft which I passed through a hole I made in the bottom of the box down to the floor with a loop to go round the foot. Then with a slight motion of the foot I could pull the string and cause the long end of the hammer to strike against the roof of the box and by relaxing the foot allow it to strike on the bottom. Then while my arms with apparent innocence were visible on the desk, I could add the clatter of my triphammer to the general confusion, whenever the occasion seemed to invite, without being suspected. But although this noisy experiment was mechanically successful, I did not enjoy it. I felt guilty and soon took the triphammer down and left the work of turmoil to others who by uselessness allowed it to happen, or willfully produced it.

Derby School

In the winter of 1834–35 there was a marked instance of the power and temper of the masters to have a riotous or a quiet and orderly school in the Derby District, now No. 4. The first master began as usual in the early part of December and proposed to govern with severe discipline. This seemed to provoke the boys to opposition and all sorts of riotous conduct. He endeavored to reduce them to order by force. He feruled and flogged 10–12 a day. The parents made great complaints to us of the committee. At length about the 1st of January the committee went there in a body. The master, the complaining boys, and parents were asked to be present. There was a very large meeting. The people and children presented their complaints. There was clear proof that all the charges of frequent and severe punishment were true, and on the other hand it was manifest that in no instance was a boy chastised without deserving so to be treated. An evil spirit seemed to have entered them and governed them. They were disobedient, insolent toward the master, and no severity reduced or corrected them. As this had hitherto been a very quiet and orderly school, it was apparent that the master and his ideas of government were not adapted to their wants. He was advised to resign. This was Friday night. He then left. The next day, Saturday, Mr. Josiah Stearns of Bedford (now for about 40 years the excellent and beloved head of one of the city schools of Boston) was employed. He entered upon his work on Monday morning. The boys, all at once, fell into their former habit of good behavior. He appealed to their self-respect and love of propriety. He was naturally a gentleman and treated his school as such. No more punishment was inflicted. No more was needed.

I have written this about the severity of the discipline not from any personal grievance, for I was always treated kindly by the masters. I was never struck a blow or otherwise punished in school. But it seems proper, in the progress of human culture, to show the hardships to which the children were subjected from the faith of the fathers in the principles of Solomon's government. Moreover, in these days of ameliorated ideas and manners, when love and persuasiveness and reason have so largely taken the place of willful authority and physical force on the part of the masters and parents, and when in the children fear has given place to self-respect and confidence in those who should lead them, and mutual courtesy has entered into the relations of the older with the younger in families and in school, it would hardly be believed that such scenes and events as I have described could have existed in any of our schools except from the evidence of an eye witness or one who had received it from reliable tradition.

Teaching

The teaching has ever been far better than the government of the schools from the very early period. The masters of the grammar school were educated at college, and most of them were recent graduates fresh from their studies. Unfortunately few of them made teaching a business but gave only one or two years to the work in order to obtain means to pursue their professional studies. Nevertheless they brought a large endowment of learning and general intelligence to their work, and they were conscientiously faithful and generally successful as teachers. They were required by the law of the state and the regulations of the town to teach reading, spelling, writing, grammar, arithmetic, geography and also Latin and Greek languages.

The reading books, in my earliest day, were Webster's spelling book, American Preceptor, Columbian Orator, and also the Bible used mostly as devotional exercise. Afterward the English Reader was substituted for American Preceptor, the Columbian Orator gave place to Scott's Lessons, and the last at a later day gave place to Pierpont's First Class Reader.

Usually the morning exercises in school began by the members of the first class reading the Bible, by turns, one or two verses each. This was followed by prayer by the Master. The first class, usually standing in their seats, read both in forenoon and afternoon. The second and lower classes were called and took their places on the floor, usually twice each half day, and there read and spelt.

Writing

The writing books in my earliest day and previously were of domestic manufacture, made of sheets or leaves of foolscap paper doubled so that each half sheet made two leaves of the book. These were sewed together with a cover of house paper, sometimes coarse blue paper that had been used as a wrapper for loaf sugar, or other coarse paper was used for this purpose. As the pages of this book were entirely blank, it was necessary to rule it to guide the lines of the writer.

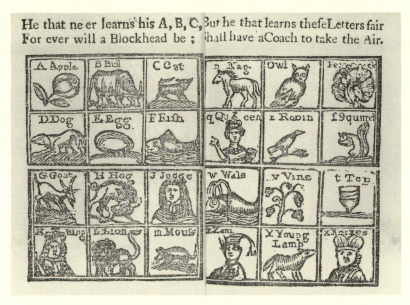

A page from *New England Primer*

For this purpose, every scholar was provided with a ruler and plummet. The ruler was simply a straight piece of mahogany or other wood, 10 or 12 inches long, one or two wide. The plummet was a piece of lead, usually 1½ or 2 inches long, about half an inch wide and one-sixteenth of an inch thick, sharpened at one end, to make a fine mark on the paper. Usually it was fixed by a string to the ruler, long enough to allow the lead to move across the page of the book.

Mr. Munroe had a little foundry near my father's, where he cast the brass wheels and other parts of the clocks that he made. I copied his processes to make lead hatchets for my plummets. I made a model in wood, used flour for the bottom of the model, and then melted the lead in a fire shovel and ran it into the model. This I scraped and trimmed into the desirable shape. The edge of this hatchet made the desired marks or lines in my pages. As some other boys were pleased with my hatchet plummet, I made such for them and felt well rewarded by their praise.

The boys generally ruled their own books for coarse hand and fine hand. It was not easy for them to make their lines parallel with each other or with the upper and lower margins of the sheet, and some exhibited singular difference in the width of the same space for coarse hand at the two ends, and some pages were very manifest violations of geometrical rules. Some could not rule. For these the Master did this work, or their parents did it at home for them.

It was the business of the master to set copies for the young writer. They began with straight marks at the beginning of the lines which the learner imitated through the lines. Then these marks with a turn or hook at the bottom as part of or at the top or part of *n*, then *o*, then *a*, etc., through all the alphabet. Next one word as *cat*, *pit* at [the] top which was in like manner copied through the page.

Next came sentences—mottoes, often moral sayings—which were copied. Afterward (later in my day) such copies were printed in various copy books containing all the series of lessons from the above first elements to full lines of fine hand which were to be copied into the writing books. It was the constant injunction of the masters to mind the copy and write as nearly like it as possible.

Early in my school days, writing books were made by the book-binders and sold at the stores. These were ruled by machinery in exact measurement and parallelism, for the various sizes of letters. Some of these had the copies in various stages of progress and sizes printed at the tops of the pages, so that the boy or girl, learning, would not miss the model which was ever before them. These were slow in reaching the body of the school, as many parents preferred their own simple manufactures to the more costly writing books made in shops and sold at stores. Especially was this the case in some of the district schools, as for 6 cents cost in money they could make a writing book of 48 pages, whereas one made and ruled at the shops would cost 10 or even 12 cents.

There were no steel pens in those days. Quills were universally used. The best, prepared I suppose in Holland, were called *Dutch quills*. They cost about one cent apiece. They were yellow, hard, elastic and made good and somewhat durable pens, but a cheaper kind, less durable and less easy to write with, were generally used. A few brought *goose quills* fresh from the goose, which were coarse, somewhat soft and could not make a fine or clean mark. The master always had a *pen knife* and was expected to make and to mend all the pens. A pen of the best class of quills might be used to write two or three pages, those of the second class not more than half as much before they needed repairing. A few of the larger boys owned pen knives and made their own pens (and sometimes [also] for some of the smaller boys), but for the great majority of those who wrote, the Master probably made for each boy and girl one or more pens every half day. Some masters required all the writers, at the end of the session, to bring him their pens, which he repaired after the children had gone home, each one being marked with the owner's names. Some masters carried these pens to their homes and mended or made them there. But at any time in the writing hour, the pen was liable to fail and was then carried to the master for repair.

In most schools, some definite time was devoted to writing, when the master gave his exclusive attention and instruction. In this way, almost all the girls and boys learned to write a hand of various degrees of legibility by which they could write their own letters, and some acquired a clear and beautiful style of writing. Every scholar had an *ink stand* which was supplied with ink from home.

Arithmetic Ciphering

In the early times—my father's day in 1782—there was no arithmetic [book] in school except the one owned by the master. Every cipherer was required to have what was called a manuscript made like the early writing books before described. They were of the size of the foolscap sheet. The printed arithmetic contained the rules and explanations of each part, Addition, Rule of Three,[3] Interest, etc., followed by sums wrought out and explained under each part or principle. After this were several sums or examples involving the same principle or rule for the cipherer to work out. Each cipherer copied into his manuscript a description of each part—as Addition, Subtraction, Rule of Three, Interest, Square Root, etc.—also the rules of working, the example given for explanation, and a detail of the process. This was to be his model for doing the sums and solving the problems. Under the several heads he copied also the several sums or examples given in the book. He had also a slate and pencil, and with these he did each of these sums that he found in the printed book. If by his calculation he came to the same result as that which was printed, it was presumed that he had done it correctly, and he copied all the details into his manuscript. But if, after all his labor, he could not obtain the result that was printed, he sought the assistance of the master or one of the more advanced

3. Ed.: A mathematical rule according to which "the product of the means in a proportion equals the product of the extremes—used for finding the fourth term of a proportion where three are given" (*Webster's Third New International Dictionary* [1986]).

scholars, who would find the source of error and put him in the right way. In this manner, all the rules of the arithmetic, and the sums and their details of process, as far as the learner went, were transferred to the manuscript and presumptively to the mind of the scholar. Most of the scholars had a special ambition or a definite idea of what they wished to accomplish—to cipher as far as the Rule of Three, Cube Root, or through the whole book; but the good scholars (those who enjoyed the best opportunities) generally accomplished the whole and were to that extent well fitted for the business of life. When I entered school, a copy of Adams's Arithmetic was in the hands of every cipherer, but the manuscript was still retained. Every arithmetician had his manuscript, as his father had before him, and copied into it all the rules, statements, sums, and details of calculation, from his own printed book, also all the sums which he wrought out on his slate. The school regulations adopted by the town fixed the time to commence the study of arithmetic at the age of 14. Although some were allowed to begin much earlier, this restriction of age was applied to no other study.

Algebra

Algebra was not taught in my day. Some time between 1822 and 1826 Colburn's mental arithmetic was introduced and taught with very great success. Children of very early age were allowed to commence the book, and it had the wonderful effect of opening their young minds to the first steps in the science of numbers, and the older ones were easily led to a clear understanding and ready use of the higher numerical calculations. The principles of Colburn have not been superseded, but many improvements have been made in their details and presentations. Some other and higher mathematics were taught in school to those who wished. I studied trigonometry and surveying when I was 14 or 15 yrs. old.

Geography

This branch seems to have been considered a secondary matter and did not receive much attention in my early day. Morse's geography, a duodecimo volume of about five hundred pages, was used. This was an abridgment of Dr. Morse's larger work of two octavo volumes. Each country was described singly showing "the situation and extent" and extremes of latitude and longitude, the extremes of length and breadth, also the countries which were on the east, west, north and south. Then followed the description of the country as to its soil, mountains, lakes, rivers, etc., and its productions, populations and general occupations. Next was described its government and its history. All this gave but a meager account of the countries and offered to the scholars very little of interest or satisfaction. There were few maps, very meagre and indefinite, which gave the scholar very little help in his researches. This book was sometimes used as a reading book by the first class.

About the year 1817 or 1818, Cumming's Geography appeared on a new and greatly improved plan. It was accompanied by an Atlas of clear and distinct maps, with the boundaries of the countries painted so as to be easily recognized by the scholar, and the mountains and other geographical elements were clearly represented. This book made this study easy and profitable, and many more engaged in the study than had previously.

Grammar

This study was considered as a paramount element in education. Some children were put into it almost as soon as they learned to read. Master Paige put me into it when I was 7 yrs. old. The central or town school was called the *Grammar* school. We had our lessons twice a day in the grammar, and afterwards in parsing. Very great pains were taken to make us understand the constructions of sentences, and to enable us to comprehend the most difficult and complicated lines of poetry, and to show the grammatical relations of the several parts. In consequence of this faithful and careful instruction, most of the scholars, then and thereafter, rarely (and some of them never) used ungrammatical or unintelligible language in their speaking or writing.

Composition

Composition was required from the older scholars by most masters, periodically, usually once a week. This gave them a facility of expressing their ideas in writing letters, etc. during their lives.

Declamations

The older boys were usually required to speak either single pieces or parts of dialogues. In this matter, there was a very great difference in the boys. Some spoke with great facility and impressiveness and interested the audiences, as I well remember George W[ashington] Hosmer, now Rev. Dr. G.W.H., when a small boy spoke one of Addison's Hymns and commanded the attention of the whole school. The dialogues interested the audience most, and we all looked forward with great satisfaction to some dialogues in which John Flint took a great part and in which he manifested much dramatic power. He afterwards became an eminent and successful teacher in the City of New York.

Latin and Greek

It was the original intention of the law requiring these grammar schools to be established, that Latin and Greek should be taught, and boys fitted for college in them. The masters were all graduates and competent to teach these languages; probably most of the boys who went to college from Concord during the last and early part of this century were fitted wholly or in part in this school.

Other Studies

Chemistry was taught as early as 1819. Astronomy, Rhetoric, History, Algebra, Geometry had their students, probably most of the time since then.

Manners

One of the masters (1780–85) could play upon the violin. He asked the older boys and girls in the summer time to stop, after the school was dismissed, in the hall below, and there he taught them dancing for an hour. This great innovation upon the old custom was received in a different manner by the people. Most approved, and a few thought it a perversion of the functions of the school master. One of the aggrieved class went to Mr. Ripley, then a young minister, and stated to him the fact, with her views of the impropriety. Mr. Ripley heard her patiently and quietly through all her complaint, and then he said that he had noticed the fact and felt interested in the plan. He thought that this method of teaching manners had improved the deportment of the children, and he hoped the master would be allowed to continue it.

It was the universal custom, when children met their elders or superiors, for the boys to bow and the girls to courtesy [*sic*], and this mark of attention was universally returned. It was the rule of the school that a boy or girl on entering the school should bow or courtesy to the master. This was very easy. The scholars were then facing the master, but the same rule required that when the scholars left the school room, they should turn round and perform the same ceremony. When they left individually or singly there was no inconvenience in this, but when the school was dismissed and the scholars crowded at the door, they could not properly turn round to the master. Some turned a little to one or the other side and bowed hastily in any direction and sometimes interfered with each other. After a few years this custom, which caused more confusion than order, was given up.

District Schools

The grammar school was usually called the Town school; for most purposes it was mostly a district school open chiefly for those living in the centre district. Yet it was always open to any scholars in the outer districts when their own schools were not in operation. Moreover, any pupil in any district who wished to pursue any branch of study which was not taught in their own district had the privilege of going there. Many of the masters of the district schools were young men in college who were allowed to go out to teach during the long winter vacation. The centre school in its administration and teaching had an important influence on the purposes and aspirations of all the youths of the town. By these means of more liberal educations, many boys were prepared and developed for a broader and larger field for the business of life than they could find at home. Hence many sought fields of employment in other towns and some far abroad, where they grew to be men of business and have done justice to the schools that made them what they are.

Schoolhouses

The old schoolhouse, as I first knew it, was of wood, two stories high, and 30 by 40 feet. It stood where now stands the engine house, next to the house of Mr. W[illia]m Heard. The school room was in the second story, 30 feet square. The door opened in front, upon an open floor, about 9 feet wide which ran to the Master's desk, on the opposite end. On each side the floor was raised on an inclined plane from the level floor in the centre to the wall on each side. There were four rows of seats for the accommodation of ten scholars in each row. The end seats against the wall were single and between these were four pairs of seats for two each with alleys running between the seats to the back or upper seats. Every seat had a box with a lifting lid. The architecture and joining of the room was coarse and imperfect and commanded little respect from the boys. Many boys had a lock on their boxes with the idle fear that their books were unsafe. Some boys had two locks on their boxes of which they were very proud, and one boy had three locks on his box. These duplicate locks gave their owners great satisfaction, and [upon] coming in, they took out their keys from their pockets and ostentatiously turned the locks and opened their boxes apparently thinking that thereby they manifested their superiority to other (and little) boys who had no locks. If the boy changed his seat or left the school, he took off his locks and left the box much cut in front. Very many boys had pocket knives, which they freely used cutting paper on their boxes, thus the boxes became very much scratched. Some cut out their initials and some their entire names on their boxes, so that the lids became so rough that it was not always easy to write without several layers of paper laid on the box. Even the seats were subject to the wanton depredations of the boys' pocket knives.

Heating

The school room was warmed by an old rickety stove which had formerly been used in part for cooking purposes. It was about four feet high, with a hole through the middle, which had been used as an oven but now [was] used by the boys to warm their feet. The doors to the oven having been taken off, the stove was loose-jointed. It stood on legs of similar character, and the funnel was also loose and imperfect. Consequently, the stove frequently smoked, and sometimes it fell down by the pressure of boys trying to warm themselves. Then the school was dismissed till the stove could be righted.

The room below was used as [a] woman's school, and it was here that, as spoken of before, the Master taught dancing. There was a bell in the belfry to notify the scholars the time for school hours. This building was burned in the winter of 1819–20, having caught from the stove, and another was built of the same size and on the same place of brick with the school room below and Masonic hall above.

Ventilation

There was no ventilation nor means of purifying the air in any schoolhouse in Concord in my early day, nor even as late as 1837, when I was on the school committee. Then the most painful part of my official visits was in breathing the foul and oppressive atmosphere of the school room.

The grammar school room was 30 ft. square and about 10 ft. high, making 9000 cubic feet. There were seats for 80 scholars.

The district schoolhouses were about 20 ft. to 25 feet square and 8 feet high. They offered 3000 to 5000 feet of air for 30 to 50 children.

When they entered the house, the air was fresh and healthy. But as the air became foul, it vitiated their sensibility, and neither they nor their teachers perceived the difference and did not complain. But when one entered from the fresh air abroad into this corrupted atmosphere it was very oppressive and offensive. It must have been equally injurious to those who had been in it and breathed it during the hours of the school session.

I am not aware that even now, 1878, these houses are any better ventilated than they previously were, although the rooms are larger and have more air to begin with.

CHAPTER VII

Books and means of knowledge. Small supply in former times. Library.
Old. New. Magazines. Newspapers 1810 to 1820. Now.
Post office. Mails.

Books

Within a hundred years, there has been a very great change in the supply of books, both as to their character and their abundance. Those of the earlier period were, in large proportion, of a religious and moral nature and history. There was a plenty of novels, and some of these were of low moral tendency—Smollett, Fielding, etc., but I have no recollection of ever seeing these in Concord. There were no novels in the Concord Library, yet some of these I found in friends' houses, and I read them in my boyhood. Dr. Ripley and the Physicians and Lawyers had their professional libraries and works of history, travels and other branches of literature such as the market supplied. A few families of culture or taste also had books of the latter class, but except the above, there was no collection that could be called a library. My father had what we called a "book case" in which were about 25 feet of shelves, filled with books, and others were scattered about, perhaps 200 or 250 in all. He used to intend to expend about twelve dollars a year for books. Probably in every family one or more bibles and testaments and school books were found. Some had histories of the United States [and] of the Revolutionary War. Many families [had] Thomas's Farmer's Almanac hanging on a string in the kitchen or sitting room chimney. The Social Library was small and had a limited variety of book.

Yet there were some very diligent readers who read and pondered on the matters learned. Those who had books lent them freely; there was, consequently, much general intelligence among the people especially in respect to American History and politics.

Library

Connected with the moral advancement of the town, several associations have arisen and flourished for various elements of culture. These have been both consequences and causes of the moral growth. They naturally arose out of a certain degree of elevation and a fitness and craving for more, and when formed they at once became active aids to further progress and means of still greater culture. The old Library was begun in 1786 and lived in various forms and organizations to the present time with its magnificent collections and its fitting home. The early library was very different from the present, but not more [so] than the supply of books in the world at large differs from what is now offered. I can well remember the small case of books kept in Mr. Stephen Wood's store on the dam and the huge volumes (octavo almost all of them) and almost the whole beyond the comprehension of boys. They were the best books in the English language—Sermons, Divinity, History, Philosophy, with a few travels and very few tales, that I could venture upon. I hungered for[the] opportunity of reading. I took out *Robinson Crusoe* several times; Custer's sufferings, Cook's and another book of voyages. Those are all I now recollect. And once, when I had taken out a book for the fourth time, my mother told me I must not do it again, for four times was enough to read any book. So I had to go hungry again. There was no such mental food for children and youth as now. I read [M. R.] Robinton's histories of Charles V, America and Scotland in my father's library and Bigelow's *View of the World* in my 12th year and then went back to the town library and got [J.] Burgh's *Dignity of Human Nature* and then Faber on the Prophecies. But they were hard reading for a boy and not profitable. Nevertheless I heard my father and Deacon Hubbard one Sunday noon discussing books and both agreed that Burgh's *Dignity* was an interesting and valuable book for young as well as old people.

Such men read and digested such books and were stronger in mind and warmer in heart. Those books are in the library now (1877) although probably rarely taken out, for the last 50 years. They did a good work in their day, as will be seen by looking at their conditions,

Concord Free Public Library

much used, worn perhaps, but not abused. As early as 1815 to 1820, books were more plent[iful] and better adapted to the living and to the younger, as well as the new mature, generation, so the library grew in comprehensiveness. A larger number—and more frequent readers— borrowed, and [the library's] usefulness was extended. So it continued to grow until now it has over 1200 volumes and these [numbers are] constantly increasing. The present library now sends its treasure into a very large part of the families of Concord. During the year 1878, 26,356 books were taken out. This is eighty-five books a day when the library was open.

Magazines and Newspapers

The Christian Disciple began in 1809, and a few copies were taken by people in Concord and continued by them as long as it bore this name, and its successor *The Christian Examiner* [was subscribed to] as long as it was published. *The North American Review* was also taken by some from its first [publication] for many years. The library early took *The London Quarterly* and *The Edinburgh Review*. Few or no other magazines were taken in Concord, previous to the War of 1812. In the times of Presidents Jefferson, Madison, and especially during the War of 1812–1814, political parties were very earnest and jealous for their own principles, and bitter towards each other. Each took its own papers from Boston. The Federalists had the *Centinal* (near always thus spelt and printed for reasons not known. Mr. Benjamin Russel the proprietor and editor was an intelligent man but preferred this way), and the Democrats the *Patriot* and the *Chronicle*, and each put unfaltering faith in the teachings and statements of its organ. The *Centinal* was printed Wednesday and Saturdays, the others Mondays and Thursday. They were brought to Concord by the morning stage in large packages. I used to see them as they were thrown down from the stage when I went to the tavern for my father's *Centinal*, 60 or more years ago. As nearly as I can now guess, there were about 40 of each class of politics. There were a few *Repertories* and *Palladiennes*, other federal papers perhaps, but I believe these were all that came to town. There were then no religious nor agricultural nor literary papers. I think the whole papers taken in town did not exceed a hundred of all and every kind. Later the *Recorder*, *The Christian Register*, and *The New England Farmer* sprung up and had good lists of subscribers in town. Still later, the *Traveler*, *Courier*, *Transcript* among other appeared and were taken in Concord.

Newspapers and Magazines: Papers Received in Concord At the Present Time, 1878

By the courtesy of Henry Whitcomb, postmaster, and of Mr. Edward W. Smith I have received the following accounts of the papers and magazines received in Concord through the post office and the newsdealer, Mr. Davis, in the centre village and the dealer at the junction. They show that there are 291 daily papers, 3 semiweekly papers, 647 weekly papers and 118 monthlies, principally magazines, now taken and read in the town. Comparing these with the 60 or 80 papers taken twice a week 60 years ago shows great progress. Besides the preceding, many papers are taken by residents of Concord at their places of business in Boston and brought home to their families. [See Appendix III.]

Previous to the establishment, thirty or more years ago, of the cheap rates of postage, 3 cents pr. letter to all parts of the United States, these rates were 6 cents for 30 miles or less, 10 cts. for 30 to 80 miles, 12½ cts. for 80 to 150 miles, 18¾ cts. for 150 to 400 miles, and 25 cts. for over 400 miles.

There were heavy burdens on correspondence, and people sent a large part of their letters by private hands. Travellers everywhere took letters for their friends and acquaintances. Very many letters were left at taverns for the casual travellers to take and carry with them. At all these public taverns that I remember there were boards fixed to the wall by the barroom fireplace across which tapes were fixed with spaces between the tacks wide enough for the insertion of letters. Here writers deposited their epistles, and the depositions usually presented quite an array of them. Then travellers, teamsters, etc. [who were] stopping would look at this board and if they found letters directed to their town or on their way, they carried them to the tavern of that place, and the tavern keepers would keep watch of the letters and of their customers and send them as opportunity offered. Much of the correspondence of some people was carried on by writing on the margin of newspapers. Such they sent for one cent each. It is true the law forbad this and charged letter postage on the paper when discovered. Yet, as few postmasters opened and examined the paper, probably most escaped detection.

As far back as I can remember, certainly to 1817 or 1818, one mail was brought daily from Boston on the line of stages that ran to Keene, N.H., and Burlington, Vt. It arrived at 5 to 6 o'clock a.m. One bag held all the letters, papers etc. for all the post offices on the line from Boston to Burlington. This bag was put into each successive post office. The postmaster or his clerk took out all that were directed to his place and put in all that he had directed to the offices beyond him. Then the stage carried the bag to the offices beyond. The stage brought the mails down from the upper country late in the afternoon or evening according to the state of the roads. The postmaster did the same with this mail as with that which came up from Boston, and put in all the matters [sic] which were to go to or through Boston or the intermediate towns. Then Concord received one mail a day from Boston and one from the upper country. Sixty or seventy years ago Deacon Parkman was postmaster. He kept a little store on the ground where the Library now stands. Afterward Mr. John L. Tuttle was postmaster, and when he went into the army in 1812, Mr. John Keyes was the official postmaster, but the business was done by Messrs. Burr and Prichard, who kept the green store which stood where now, 1878, the Catholic church stands. In 1835 or 1836 Mr. Charles Davis succeeded Mr. Keyes and kept the office in his store on the Mill Dam. Then [came] Mr. Stacy and now Mr. Whitcomb.

Now Concord receives five mails from, and sends as many to, Boston [in] a day but none directly from or to any other place. All the mail matters from or to any post office in this region are sent to Boston and there distributed. A bag is made up for each post office and sent there only, and the same is sent back to Boston containing all the letters, etc. for every place. Thus a letter directed to Acton or Lincoln and left in the Concord post office is sent to Boston, and it is put in the bag there for the office to which it is directed and sent to that place. I have no means of knowing the amount of business done by the Concord post office early or even in the middle of this century. Mr. Whitcomb, present postmaster, wrote me in January 1879 that the gross receipts were $2,029.93 in 1869, when there was only one office. Since that time, there have been established two other post offices, one at the factory and the other at the junction of the Fitchburg, the Lowell and Framingham Rail Roads, which have taken off some of this business. The gross receipts were in 1878, $2575.02.

In 1867 about 40,000 3 cent stamps and in 1878 about 60,000 were sold and about 1800 postal cards. There are also foreign letters at 5 cts. and drop letters at 1 ct. These give the approximate number of letters sent, and Mr. Whitcomb says they receive about the same number. This would make 200 or more a day sent out and as many brought to Concord. It may be added that about 70 persons have their business in Boston. These include the most active business men, who have the largest correspondence. They send and receive the greater part of their letters through the post office in Boston.

CHAPTER VIII

Social Club

The Social Club began about 1786. It included the elite of the moral
and intellectual element of the town. Now for 100 years it has maintained its constant life. Twenty-five members belong to it. They are
usually chosen for life. That is, the membership is only terminated by
death, removal or migration. My father was elected in 1789, and in
1838, when he was 70, he wrote me ([I was] then in Louisville,
Kentucky), "I have left the club. I do so with a clear conscience for I
have attended its meetings constantly for forty years." Dr. Josiah
Bartlett was elected in 1822 and is yet a member, having held his
connection for 56 years. He died Jan. 5. 1878. Dr. Bartlett came to
Concord in 1820. He soon was in business and continued his professional activity and usefulness until 1st Jan. 1878. In his long life in
Concord he was a zealous promoter of every good work and shed a
holy influence on all around him and left a mark in the elevated
character of the town. I know of no other who has been connected
with it as long.

[The Social Club] met weekly at each other's houses, through 26
weeks of the cold season, for conversation, discussion, or business.

These are eminently the "Conscript Fathers" of the town. In all the generations this club had a leading influence in the management of the town and its offices. They took a deep and lively interest in all the movements, and generally the lead in their initiation and program. Nearly every plan and measure was first introduced and discussed here, and if thought advisable, it was put into the warrant for the town meeting. Then and there the members were sufficiently influential to carry it. I remember that in the winter of 1834–35, I suggested the celebration of the bicentennial anniversary of the settlement of the town. The matter was favorably received and, after conversation upon it, referred to a committee for consideration. They reported favorably at a subsequent meeting, and the club voted to ask the selectmen to put it into the next warrant for town meeting. [Similarly,] in this manner the new [fire] engine was brought forward in 1817. So my father told us at the time. So also, projects for roads, bridges, the poor, schools etc. had their first inception in the club. This association is still as full of life and good purposes as ever. It has similar characters for members and they hold similar positions in society and the whole have the same sort of elevating influence on the town. The club [members] were entertained with some refreshment at the end of the evening. This was very simple at times and, at others, luxurious.

Members and meetings of the Club 1879–80.
Social Circle 1879

H. M. Grout	Oct. 7	1880	
R. N. Rice	14	H. J. Walcott	Jan. 6
Samuel Staples	21	R. W. Emerson	13
E. W. Bull	28	H. J. Hosmer	20
Lorenzo Eaton	Nov. 4	Geo. M. Brooks	27
E. R. Hoar	11	Grindall Reynolds	Feb. 3
Geo. Heywood	18	J. M. Smith	10
E. C. Damon	25	J. S. Keyes	17
Elijah Wood	Dec. 2	N. B. Snow	24
F. B. Sanborn	9	H. F. Smith	Mar. 2
Geo. P. How	16	Jas. B. Wood	9
J. F. Barrett	23	Richard Barrett	16
Geo. Keyes	30	E. W. Emerson	23

Lyceum

This Society began [in] December 1828 and now, for nearly 50 years, has had its meetings and lectures through every winter. These lectures have been on all the varied topics that are presented to popular audiences, and have always been well attended. Dr. Ripley was the leading spirit in the beginning, and to his death his interest continued. Mr. Emerson as a lecturer has ever been a ready friend [who] always gratified and instructed the people.

These courses of lectures have been given in every winter including this of 1877–78, for fifty years, varying in number for 12 or 15 to 32 or 35. The lecturers have been generally persons of high education [who are] profitable for the people to hear. Their topics have been widely diversified but never trifling—moral, religious, philosophical, political, historical, scientific. The audiences have ever been good; in some seasons large and sometimes crowded. The people generally seemed to consider the institution as theirs and for the benefit of the town. In the early stages it was an organized society, consisting of all who subscribed to the funds, and (as in those days lecturers charged only their expenses of travel) the whole cost of the course was small for any season. But the lectures were offered free to all without further cost.

In course of time lecturing became a profession in some degree. Men, and some women, especially prepared themselves for this work and charged a fee, sometimes a large—even a very large—fee, for their lectures. It then became necessary to raise more money and to require all the attendants to contribute their part of the cost, and the amount of this subscription now determines the number of lectures that can be offered.

The subscribers and attendants are from most of the families who are thus represented at these meetings. They thus obtain the best ideas of the time on a great variety of topics, and these they carry to their homes for the secondary instruction of their families and their neighbors. Here meet all these peoples of all degrees of cultures, except perhaps the very lowest, all on terms of good fellowship and equality, and thus the social as well as the intellectual nature is receiving a new elevating and refining impulse. And the whole town is in a degree improved thereby, made wiser, more loving, more generous in spirit and in affection.[1]

1. Ed.: Jarvis inserted into his text a newspaper report of the address delivered by the Hon. E. R. Hoar celebrating the fiftieth anniversary of the Concord Lyceum. In the speech Mr. Hoar recalls that the roots of the organization lay in the hope of a man named Josiah Holbrook of Boston, who "was interested in geology and mineralogy, and went about the State delivering gratuitous lectures upon those subjects, and urging the people of the cities

Farmers' Club

Concord has ever been a good agricultural town. The farmers have been as intelligent professionally and generally as those of any town in the state. There were [in 1878, eighty-five weekly agricultural papers and six monthly magazines devoted to the same purpose] taken in town and read profitably.

Fortunately, Mr. Simon Brown, late lieutenant governor of the state, a gentleman of rare intelligence especially in all matters of agriculture and horticulture, proposed the formation of a Farmer's Club for mental instruction. This proposition met with a ready response from the farmers. It was seed sown in good ground, all ready to give life, growth and fruit.

The club was organized and included most of the farmers of the town. [It has] gone on increasing in strength, and in numbers, in the interest in its purposes, and their own work at home.

They meet weekly at each other's houses. They have an essay on some agricultural topic, and then a discussion upon the matters thus presented and suggested. At first the members were diffident, self-distrustful, and wrote unwillingly and spoke hesitantly. But practice has worn off these objections. They became more thoughtful, more concentrated, better observers, and had more to say, and spoke with more and more readiness, so that now the discussions are rich with their experience and observation and never falter or fail of interest.

Capt. John B. Moore, at first, was the most retiring and uncommunicative of the members. But being a man of talent and quick

---

and towns to form lyceums for popular education." The Concord Lyceum "absorbed into itself" the old debating society, and "with that persistency, which we flatter ourselves is somewhat a characteristic of Concord, we have steadily maintained our courses of lectures and kept up the Lyceum, until now it has rounded its period of fifty years." The list of lecturers includes noted clergymen, two presidents of Harvard (Felton and Hill), "Agassiz and Holmes and Lowell and Dana," Edward Bliss Emerson and Charles Chauncey Emerson, "who gave to us loftier truths from sweeter lives than this generation knows," and notable townspeople. "Mr. Thoreau gave us 19 lectures . . . Dr. Jarvis 17, Deacon Nehemiah Ball 17, of which I well remember a course in natural history illustrated by a magic lantern on a very large scale, and the delight with which the young people viewed the representations of every known species of ape, monkey and baboon, accompanied by a very precise and accurate statement of their length from the tip of the nose to the insertion of the tail." Finally, Judge Hoar celebrates Emerson's contribution made to the town by way of his 98 Lyceum lectures. "The presence of Mr. Emerson in Concord has been the education of the town. It has given it its principal distinction to our generation." Mr. Hoar's graceful speech concludes, "I had nothing special to say to you, but there is a great deal that comes into my thoughts as I look back over this fifty years; the heart is full of ghosts and of memories, many of them very tender and pathetic."

observation, he was led to see and think more and more, and to give forth his thoughts, and he grew in power and wisdom. He became one of the best and most productive powers, and gave to the Club the results of his observations and experiments. He communicated to others and [to] larger associations of cultivation. For several years his contributions to the reports of the State Board of Agriculture [have been] among the most valuable parts of the annual volumes.

Other members grew in the same way, in power and instructiveness, so that now it's not the question who shall be prevailed on to speak but how they can find opportunity to speak. These discussions, reports and conversations—all these means of mutual culture—have a great and beneficial effect on the minds and mental habits of the members. They increase their acuteness of observation and their habits and methods of reflection and reasoning. They are led to see the relations of the [observable] facts and their causes and consequences. They are therefore better farmers and gardeners. Year after year they cultivate their lands and care for their animals, with more skill and [indecipherable] and hence their works are more profitable to them, and they are benefited in their fortunes, as well as in their mental character. They carry their personal social cultures to their houses and their neighborhood. Their families and their neighbors enjoy their improvement, and thus the general society of the town has indirectly and remotely the benefit of the Farmers' Club.

In this way, all these associations and assemblages for the good purposes herein mentioned diffuse their blessing to the homes and the families of the members. The intelligence, and the amenities, the more cordial bearing, the confiding and the respectful manners thus acquired are contagious, and all are elevated thereby in greater or less degree.

Nightly Feastings

Nightly feastings connected with the social and the farmers' clubs are entertainments for the body after sessions are over. In the Social Club, the former entertainments were, as I have elsewhere said, simply a plate of apples and a decanter of wine which 50 years ago was hardly touched. Now they have luxurious feasts—oysters, salads, sardines, sometimes meats, turkey, or others; custards, ice cream, cakes, foreign fruits, tea, coffee, etc.

The Farmers' Club has similar feastings. These are burdensome to the housekeeper for preparation and to their husband for cost, and being at night after the three meals have already been eaten are not only needless for nutrition but somewhat exhaustive to the digestive powers and so far, weaken the animal frame.

Farmer's Club Supper—Concord Mrs. C. A. Hubbard

Raw Oysters
Escalloped Oysters
Pepper, Salt, Pickles
Crackers and Rolls
Sponge and French Cake
Cocoanut Pies
Cream Cakes Ice Cream
Apples, Oranges, Grapes, Nuts and Raisins
Tea and Chocolate.

This was the general character of the suppers in 1877. Yet it was varied in some of its elements, according to the taste or convenience of the families with whom the club met.

Salads
Cold Meats
Tarts
Jellies, Gelatine

Concord
Oct. 26, 1878

Edward Jarvis M.D.
Dear Sir,
Enclosed find the exact list of articles furnished at two suppers of the Social Circle.
The first I should consider one of the most expensive. The second medium.
I received and read with great pleasure the extract from your diary. I remember when Dabney was considered the best.
Very truly G[rindall] Reynolds.

Supper of the Social Club 1878

Raw Oysters, Frozen Puddings, Fancy Sherbet
Concord and Almeria [Spanish] Grapes
3 Kinds [of] Pears
Apples (Hubbardston)
Currant, Sponge, Chocolate and Cup Cakes
Macaroons
Cocoa Nut Cakes
Preserved Ginger
For drink, Chocolate

Supper of the Social Club 1878

Raw and Escalloped Oysters
Pears
Apples
Sucro Pudding
California Grapes
Nuts and Raisins
Pound and Sponge Cake
For drink, Coffee

This and the preceding were given by different members of the club. They may be taken as specimens of the most elaborate and the medium. The articles were varied in different families according to the taste and convenience of the entertainer.

I regret here to add that these entertainments of the Farmer's Club have become so ponderous that at the beginning of this season, October or November 1878, there were not sufficient members or families willing to continue its existence, and consequently no meetings have been held. But I trust that the club is not permanently dead. It has done a great and a good work, and I hope that it will be again revived without the useless and destructive burdens of social hospitality that do not increase but lessen [the members'] powers of labor on the next day.

These nightly feastings had become the custom of the age in the cities and other places of wealth of social culture and ambition. All classes to greater or less extent indulge in them.

The American Academy of Arts and Sciences

The American Academy of Arts and Sciences in Boston includes men of the highest literary and scientific culture, [and] the philosophers and scions of Boston, Cambridge and other towns of the state. They meet monthly usually at their hall but occasionally at the houses of some of their wealthy and hospitable members. There, after the scientific labors of the evening, they are invited to the banquetting room, where is spread a luxurious feast of the most tempting order such as I have described, differing only in the better opportunities of the city market and the addition of wine of more kinds than one. Although I never eat or drink on the[se] occasions, yet I go with the company who are usually most social and agreeable in the dining room. I find myself alone in my abstinence. All others, the servers and all, partake of and enjoy [the] opportunity with good relish, [and] the pleasant bounties of the host at this late hour of the night.

Effect of Extended, Social and Business Intercourse with the World on Concord

The increase of wealth and income, the very greatly increased intercourse of Concord people with Boston and the world abroad, [and] the immigration to the town of families of culture, fashion, and wealth have had their natural effect on the tastes and customs of the town. The progress of civilization carries with it much—very much—that is good, elevating and refining to the mental and moral character, and some that is questionable and even more that is evil in mixed society. In people of mixed nature, corporeal and spiritual, these cannot easily be separated, and we can only hope that the physical indulgences shall be so tempered as to leave little or no injury to the total numbers.

Intercourse of Concord with Boston etc.

In my early day the mail stage ran from Keene and towns beyond to Boston through Concord. I now forget whether at first it was daily or every other day, but within my distinct recollection it went up from Boston every morning leaving the city at 2 or 3 and arriving in Concord at 5 or 6. The passengers took breakfast at the upper tavern. The stage came down from Keene from the upper country in the afternoon at 5, 6, 7 or even 8 o'clock, according to the state of the roads.

This offered but little convenience to Concord people who wished to go to Boston merely for the business of a day. [Therefore] most men who had sufficiently frequent occasion to go to Boston kept horse and chaise. My father used this method. Usually he started as early as 5 or 6 and returned in the evening. Three hours was the time required for the passage either way. Those who did not own horses, hired for the time. Sometimes they went three in a chaise.

Later, while I was in college, 1822 to 1826, the stage went in the morning at 6 and returned at night. This was the Concord accommodation stage and was the usual way of travel to the city. But often the stage would take 4 hours for the journey either way, which would leave but little time for business in Boston. The *railroads* changed all that. People began to do business in Boston and dwell with their families in Concord. The trains now run nine times on each road a day.

Train passing Walden Pond, Concord. *Courtesy* Thoreau Society, Concord, Massachusetts

18 daily trains up and as many down. They go early and return late. The longest passage is one hour. The express trains run in forty-five, sometimes in forty minutes.

There are now about 50 men and 80 boys who pass all their business hours in the city or elsewhere and have their houses in Concord. Besides these constant workers in the city there are many who go for light occasions, visiting or trade. The cost of money and fatigue is so much less than formerly. Probably the intercourse between Concord and Boston has increased fifty fold within 50 years.[2] This constant

2. There are now (1878) 57 season ticket holders on the Fitchburg railroad and the ticket master estimates that 20 others go daily, making 77 daily passages to Boston on that road.

communication of Concord families through their representatives in Boston brings home the ideas, the thoughts, and the sympathies of the city to them directly, and to their associates and neighbors indirectly, so their minds are expanded and their hearts warmed and they become renewed moreover with the wider and more cultivated world, and Concord society is less and less segregated in feeling and intelligence.

Children of Concord Abroad

The schools of the town and the general tone of society have educated many of the children to a higher purpose than the business of home would gratify, and [they have] developed capacities beyond the means of Concord to occupy. Hence there has been for generations a surplus of mental and moral power and of physical energy beyond the wants of the town that must seek fields of employment elsewhere.

The youth, thus trained and prepared for active life, have gone to other places far and near, to Boston, to Lowell, Worcester, and other towns in Massachusetts and New England, [and] to the middle and the western and southern states. Concord has her representatives in most of the states of the union. When I was in New Orleans in 1841, there were seven Concord men there. Five were settled and doing business there. Two were officers of Merchant ships there on business. I was a visitor to two of my brothers in the wholesale drug trade.[3] I have met our Concord emigrants in New York, Baltimore, Washington, Louisville, Cincinnati, Buffalo, Rutland, Burlington, and manifold other places. Generally, almost always, they carry the character and energy of their nativity to their field of service in the world and have become respectable and successful in their after lives. Merchants, men of business, professional men, farmers, mechanics, manufacturers—they do good in their several ways and are in various degrees honors to the town that prepared them for active life.

Looking over the houses and the families, we find comparatively few that have not sent forth their representatives to live in these other places, very few that have not some relatives, brothers, sisters, children, cousins, uncles, aunts or other loved connection abroad who send forth their sympathies and hold frequent or occasional communication with friends at home.

3. Ed.: Stephen (1806–1855) and Nathan (1808–1851). Nathan was blown up in a boating accident.

Their interchange of visits, their correspondence, more or less frequent, their communion of ideas and of affection carry the sympathies and interests of home to the loved ones and their circumstances in these manifold regions in and beyond the state. Then they become in various degrees cosmopolitan. They include much of the outer world in their sympathies, and while Concord is no less dear, the wider realms of humanity are included in their vision and they are broader men and women, who give their children larger notions of life and interest [and] more elevated and liberal ideas of duty and hope.

Concord Travellers in Europe

Besides this large and frequent intercourse of Concord people with other parts of our own country, there has been much with foreign countries. Many of the merchants of the town have travelled in Europe of various purposes and some have resided there for considerable periods.

As far back as I can remember, Mr. Tilly Merrick, who went to Europe in the last century and dwelt thereafter in Concord, was thought much of and held in high respect on account of this opportunity of foreign observation. Mr. Abel Barrett went to England in the first of this century on business and remained until his death in Liverpool. Mr. Jonathan Wheeler also went about the same time for the same purpose. Capt. Caleb Bates was a shipmaster and went many times to Europe. His son, John D. Bates, went as a boy to a mercantile house in Holland, and there remained until his fullness of manhood, and returned about 1820. Capt. Stephen Jarvis was also a shipmaster. He went to Russia, England, France, Germany, Scandan[avia], Italy, Spain, Portugal, Turkey, [and] the East Indies. All of these spent their vacations at their homes in Concord.

Mr. William Munroe, the giver of the library building, spent most of his time (for twenty years or more) in Europe, Great Britain, France, Germany, Italy etc., on business and in travel. He was at home at intervals. In the latter part of his life he spent the warm season in Concord and the cold months in Boston or New York; the very last one or two years were spent entirely in Concord. He died in 1877 at his home. Mr. Nathaniel Hawthorne was for several years the American counsul at Liverpool, and while there travelled much in Europe and afterward spend two years in Rome and Florence. The last years of his life were spent in Concord. Mr. Ralph Waldo Emerson has visited

Europe several times and [has] had very great intercourse with the foreign scholars and men of note.

Hon. Judge Keyes sent me in March of this year, 1878, the following list of persons who had visited Europe and afterward dwelt in Concord.

William Monroe

R. W. Emerson and daughter

T. B. MacKay and sister

E. R. Hoar

David Loring

Geo. M. Brooks

R. N. Rice

Edward S. Hoar, ux and daughter

J. Fay Barrett   ''   ''

E. C. Damon   ''   ''

William LeBrun   ''   ''

Henry F. Smith

Henry N. Wheeler

George P. Bradford

C. G. Ripley and wife

Edward W. Emerson

Charles Emerson and wife

Charles Fuller and wife

Capt. Kelley and wife

Daniel C. French

Marcellus Houghton

George Hunt

Randall Lufkin

William M. Hunt ux & daughter

Alfred Munroe

W. E. Channing

A. P. Chamberlain and wife

J. B. Tileston

Thomas E. Whiting

George E. Bigelow

George Lombard

N. Hawthorne and wife

Msrs. Mann and sister

Dr. Wood and wife

Mrs. Damon 3 daughters 1 son

Miss Elizabeth Hoar

Miss Caroline Hoar

Miss Amelia Prichard

Misses Alcott

Miss A. M. Wheildon

Miss Mary C. Wheeler

Miss Alice Wheeler

Miss E. B. Ripley and father

Mrs. Waldo and daughter

Miss Carrie Moore

Miss Angeline Ball

Miss Pratt

H. G. Holland

[There have been] 75 in all, 60 now living, who have been to Europe within Judge Keyes's remembrance and afterward lived in Concord. [indecipherable]

Election Day

At my earliest observation there were very few holidays. The town school was kept all the days of the year, except Sundays, Thanksgiving and Fast days, Election day (the last Wednesday of May), 4th of July, the days of the general training of the military companies (1st Tuesday of May), and the Day of Muster when that occurred in Concord. The rest of the year was devoted to study by those boys who attended the town school and, by others, to labor. Of all these days, Election Day was held in high prominence by the boys. There was no public celebration or demonstration except in Boston, where the Governor was escorted by a procession to hear a sermon and to be inaugurated, and many went from the country to witness the pageant. But in the rural districts, nothing was done by the authorities or the people to distinguish the day. But for the boys, it was a day of great expectation and exhilaration. They looked forward to it with fondness and yet with anxiety lest the weather should be unfavorable to out-of-door sports. A large part expected to go hunting birds in the woods and fields, or fishing in the ponds and rivers. The bird hunting was the most attractive and exciting. Most of the boys 14 and over owned or borrowed guns and powder horns, or flasks and shot and pouches. These were prepared for a day or days before, and early on the Election Day they went forth on their cruel and wanton amusement. My brother Francis owned a gun. Charles and I borrowed. Our father furnished us with money to purchase ammunition, apparently cheerfully. This habit had the sanction of age, and the oldest and gravest did not condemn it. I was young and always went with my brothers. I was a poor marksman and unsuccessful hunter. I am not sure that I ever killed a bird. This was not my virtue but my fault. I was young and my arm [was] too weak to hold a gun firmly. I could not take aim steadily nor see clearly the bird. My hands trembled and when I fired the bird flew away. I felt ashamed of my ill success but did the best I could. Sometimes these hunters formed themselves into an association and divided themselves into two parties to test their skill by trial on this day. Two of the larger boys were made captains, probably self-appointed. They chose sides, each selecting alternately one among the boys in the town who would probably hunt on that day, beginning with the most skillful and going down to the least. I suppose I was the last chosen. With some rude discrimination, the birds were divided and classed according to their supposed value, each having its assigned rank. The crow was considered the highest, afterward the hawk and down to the smallest; the eggs were counted lowest. Each hunter was to go to his work in his own way and place, to kill as many as he could and also to rob all the nests of their eggs. In the afternoon all were to assemble with their ill-gotten trophies at some appointed place. The only one I ever attended was on the Nine Acre Corner road opposite the present situation of the high school. There the birds of each side were laid in separate heaps and sorted out and their individual and collective value determined and the sum total of each side ascertained. That [team] which had the most was considered the victor.

Last of all as a trial of skill, the eggs were placed one at a time on the smooth walk. Then each hunter who wished, holding a willow or other wand 5 or 6 feet long in his hand, was blindfolded and placed a few steps from the egg, facing toward it. At a given signal he walked toward the egg and when he supposed he was near enough to it, he struck at it with his wand intending to crush it. If he hit it, he was esteemed a good and successful fellow, but if he failed, as generally happened, another took his place and made the pitiful attempt to destroy the bird's egg. Fortunately for the morals and sensibilities of our boys and youth, Election Day with its corrupting and demoralizing influences occurred but once a year, and in 1821 it ceased entirely. Happily this single day's indulgence in cruelty had but little influence on [the boys'] tastes and character and daring. The rest of the year they spent their time in other and more gentle amusements or in work, study, or business.

Sportsmen

There were always a few, however, whose paramount desire was hunting or fishing. They worked but were ever ready to quit business and betake themselves to their guns, or poles and lines. Some gained a part of their living by this means, either directly for food for themselves and families, or for sale. But all of these became, in various degrees, unthrifty and in so far as they held their sporting apparatus as their first and most ready means of enjoyment, they neglected their only sure means of success, prosperity and respectability. There was more of this in former time than now. The few that are now in Concord are, I trust, dying out and their places are filling with men of higher aim and greater usefulness.

Shootings

Of similar nature and destructiveness of high moral character were what were formerly and are now called "shootings." These were and are in the beginning of the winter season. Some men propose to set up turkeys, hens, chickens etc., to be fired at by the gamesters at a fixed price per shot. If the marksmen hit the bird it was his; if not, he lost his fee. This method of game is based on the principles of all other gambling. The shooter pays the fee—10, 12, 15 cts. more or less—and takes his small chance of gaining a bird worth 25 cts, to a dollar or more. The manager of the matter calculates that the many chances of the small fee from failure to hit the bird are more than equal to its worth when it is hit. So he expects to gain and the deluded shooters hope at each shot to gain a dollar's worth of poultry for the small fee paid for the shot. These sports were common in very early days. They attracted that class of men who delighted in gambling and others who had a similar taste but hoped that their respectability would bear a little mixture of the vulgar element without material deterioration. I had not heard of them for years and had supposed that they had lost their hold on any class of the community, but I regret that they have been, within two years, in Concord or on the border of Acton, and men who should have higher aims of life and its responsibility were drawn to them.

Politics

People as intelligent and public spirited as the men of Concord could not fail to take a deep and active interest in the affairs of the state and nation. Differing individually in temperament, and in their habits of viewing matters, they necessarily took different views of the methods of managing public interest. They therefore took sides with Washington and Hamilton as federalists or with Jefferson as democrats.

The town was nearly equally divided between these parties. Both were convinced in their own minds that they were themselves right and that the others were wrong. They were earnest and some were bitter and even denunciatory, but never, that I have heard, did they go so far as to personally quarrel. On the contrary, many who were decidedly opposed in politics were mutually agreeable friends and neighbors. My father was an earnest federalist and yet was on very cordial and even intimate terms with some democrats. He took the *Centinal*, the organ of the federal party. Col. John Buttrick, equally earnest as a democrat, took the *Chronicle*, which was the organ of his party and principles. Both of these papers were brought to Concord by the morning stage and left at the taverns. My brother or I went to the tavern for the *Centinal*, and by Col. Buttrick's request we got his paper or brought it to my father's, where the Col[onel] could get it easier than at the public house. It was kept there until Col. B. could conveniently send for it. On

Samuel Hoar (1778–1856)

each side the papers scolded and said many hard things of each other and of the opposing party, and probably the zealous politicians of Concord did the same. Yet I think there was less bitterness in Concord than in most towns. By general consent, the selectmen were divided between the federalists and democrats. Dr. Heywood, a federalist and an excellent, wise, faithful officer, held the offices of chairman of the selectmen and town clerk for thirty-nine years, and in this long period rendered good service to the town. He usually had one and sometimes two democrats associated with him. All of these acted in harmony for the public interest.

For many years there was always a perfect agreement in the choice of a moderator of the town meetings. There seemed to be a universal determination to elect Hon. Samuel Hoar to this office. He was so prompt and graceful in discharge of this duty, so impartial and so true to the interests of the town that everyone seemed to wish him in the chair and also thought that every other voter had the same desire. So when Dr. Heywood called for votes for moderator, if one, two or three went up with their votes, all others considered their work as done and no more offered to vote and Mr. Hoar was declared to be unanimously elected and everyone was satisfied.

Representative

There was always a struggle by the parties for the choice of representative in the Legislature, and it was generally doubtful until the vote was declared, which party would gain the victory. These antagonizing parties continued unbroken through more than one generation. The sons usually inherited the principles of their fathers. From the last years of the 18th century (from the presidency of the elder Adams) to 1829, when his son John Quincy Adams was elected, these parties held their ranks unbroken. Then the old lines were lost in Concord as well as elsewhere, and old opponents found themselves working in harmony to effect new political purposes.

Antimasonry

Next followed the Antimasonic Party, manifesting a degree of energy and recklessness that were rarely known in any political strife. All the misrepresentation and sophistry and distrust of opponents that had been used by any previous parties were intensified in this struggle. Men seemed to have lost their usual habits of judgment and to reverse their opinions of men whom they had ever before trusted with unfaltering respect and confidence because they now stood on opposite sides on the question of Masonry and Antimasonry. There seemed to be a moral blast that swept over their relations of affection and time-honored faith in each other. One of the staidest farmers of middle age—a man of very sober judgment who had been a life-long and constant attendant on Dr. Ripley's preaching, and had leaned on him as his unfailing spiritual guide—became an Antimason. Dr. Ripley, at a public Masonic celebration, said that the charges against the lodges were not true and that no such scenes as were reported by the Antimasons had been enacted at their meetings in his presence. This old friend of the doctor said that he, Dr. Ripley, had stated falsehood and could not be trusted. At this time I said to my father that it seemed to me that political strife had never reached such [a] height of bitterness and mutual distrust, and that politicians had never been so sophistical, false and abusive. He said that in the times of Jefferson, all these were much worse and more destructive to social faith and honesty. There was much said in the paper that adopted this new political principle much against the character of our best men who, though neither Masons nor Antimasons, could not agree with either party. The Antimasons were intolerant and demanded that all should take their part and be active fighters against the Masons and their friends.

Very many pamphlets were published, mostly on the Antimasonic side, and had varied influence for good or evil. In 1834 or '35, Mr. Goodwin and I—both being on the library committee [and] finding a great quantity of loose pamphlets in the library—proposed to arrange them according to their natural affinities and bind them in volumes. We found so many in the library, though many were incomplete, that we thought it best to collect others from the dwellings and offices in town. These were very many. Their owners having read or examined them had put them away in closets, attics, barrels and boxes. They did not want them but did not wish to destroy them. They were very glad to find a new and permanent home for them and gave them freely to the library. We made 150 volumes of this transient literature. Capt. Stacy bound them in proper covers, not expensive, but sufficiently strong for all the use they would ever be put to. And thus, this part of our history which otherwise would have been lost was saved. Among these pamphlets were found enough on Masonry and Antimasonry to make three good-sized volumes. They are labelled Masonry and Antimasonry. This delusion has long since passed away and left no trace of its existence behind. People generally only know that it existed as a political party about forty years ago and more, and that the Antimasonic Party cast a large vote and carried some towns and even some states. But in these three volumes is the history of the agitation and the monuments of the party, which shows how deeply it entered the heart and the life of its partisans, how it affected their grounds of faith and confidence and their motives of action. It seemed to absorb their reason, their affections and their conscience.

CHAPTER IX

Intemperance. General habits of the people. Irish population. Spirit supposed needed for hospitality and for labor. Effect of Revolutionary War. Laborers. Haymakers. Cider. New Rum stores selling spirit. Drinking in taverns. Middlesex Hotel. Religious meetings and rum selling. Bigelow's Tavern. Shepherd's Hotel. Hospitality. Flip. Loggerheads. Domestic beer. Funerals. Bearers. Boy bearers. Representative treats. Auctions. Clubs. Trainings. Public opinion. Cider. Private drinking. General. Common drunkards. Bread. Effect of spirit on vital powers, loss of working powers thereby. Loss of earnings. Temperance societies. Drinking by laborers. Grog rations on farmers. Col. Cyrus Wheeler. Sheriffs and constables. Sales of spirit diminished. Spirits sold in Concord and the cost thereof to sellers. Statements of storekeepers and taverns. Cost of spirit to Concord people. Spirits sold by Concord stores to people of other towns. Spirits bought by Concord commerce in Boston and elsewhere. Spirits sold by taverns to travellers. Summary of all sold to Concord people. Population of Concord over 19 yrs. old. Depreciation of vital force by spirit. Consumption of spirit in England, Scotland and Ireland. Proposed discontinuance of sales of spirit in Concord. Taverns closed. Condition of temperance in 1877–78. Moral and financial effect of reforms. Some drinking still continues. Fashionable. Irish. Effect of discontinuance on moral and physical power of the people of Concord.

Temperance and Intemperance

Concord, for the last 43 years, since 1835, may be considered a temperate town. The American[1] inhabitants rank among the most favorable in that respect. In its previous history the Concord people represented the general character of the country towns of New England. Most of the people were very sober. There were many who were considered both by themselves and the people as temperate drinkers—certainly deemed sufficiently temperate in the last century and the early quarter of this century—but who now, and for the last 40 years, would be considered as intemperate. There were others who were decidedly intemperate, even drunkards, and were so accepted by their neighbors and townspeople.

Spirit—Agent of Hospitality

There was a notion almost even quite universally prevalent that hospitality and generous fellowship included the offer of food and stimulating drinks—wine and spirit. Hence these were kept in most houses, certainly in those families that could afford the cost or wished to seem to be so able. These were offered to friends and visitors. My father always had wine in the house. We knew very little of its quality or even its name. We never drank of it, but my mother always offered it to visitors in their calls. We had also in the parlor closet, West India rum, brandy, and gin which were offered to such as were supposed not to be satisfied with wine.

Rev. Mr. Stearns of Bedford told me in 1834 or '35 that he had always kept them in his closet, and it was a rule of the house always on Saturday night to examine them to be sure that the Sabbath should not find them unable to meet the due demands of hospitality if visitors should come, and especially, he added, did they do this if he was to exchange and have a strange minister in the house. There was not much thus drunk, but it was supposed to be proper to allow each one to take his choice whether to drink or not, in accordance with his habits and tastes.

1. In this account of Concord temperance I have exclusive reference to the American population. Within thirty years, there has been a great addition of foreigners, mostly from Ireland. The last were 424 in 1855, 382 in 1865, and in 1875 the foreigners of all nations were 535. Among the Irish are many who are prone to drink freely, and even intemperance in beer, rum and whiskey is very common.

Labor and Spirit

There was then an almost universal opinion that labor, exposure, or privation could not be sustained without the aid of spirit. The government made an allowance of a small portion of rum as a part of the daily rations for soldiers and sailors. Merchants allowed the same to sailors in their vessels. The war of our revolution, 1775–1783, is supposed to have been and probably was the cause of much intemperance among the soldiers and people. The hardships, privations, and labors of that severe struggle seemed to call for the free use of spirit to sustain the men. This created an appetite for it which they carried to their homes and indulged for the rest of their lives. In civil life, laborers, hard workers in mechanics' shops, some farmers through the year (and especially in haying time) thought rum necessary, and the grog [rum diluted but not sweetened] [and] toddy (rum and water sweetened) was sent out to the men in the field at 10 to 11 and at 3 to 4. Even the rigid temperance families would not deny this indulgence or apparent necessity to their men if they wanted it. My father and all his family drank no spirit, yet it was given to the workfolk in the field, and I have many a time mixed the grog and given it to the men at home or carried it to them at their work. Indeed a man who would not give this to his laborers would be considered mean and lose the respect of his neighbors.

Haymakers

In haying time, which was intensely absorbing, the most careful and provident farmers—in order to save the time needed for frequent visits to the stores for this purpose—were accustomed to procure their rum in advance for the season. The largest employers thus bought a barrel or more, and others as many gallons as they supposed to be needful, for the whole hay harvest. I found this custom in my earliest childhood, and it was spoken of as having been established from time immemorial. There was no discrimination as to age in this supposed necessity on the part of the employers. The grog was offered alike to the boys and the men and was drunk by the laboring children as well as their fathers. So the youth early began to take steps that might generate an appetite that might, from indulgence, become a power of evil to control the future man.

Cider

It may be safely said that every farmer made cider. Apple orchards were cultivated principally for this purpose. A very small part were russets and blue pearmains, and these included nearly all those raised for eating. The greater part were sour, unpleasant, and unfit for cooking or eating. It was sufficient that they had juice, which could be pressed out of them. All these of every sort and condition—sound and rotten, the fair, and those having worms within them—were all poured in one mass into the mill and there ground together (the sound and the decayed, the pulp and the worms) and then pressed, and the juice poured out into the great tub to be thence transferred to barrels for storage in the cellars for family use. Probably every farmer and all others that could afford the cost laid in their store of cider for the year's use. They varied according to their size, taste and habit. My father usually made, and put in, eight barrels, much of which was made into vinegar. Some families would have only one or two barrels. One large, wealthy, and hospitable family put in twenty barrels a year. Cider was (generally among farmers) universally put on the dinner table in large mugs from which each one drank with his or her food. None of my father's own family drank cider, but the mug was set before us for the hired men who sat at the table. My father would not confine their diet. It was also offered to visitors.

Stores

There were nine stores in Concord in which spirit of various kinds— West India and New England rum, brandy, gin and wine—were kept for sale. These stores were Jonathan Hildreth's (who died in 1818; afterward George Hildreth's) on the road to Westford one mile from the village; Deacon White's (afterward Col. Shattuck's) [at the] north-west end of the square in the block where now L. Surette lives; Daniel Smith's for a few years on the spot where the Town Hall now is; the green store where is now the Catholic church kept successively by Abel Barrett, Jarvis (my father) and Hammond, Isaac Hurd, Burr and Prichard, L. Bascom and J. P. Hayward; [a] store [at the] corner of the Lexington road and the Common, kept by John Adams and afterward by Moses Davis; [a] store southeast of the Common kept, 75 to 80

Haying at J. A. Smith's farm, Concord

years ago by Richardson and Wheeler, [by] Jonathan Davis who died in 1815, Ebenezer Woodward [who] died in 1820 and Cyrus Davis, successively; [the] store on the northwest side of the mill dam northeast of the brook, kept by Stephen Wood till his death in 1820; [the] store of Tilly Merrick afterward of Phineas How where now is the front yard of Judge Brooks. Josiah Davis's store stood where is now the barn of Mrs. Calvin Damon. This was opened about 1812 to 1814 and continued until about 1836. These were all miscellaneous stores keeping everything wanted in the country, [and] spirits and wines were included. New rum [colored with caramel and aged] or New England rum constituted the far greater part of the spirits that were sold. This was used by work people, by those who loved it, and by the self-indulgent. West India rum, brandy, gin and wine were kept in families for company, but not used by the work people in fields or mechanics' shops nor by the topers.

New Rum was what was called by the traders a *leading article*, and on this they based their competition. It was called for much more frequently than any other article and generally the first in order of the customers' wants. People generally knew its cost and first inquired the price, and if it was satisfactory, the purchasers would take it and then ask for other matters that they wanted, with the value of which they were not so familiar, and took these with less care as to the price to be charged. It was the object of the trader to make this leading article as attractive as possible, and therefore it was generally retailed by the gallon and the quart, at the cost by the hogshead in Boston and transportation to Concord. Besides the quantity of spirits sold to be carried away and used at houses elsewhere, all these stores sold liquor by the glass to be drunk on the premises. They all had on the counter near the spirit barrel or hogshead a tin shallow pan one or two inches deep, 12 to 18 inches long and 10 to 12 inches wide with a wine grating over it. On this grating stood the tumbler to drain into the pan below. Close by stood a pitcher of water and a bowl of sugar and spoons. Thus it was easy to mix a glass of grog for any caller. It was not the general intention to sell grog in this manner to all or any merely thirsty person, but mainly to purchasers of other goods, some of whom wanted and claimed a treat gratuitously from the merchant in consideration of this gain from his other and profitable sales. More frequently it was probably offered voluntarily by the traders in gratitude for the opportunity of satisfactorily dispensing other goods, and in some stores, especially the one on the dam, grog was freely sold to any who wanted it, and thirsty men and topers resorted hither to gratify their desire for rum at probably a cheaper rate than at the tavern. Yet I believe that generally the drinkers independent of other purchases were unacceptable to the traders.

Taverns

From my earliest recollections and from tradition that went much farther back, there were three taverns in the village. They were all in their several ways respectably kept according to the ideas of the time and held in good esteem by the people and the classes of travellers that went to them. All the taverns in those days had a bar, and the public room was called the *bar room*, which very hospitably opened its doors and in cool weather offered its great fire and comfortable seats to all. The bar was in one corner, a place of varying size sufficient for the bar-tender, landlord, or his assistant, whose most frequent work here was to prepare and deal out the liquors to the drinkers according to each one's wish. He was [also the] clerk [whose job it was] to make out the bills and receive pay from the customers. On the shelves were conspic-uously displayed the decanters of spirits of different colors—brandy, rum, gin, whiskey, wine and some kind of bitters that were in use. Stoughton's elixir was prominent 50 to 60 or 70 years ago. There was a bench or sort of counter inside the bar on which was a pitcher of water with tumblers, a bowl of sugar and toddy stick all ready for use. The bar was a very important element of profit to the tavern and probably in many, a necessary part of the business, the profits on all other matters, food, lodging and stable being insufficient for the support of the house.

The oldest is now the Middlesex Hotel near the courthouse (by some in former years called the jail tavern). This has ever been more a town tavern than the others. The selectmen and other town officers meet here, if in any public house, it being near the courthouse where the town meetings were held until it was burned and the town hall built. The people who had occasion to stop and wait to warm themselves, or for other purposes before they went to the public meeting or had appointments with each other, went into this place.

This had the custom of travellers of all sorts of those who went in their own carriages and wanted to live genteely and men with teams who desired a plainer entertainment for themselves and their horses and cattle. Early in this century, Mr. John Richardson enlarged the house by adding a width of one room on the southeast side and one story to the whole including a hall for dancing and other assemblages. After this, balls and other gatherings were held there.

In some winters, 1820 to 1825, Mr. Thompson then the keeper of this house—wishing (as the biographer of his son Richard Thompson said in his book) to offer to the people a purer religion than Rev. Dr. Ripley offered in the meeting house—had Methodist meetings and preaching in this hall [on] Sunday evenings. Many came and heard these preachers. I was told that the hall was filled every evening. But it was made a public occasion and drew many to the tavern who were not attracted by the religious services. The bar was kept open and its wares offered as invitingly as ever. The thirsty had their opportunity of indulgence. The bar room assemblages increased, and the toping element became more active week by week. These men were social, buoyant, and drink made them noisy—so loud as to be heard through the neighborhood and to disturb the peace of the people. My father and others were aggrieved and remonstrated without effect. The keeper thought the religious meeting good and profitable to the souls of the people, and the work of the bar room one of the necessary duties of a tavern which he was licensed to keep. The selectmen were appealed to and took the matter up. On inquiring of the bar keeper, they learned that the sale of liquor had been very greatly enlarged since the meetings began in the hall and were weekly increasing, so that on the Sunday evening previous the receipts were twenty-four dollars. The selectmen then ordered that Mr. Thompson should close the religious meetings or his bar. He chose the former and the noise and rioting on Sunday evenings ceased, and there was no special ground of complaint thereafter on that account. This tavern is now the Middlesex Hotel and is the only house of entertainment in Concord for men and beast, and sells no spirits openly. The tavern on the main street on Groton road next above the burial ground and where now (1877) the house of Mr. Reuben N. Rice stands has ever been, and was until the death of its late proprietor Hartwell Bigelow, the home of teamsters, people who were contented with a coarser fare and at a lesser cost, but it had a larger bar custom than either of the others. It was more the resort of those who were in the habit of drinking spirit and especially of those who were given to frequent indulgence and even intoxication. This was the tradition and my early observation from the beginning to my final removal from town in 1837. There were constant gatherings of these dissipated fellows in the evenings until late, sometimes very late, at night. Passing by to my house in my last years of residence there, after dark, I could commonly hear the toddy stick in its frequent work, stirring up the rum and sugar and water for the thirsty customers. They were merry, they had their jokes, their stories, their mutual banterings and their loud and merry laugh, and sometimes their quarrels, and rarely a fight. These were the lowest of the intemperate, yet most of them were required to pay the cost of their drams even when they could not pay for their bread. Yet even long accounts were run up by some who had been respectable and whose character and manners helped to draw others to this haunt of dissipation. Once there was an account swelled to $80 and over by a pleasant and very affable drinker whose company was always acceptable. All this stood on the tavern books in the charges of "to glass 6 cts." As this man never changed his habits but died of delirium tremens, it is probable that the debt was never paid. But the great profit on these sales and the effect of this man's pleasant stories and laughable wit in keeping the drinkers there were sufficient compensation for this loss. It must be said here that besides the bar, under the supervision and management of his excellent wife, the host kept a good house of his class and doubtless it was therein profitable. But the bar was a very strong element of his gains, and at his death he left a large estate.

The upper tavern, called sometimes the coffee house or Shepherd's coffee house, was the resort of more wealthy or genteel travellers. It was the stage tavern, where the passengers from Boston going to the country had breakfast. This was in my early day the place for the more cultivated assemblages for the dancing schools, balls etc. The whole style of the house and management was more refined than that of the others and of course more costly to the customer. It was more quiet, although there was a bar, and liquor was offered to such as wanted it. Yet these were mainly travellers, and very few townspeople went there to drink. There was no gathering of the low and rowdy element, none of the intoxication that the others presented. Such as these certainly in Mr. Shepherd's day were very unwelcome, and they were not drawn to this house.

Hospitality

The tavern, being always open to everyone (both citizen and traveller) with its covering for man and beast in shed or barn and a warm fire in winter, was the convenient and attractive shelter in cold and

Barroom, Wright Tavern, Concord

storm, and at all times a convenient stopping place for any to wait, or a place of meeting for such as had business together in the village. Hence the townspeople frequently centered there singly and in companies. There was no charge for this hospitality. These visitors wanted no food. They could not order a dinner or supper. The bar offered the only apparent opportunity of payment for the room and the fire thus enjoyed. Hence many called for something to drink, although they did not want or enjoy it, but they could pay the price of it and thereby acknowledge the benefits of the house which they needed and did enjoy, and thus some generated an appetite for stimulating drink. Others did want the grog and were glad of an excuse to indulge their appetite, which was thus increased to become a ruling power within them.

Flip

Sixty or 100 years ago, flip was a common drink offered in taverns. It was made of domestic beer which was a decoction of hops, roots and spruce fermented. Thus a very small proportion of alcohol, 1 to 2 and even 3 per cent was developed. This [beer] was kept constantly in taverns and very commonly in some private families. It was esteemed a very harmless as well as pleasant drink. Flip was made of this beer with rum and sugar added and the whole warmed or heated by putting into the mixture the heated even red hot bulb of a loggerhead.

Loggerhead

This instrument was a rod of iron ⅜ or ½ inch in diameter about two feet long with the upper end wound into a ring, and on the lower end was a ball about 6 inches long and 1½ inch in diameter. This was in all taverns, and to meet its frequent necessity it was kept with the bulb in the bar room fire constantly ever ready for use. The flip was made in half mugs, one pint, enough for one, or in whole mugs, one quart, enough for two. If the traveller or customer were alone, he called for a half mug, or if there were two, they called for a whole mug. The mixture was made in a moment and the ever-ready heated logger-head put into the mug. The drink was soon warmed and made very pleasant to the drinker, especially in the cold days or evenings of winter. So when one came to the village in the cold season, he was strongly induced to call at the bar room and warm himself outwardly, then to get a drink of hot flip to warm himself inwardly and to pay for the fire, the room, and the drink all in one bill. Many travellers also found the flip a pleasant and convenient means of protection from cold. The heated alcoholic fluid in the stomach would send its heat through the frame when they should be exposed to cold abroad. My father in his early day stopped one cold winter's noon at a tavern in Groton to refresh his horse and himself. After eating his dinner while waiting for his horse to finish his repast, he talked in the bar room with another traveller who had fed his horse but not himself. The stranger called for a half mug of flip and then proposed to my father to join with him and take a mug together. My father declined. The stranger said, "When I go out in the cold I always take a half mug of flip." My father said, "When I go out in the cold I get a good dinner."

Loggerheads were frequent in private houses usually hanging in the kitchen on the jamb of the chimney beside the fire. In my father's house this was its constant place. We never had flip, yet we used, now and then, to have a mug of small or domestic beer which was frequent in private families. [We] sweetened it with molasses and then warmed or burned it by putting the heated loggerhead into it. If however we did not care to heat this instrument, we found a ready substitute in the leg of the andiron that stood in the coals and was always hot.

Funerals

Before my day or observation, it was the custom to set out decanters of brandy, rum etc. at the funerals, for all who would partake. It is impossible to say now how many or what proportion of the people drank, but tradition said that many did so, and the weak-headed and lovers of spirit often became intoxicated on these occasions, and some were supposed [presumed] to attend for this purpose only.

Bearers

The custom of offering spirit to the bearers, who had a separate room for themselves, was continued unbroken certainly until April 1826. At my mother's funeral in that month, I proposed to my father that no spirit should be put in the bearers' chamber. My father was full of grief and felt grateful to these friends for coming to do this last office for my mother, and felt disinclined to withhold this mark of hospitality. He said they were old men and accustomed to the occasional use of spirit especially at funerals, yet he saw the propriety of my proposal and wished me consult Dr. Ripley. I went then to Dr. R. and laid the matter before him. He, like my father, was pleased with the plan, yet he said it was new; spirit had always been given, and it might be considered a mark of unkind inhospitality to withhold it. He asked the names of the bearers who were invited. Then he said, "Perhaps they may think it strange, yet they are all sober men and not in habit of drinking, I think they will approve the measure. It requires some courage to make this innovation but you can take the responsibility; it is known that in this matter, your father leaves the whole management to you. You are in college, you are of age and can bear any odium that may come from it." No spirit was then offered, and I never heard any complaint of our want of hospitality. I do not know that this example was followed immediately and generally, but I think that soon thereafter the practice was discontinued.

While [I was] writing this account, Rev. Dr. Geo. W. Hosmer told me that early in December 1815, when he had just completed his 12th year, a child of Mr. Abel Conant died in the house where now Elijah Wood lives (and where his father Elijah Wood and great-grandfather Judge Wood lived). He, G. W. Hosmer, and other boys of his age were called to be the bearers at the funeral of this child eight years old. These young bearers were like their elders put into a room by themselves, and as with older bearers, they had decanters of spirits of several kinds—three kinds he now thinks—with sugar and water with tumblers for their use. None of the boys touched the spirit. This indicates the universality of the custom.

Representatives

I have elsewhere spoken of the custom of the Representatives treating the town at the taverns with toddy and crackers. I think Mr. Merrick, in 1813, was the last to offer this mark of gratitude. Certainly my father, in 1817, did not treat the town for electing him.

Auctions

I do not know that it was the custom in Concord to offer spirit at auctions, but it was in some other towns [not unusual] to place decanters of rum, brandy etc. for all who would partake. An old auctioneer told me that this had a marked effect on the sales. People drank and some became exhilarated and happy; they set higher value on the articles offered and on their means of payment and bought things that they did not want and at prices beyond their value. It was a profitable investment for the sellers.

Clubs

The club[s] in the last century became extravagant in their entertainments and at length so burdensome that they resolved entirely to change and voted that "the entertainment should be moderate with nothing but flip, grog or toddy"! How long this continued I do not know, but in my earliest recollection my father offered wine and apples. When I was a member of the club, 1832 to 1837, this was the usual and I think the universal means of hospitality. Very little wine was drunk, not a pint at an evening. The apples were used more freely.

Trainings

The military companies all had toddy carried out in pails to them. All drank freely out of tin cups. This was offered once or more in a half-day's parade. I do not recollect that any one became intoxicated, although each had as much as he desired. It is probable that in the militia company, which included all that were not in the infantry and artillery and some that were prone to excessive drinking, some were overcome with the spirit and unfitted to do military duty in the rest of that day.

Public Opinion as to Drink

All these customs had their natural effect on public opinion, with many [of the opinion] that the use of spirit is needful for men exposed to privations, to cold and fatigue, and to those engaged in great labor, with most, even those who personally avoided or were even averse to this habit, tolerant of its use in others, and even [unconcerned with] the remote effect of intemperance.

Cider

The frequent and the constant use of cider in many families prepared the way for the use of stronger drinks. Within my knowledge there were but two who had the reputation of being intemperate in cider. The occasional or frequent use of spirit had its natural effect of lessening or overcoming that sensibility both physical and moral that creates an aversion to its use in some. In others it excited an appetite for it, and this grew in many to be desire, even an overpowering want, which they could not resist. With their taste, it required but slight temptation to induce one to drink, and sometimes more than was intended, more than the nervous system could bear without disturbance. Some men otherwise of character, of substance and influence, calling at the taverns for rest, warmth, or business alone or with each other at times of public gatherings, town meetings, trainings etc., indulged their social nature and drank with each other so their brains were sometimes exhilarated more or less, their judgment and conversation unbalanced, even their muscles not under their usual control so they sometimes staggered.

Private Drinking

Some drank at home, alone or with company, not to intoxication but sufficient to disarm their resistance and destroy the natural repugnance and thus to create an appetite for spirit. Some drank thus frequently, some drank constantly, and they were less able to labor skillfully and effectively. They produced less by their physical exertions, and they managed their affairs with less discretion and profit.

Common Drunkards

Some were carried farther and became acknowledged inebriates and lost power of constant labor and proper administration. These were drunkards. It surprised nobody to see them intoxicated, excited, boisterous, or noisy in the bar-room or reeling in the streets. These exhibitions were too frequent to be matters of anxiety or mortification. There were a few drunkards in town, lost to all sense of self-respect, who might be seen, at any time, intoxicated, staggering with difficulty in the road, or even lying powerless on the ground. Chief among them was Breed, the barber, with whom rum was the all-absorbing want and motive of action. He would do anything, try every art, to get it. Regardless of health, of home, duty, rum only affected [attracted] him. If he could get a chance to shave or cut hair and thus earn six cents, he would expend one cent for a cracker and five for rum. It was a frequent sight to see him lying dead drunk in the highway, and if in the carriage path and in danger of injury, people would haul him to the grassy side, as they would a log or any other obstacle to travel, and then leave him to recover consciousness and power of motion sufficient to carry him home. He was found dead in the road, Sept. 1824, died of drunkenness. All this temperate and intemperate drinking reduced men's vital force, increased their susceptibility to disease, and lessened their power of recuperation, and hence their lives were shortened and mortality among them increased, and some had delirium tremens and died, others were by their intemperance wasted away and destroyed. Dr. Josiah Bartlett, who practised his profession in Concord from 1820 to 1878, 57 years, used frequently to speak to me of the destructive effect of alcohol on the human constitution, which reduced its power to resist the attack and ravages of most diseases. In proof of this opinion he spoke of the results of his own observation and experience among the sick. He told of many who had not been acknowledged drinkers but had drank sufficiently to reduce their vital power, so that when attacked with fever, pneumonia, consumption and/or suffering from injury or surgical operation which would not have destroyed a sound constitution in other men or from which they would have recovered if theirs had not been vitiated, yet they died because their power of

Dr. Josiah Bartlett (1796–1878)

resistance was gone. Their disease was not called alcoholic, yet alcohol was the prime cause of their death. Dr. George Vorrentroff of Frankfort in Germany, one of the most beloved and judicious physicians in his country and authority on all medical and physiological matters in Europe, writing to me a few years ago on the effect of alcoholic stimulants on the human constitution adds, "In the case of attack by fever or inflammation of any kind, Typhus, Typhoid, Gastric, Lung, Scarlet etc., I find the chance of recovery is better, for even the emaciated, scrofulous, rickety toiler than for the stout, fulfilled apparently robust beer drinker."

The same may be said of all injuries and surgical operation. Their chances of recovery are much impaired by the use of alcohol in any form—by rum, brandy, which [are used] by most, by beer [used] next [most frequently], that is, in proportion to its strength.

The records of death in the town state that intemperance was wholly or in part the cause of death of eleven in the period 1779 to 1800, of nine in the period 1801 to 1820, eighteen 1821 to 1830 and ten in the years 1831 to 1850, and four from 1858 to 1878.

Loss of Working Power

The loss of life of those who are on the record as owing their death partly or entirely to intemperance earlier than they otherwise would have died was a loss of many years that might otherwise have been devoted to labor and productive service to themselves and the country. These were the culmination of the effects of intemperance. They were the upper stratum of the pyramid of drinkers. The lower stratum included first those who drank sufficient to visibly impair their health and strength to lay themselves more open to attacks of disease and lessen their power to resist its destructive effects and thereby shortened their lives, although they did not die of the direct effects of drinking. Below these were the strata of those who drank sufficient to impair their nervous energies, to cloud their brains, obscure their judgment, weaken their muscular force or the control of the brain over its action. They would work less, and effect less and with less advantage. They were less productive, less profitable workers. They earned less, they were less able to support themselves and their families. They could contribute less to the general capital of the town and commonwealth. In all these ways (to the extent of the impairment of their vital force), in all these classes (to the extent of their consumption of alcohol), the town lost in their impaired wisdom, their diminished production force, their earning, and their contributions to their own estates and the Commonwealth.

Temperance Societies

These existed early in the century, their name described them. They allowed their members to drink temperately a little wine and spirit.

Moderately used, [it] was not harmful. They merely intended that their members should not drink to excess, that they should never be intoxicated. Very probably these societies did good in their mild, moderate way. They had no intention of going to the root of the evil nor of prescribing total abstinence; they only proposed to prevent the excessive use of spirit. The wisdom and wealth of the community sustained them. All these called themselves temperate drinkers. They felt secure as long as they did not drink what they considered as too much. To each drinker, in every stage of indulgence, the excess, the too-much, the dangerous point, was in the next stage beyond his own. Therein he considered himself safe. The danger was in each one's opinion in going beyond his indulgence. A change was coming over the public mind at this time as to the use of alcoholic drinks. The moderate restraints of the Temperance Societies did not satisfy the principles of many whose numbers were increasing and who now proposed the entire disuse of ardent spirits, (wines etc., in every form) and the formation of *Total Abstinence Societies*. These presented an absolute avoidance of every drink that would intoxicate. They had their lecturers who earnestly differed and enforced these doctrines. Independent of these societies and teachers and even among those who would not join them, there was a slow and insidious relaxing of the notions of the beneficial effect of spirit on human power, and the very strong ally of the temperance cause was found in the almost unrecognized notion of those who openly, by word and action, opposed it. They were ceasing to use spirit themselves at home or abroad for social entertainment.

Farmers Began to Stop Rations of Spirit for Their Men

The custom of sending grog to the fields at 11 and 4 began to be omitted and went gradually into disuse. At first many employers, recognizing the right of their men to the use of spirit as a strengthener in their contracts, offered them the usual spirit rations in addition to the ordinary wages or their cost in money. They did this even after they had ceased to use it themselves, and it was not unusual for men who entirely discarded rum and even joined the temperance society to give the grog forenoon and afternoon to their men, who they admitted had a right to drink if they wished. But generally, the money was accepted in commutation and the rum entirely discarded on the farms where the employer set the example, and after a while the abstinence plan became almost universal in farms and in shops. In 1834 one of our best farmers told me that he had given his men no rum for two or three years and he had never before got through his work, especially in haying time, so easily; never had accomplished so much in a given time with the same number of men that previously, with the free use of rum, had occasional troubles, bickerings, complaints, disputes, and in some days had totally lost hours of some of the men; but now, under the abstinence custom, all had worked steadily and cheerfully from the beginning to the end of the year, and no time was lost. This was the general testimony of those who had tried this experiment. But yet this man refused to join the temperance society, still less would he sign the pledge of total abstinence. He said he would not sign away his liberty. He would reserve his right to drink whenever he wished. But we know that he had not drunk spirit for years and he never did drink it afterward.

Tea at Dinner in Farmers' Families

At this time, tea began to be used at dinner in farmers' and other working families. Col. Cyrus Wheeler, of Nine Acre Corner, was one of the best and most successful farmers in Concord. He was never a drinking man, yet he had always given grog to his men and taken it himself, especially in haying time. But at this time he had discontinued it entirely for himself and men. Two years after he had ceased to have rum on his farm, his wife in the autumn said to me, "My husband has had no spirit on the farm for two years and he says he has never got along with the work so easily and so comfortably, and both he and the men feel a great deal better than they used to when they had their grog." But she added with a very pleasant smile, "He does dearly enjoy his cup of tea with his dinner." And I thought, "And you do enjoy as dearly your gratification of his taste in this respect." At this time farmers began to send coffee in the forenoon to the field with a luncheon for the men.

Sheriff and Constables

Capt. Abel Moore, the sheriff and jailor, boarded the other sheriffs and the constables and some jurymen in his house during the sessions of the courts. I was in his house one Saturday afternoon after the court had sat during the week. He called my attention to the spirit decanters in the open closet of the sitting room. They were about two-thirds full of brandy, West India rum and gin. "There," said he, "you see what they have drunk during the whole week, less than a quart of spirit for about twenty men. The closet has been open all the time and the spirit free at all times to everyone and his friends that called." I asked how it was a few years ago. "Well," he said, "I used to have the three decanters filled every day and often more than once a day. I used to average more than three decanters a day, more than eighteen a week. Now [I use] less than one in the whole week."

"Were they the same men?" "Yes, the same men, or their successors, or the same sort or class of men, and about the same number. They have almost ceased to drink, some entirely, and others drink very little."

Diminishing Sales. Spirit Sold in Concord and Its Cost

In 1834 Dr. Josiah Bartlett and I, both practising physicians in Concord, made inquiry of all the traders and the tavern keepers as to the quantity of spirits and wine sold in Concord and the cost. Here I would say that we found all these men kind and sympathetic and willing to give the information we asked. Furthermore, all the traders disliked the business. They kept these liquors only in obedience to the public demand, and they all hoped to find their way out of it. The taverns felt it their duty to supply their guests with what they wanted in this way. Mr. Shepherd disliked all mere grog drinkers and unwillingly supplied them.

Amount and Cost of Spirits Sold in Concord

I have now, 1877, here in Dorchester the memorandums of the statements of the several traders and tavern keeper of their sales of that and of some of the previous years. These memorandums are in the writing of the sellers or their clerks. Of the traders before spoken of, Messrs. Hildreth, Shattuck, Burr and Prichard, How and J. Davis sold liquor in 1828. In 1832 Burr and Prichard gave up business and were succeeded by J. P. Hayward. J. Davis gave up business and his store was closed between 1828 and 1832. Charles Davis was in business all this time, but never sold spirits or wine. The following tables contain the facts given to us reduced to systematic form for presentation.

Spirits, rum, brandy and wine sold in Concord and cost stated in dollars

	1828			1833		

GEORGE HILDRETH

Liquors	Gal.	cost/gal.	Total $	Gal.	cost/gal.	Total $
New rum	1000		$340	480		$163
Brandy	50		75	25		37
Other spirits	150		210	94		125
	1200		625	599		325
Wine	30		22	20		15

COL. DANIEL SHATTUCK

New rum	2040	40	$816	760	40	304
Other spirits	400	86	320	90	80	72
	2440		1136	850		376
Wine	200	100	200	200	100	200

PHINEAS HOW

New rum	1867		620	1227		400
Brandy	136		144	87		128
Other spirits	583		439	489		424
Total spirits	2586		1203	1803		952
Wine	150	105	225		155	

JONAH DAVIS

	1828			1833		
New rum	798	271	.02	Mr. Davis gave up business		
Brandy*	90	76	.25	before 1833		
Other spirits	211	152	.11			
	1099	499				
Wine	85	88				

* 30 gallons sold to taverns

J. P. Heywood in the green store [is the] successor to Burr and Prichard. The years are from July 1 to June 30. The quantity was not given in Mr. H's statement and total cost in dollars. Mr. Prichard gave verbally for 1828, 2500 galls. spirits 500 galls wine.

Liquors	1831–32	1832–33
New rum	1020	640
West India rum	300	250
Brandy	240	210
Gin	250	275
Total other spirits	790	735
Total spirits	1810	1375
Wine	340	450

Profits on Sales

In the preceding tables the cost refers only to the price paid by the traders in Boston and for transportation to Concord, and a profit was added to the cost to the consumer. This profit was on the New Rum only 2 cents a gallon at Mr. Davis's store; all others said it was very small. I have assumed that it was 2 cts. in all stores. The profits on the brandy and other foreign spirits were given by several and [were] much larger than on the rum. I have assumed that the others charged the same per cent and have calculated accordingly. No trader gave the profits on wine. These I assume to be the same as on brandy and foreign spirits.

Profits in Tavern Sales of Spirits

All sales of spirits at taverns are by the glass mixed with water and sugar, or grog, toddy, flip, sling, etc. The bar-tender puts one to two fluid ounces of spirit into the tumblers and fills the rest with water. There are 32 fluid ounces in a quart and 128 in a gallon. An ounce and a half will probably be the average spirit in the glass of grog, then a gallon of spirit will make 85 glasses. the price is 6½ cts. each, and the gallon will amount to $5.51.

Mr. Prichard gave only the quantities of spirits in gross but no cost. I assume that his spirits were in the same proportion of new rum, brandy and other foreign spirits as men sold at the other stores and at the same price and cost to him and to the consumer. Mr. Haywood returned only the cost of his spirits and wines. I assume that he paid the same as the others and have calculated the quantities accordingly. Col Shattuck gave all his foreign spirits for one glass. I have distributed them also in the ratio of others.

Consumption of all spirits and wines 1828, 1833

Year	New Rum		Other spirits		All spirits		Wines	
	Gallon	Cost	Gallon	Cost	Gallon	Cost	Gallon	Cost
1828	7555	$2861	2120	$2329	9675	$5190	939	$1073
1833	5463	$2138	1230	$1243	6693	$3381	987	$ 957
Decr	2092	$ 723	890	$1086	2982	$1809		
%	27.7	24.5	41.7	46.6	30.2	34.8		

Spirit and Wines Sold in Concord at Stores, 1828

Traders	New Rum		Other Spirits		Wine	
	Gall.	Cost	Gall.	Cost	Gall.	Cost
Hildreth	1000	$340	200	$285	25	$37
Davis	798	$271	301	$228	88	$87
How	1867	$621	719	$583	150	$105
Shattuck	2040	$816	400	$320	200	$200
Prichard	1850	$662	550	$511	500	$495
	7555	$2710	2170	$1927	963	$924
Profit		$151		$402		$149
Cost to consumer	$2861		$2329		$1073	

Spirit and Wines Sold in Concord at Stores, 1833

Traders	New Rum		Other Spirits		Wine	
	Gall.	Cost	Gall.	Cost	Gall.	Cost
Hildreth	480	$163	94	$125	20	$15
How	1227	$400	489	$423	225	$155
Shattuck	2040	$816	90	$72	200	$200
Hayward	1716	$640	557	$525	542	$450
	5463	$2019	1230	$1145	987	$820
Profit		$119		$98		$137
Cost to consumer	$2138		$1243		$257	

Taverns

William Shepherd

	1828		1830		1832		1833	
Spirits	Galls	Cost	Galls	Cost	Galls	Cost	Galls	Cost
Brandy	150	165	100	130	80	120	75	105
Other spirits	365	328	200	180	175	157	150	135
Total spirits	515	493	300	310	255	277	225	240
Wine	200	200	200	200	200	200	200	200
Total		694		510		477		440

Heartwell Bigelow
1833

Brandy	120 gallons
New Rum	412 "
Other spirits	100 "
	632
Wine	120 gallons

He gave no amount for 1828
but stated that more was sold
in that year.

Thomas D. Wesson—Middlesex Hotel

Gallons Bought

	1828	1833
Brandy	75	100
New Rum	350	100
Other spirits	75	100
Totals spirits	500	300
Wine	100	100
Beer barrels	30	16

Mr. Wesson gave no amount of cost.
Probably much of this statement is estimate.

Summary of Taverns 1828 and 1833

	Spirits all kinds		Wines	
1828	*Galls*	*Cost*	*Galls*	*Cost*
Shepherd	515	493	200	200
Bigelow	632	669	120	120
Wesson	500	478	100	100
Total	1647	1640	420	420

	Spirits All Kinds		Wine	
1833	*Gall.*	*Cost*	*Gall.*	*Cost*
Shepherd	225	240	200	200
Bigelow	632	669	120	120
Wesson	300	318	100	100
Total	1157	1227	420	420

Less in 1833   490   343
Ratio of diminution   29.5   21.8
Mr. Bigelow and Mr. Wesson gave no cost. I have assumed Mr. Shepherd's
rate of cost for them and thus obtained their probable cost. Mr. Bigelow
made no report for 1824 but said it was more. It is safe then to assume for
him as large [a] sale in 1829 as in 1833.

Final Cost of Spirits to the People

These were the quantities of spirits and wines which the stores and
taverns bought, and their original cost to the traders of the tavern
keepers. Besides statements given in writing, these gentlemen gave us
verbal estimates of their receipts for these liquors and wines or the cost
to the consumers. These estimates I took and recorded at the time. The
records are here now with me. I condense them into the following
tables. The profits of tavern sales were very large: 6½ cts. was the
ordinary price of a glass of grog. This ordinarily took 1½ oz. (⁵⁄₃₂ pint)
of spirits. This would give 21 glasses in a quart sold for 6½ cts each, or
$1.31 for a quart and five dollars a gallon. The wines sold by the glass
were nearly as profitable.

Spirits and wines sold at the stores and taverns and their cost to the
buyer or consumers

	Spirits		Wines		Total cost
Stores	*Galls*	*Cost*	*Galls*	*Cost*	
1828	7995	3564	1015	1130	$4694
1833	6226	1839	987	1019	$2858
Taverns					
1828	1647	5041	420	1600	$6641
1833	1157	3092	420	1680	$4772
Stores and Taverns					
1828	11,642	8605	1435	2730	$11,335
1833	7383	4931	1407	2699	$7,620
Decrease	4259	3674	28		
Percent	36.5				

The principal sales of spirits at the stores were of new rum, at the smaller profit, but
the other spirits and the wine were sold at a much larger advance on the original cost.

Spirits and Wine Sold to People of Other Towns. Townspeople Bought in Boston

Doubtless some of the spirit and wines sold by the stores were to persons in other towns who came there to trade, and these should not be charged to Concord consumers. But on the other hand, probably much more was bought by the Concord people in Boston at the wholesale stores and prices. Some of the largest farmers who laid in their large stock, a barrel, more or less, for haying, and others were in the habit of going to market with their own teams and would buy there and thus save both the profits of the retailer and the cost of transportation to Concord. It is known also that some sent to Boston for their liquors and wines to be used in their families, with the confidence that they would obtain spirits and wine of better quality than in Concord. The storekeepers all agreed with this opinion that their sales did not exceed the consumption in the town. Hence no deduction should be made on this account from the sum stated of the cost to the Concord people for spirits and wine sold at the stores in 1828 and in 1833.

Tavern Sales to Travellers and Townspeople

There is more doubt as to the quantity sold and drunk in the taverns. It is a question that cannot be settled—how much of this was used by the people of Concord and how much by travellers from other places. At Shepherd's probably more than half was taken by strangers. At Wesson's probably more than half by Concord people, and at Bigelow's probably a very large proportion was taken by the people of the town. Perhaps it may be safe to say that one-half of the tavern spirits and wine were sold to townspeople and that one-half of this cost should be charged.

Sales of Spirits and Wines at Taverns to Residents of Concord

The tables on the preceding pages include all the sales to both strangers and people of Concord. It is not possible to determine the proportions of these sales to travellers and to the townspeople. But we may make an approximate estimate. Mr. Shepherd's hotel was not a favorite resort of the Concord drinkers. It is probable that most of his sales at the bar were to strangers. Bigelow's tavern was a favorite haunt of these topers, and it is safe to assume that much the larger part of his bar custom was for townsfolk.

Wesson House was the resort of many business men, assemblies and larger gathering of Concord men. It may be assumed that his bar custom was equally divided between traveller and home patrons. Then in the following table one-half of the spirits and wines sold in the taverns were consumed by Concord people.

Cost to Consumers of Drink at Taverns

In the preceding tables of the tavern sale, the cost refers only to the price paid by the tavern keepers for their liquors and wines in Boston as returned by themselves, but they said nothing of their receipts for the same. In the calculation on page [blank] an endeavor is made to determine these receipts per gallon.

Sales of spirits and wines to people of Concord at taverns and cost to the consumer

Year	Spirits		Wines		
	Gallon	*Cost*	*Gallon*	*Cost*	*Total Cost to consumers*
1828	823	4534	210	1197	5691
1833	578	3184	210	1157	4341
Decr.	245	1350			1340
%	29.6	29.7			23.5

Total spirits and wines sold to people of Concord at Stores and Taverns

Year	Spirits Stores		Wines Taverns		Spirits Stores		Wines Taverns		
	Gall	*Cost*	*Gall*	*Cost*	*Gall*	*Cost*	*Gall*	*Cost*	*Total Cost*
1828	9675	5190	1647	1570	11322	6760	1773	2230	8990
1833	6693	3381	1157	1227	7850	4608	1797	2114	6722
Dcrse	2982	1809	490	343	3472	2152			2268
%	30.2	34.8	29.1	.28	30.6	31.8			25.3

The population of Concord was 1960 in 1828; 2050 in 1833.

The whole amount of taxes paid by the town for state, county and town purposes including the support of the ministers of the old parish and the repairs of the highways was, in 1828, $6982.46 and, in 1833,

$5268. Add the salary of the minister of the orthodox congregation $600 a year makes $7582 in 1828 and $5868 in 1833, which was $432 less in 1828 and $622 more in 1833 than the people paid for intoxicating drink. In Concord the whole population exclusive of foreigners in 1830 was 1990, 127 colored. Of the whites, 625 males and 633 females were over 15 years old. The 625 males over 15 years old were the consumers of almost all the 10,618 gallons of spirits in 1828 and 6,804 gallons of spirits in 1833. That includes all the sales at stores and one-half at the tavern. To this cost of spirits and wine should be added the depreciation of vital force, the loss of productive power, the loss of time, of wisdom, in place of management, the diminution of income and capital, consequent upon the use of these destructive beverages. These cannot be mathematically determined. But it is not unsafe to estimate if no spirit nor wine had been used in Concord for 100 years, full twice the amount of the annual cost to the people would have been added yearly to the income and capital of the town. I find in the *Contemporary Review* for June 1877, p. 74, London, this statement: "In 1873, 59,174,089 bushels of malt were manufactured into beer." 30,644,750 gallons of spirits were made during the year ending Mar. 31. 1875. There were retained for consumption as a beverage 29,821,574 gallons or about one gallon for each man, woman, and child in the United Kingdom. It is seen by the tables of the return of the traders that the sales of spirits had fallen off greatly from 1828 to 1833. I greatly regret that we could not get the accounts of the sales as far back as the first of the century or even 1810, 1815 or 1820. The dealers said it had been declining but never so rapidly as within the last five years.

Proposition to Discontinue the Sale of Spirits

At this time, the friends of temperance proposed to the traders to discontinue the sale of it. They were met kindly by those sellers. None of them liked the business. Yet they at first seemed to think this was a part of the public demand, which they ought to supply, and probably some feared that their other sales would suffer if they should fail to meet this want. They knew that some men revolted against any apparent interference with their habits. They would not be dictated to by their storekeepers as to what they should purchase and use. Some tried the temper of their customers by purposely being temporarily out of rum, and found that although they could not fill their jugs, they still bought their other articles. By this and other means the storekeepers found that public opinion would sustain them, and as all disliked it, the entire sale at the stores was ultimately given up.

I left Concord for Kentucky in March 1837 and have not lived there since. When I left, the storekeepers had not given up the sale of spirits, but had discouraged it, and greatly diminished it, and were hoping soon to discontinue it entirely, and did so within a few years afterwards. The taverns all continued their open bars, but with greatly diminished sales, excepting Mr. Bigelow's; and Mr. Shepherd's passed into different hands but was closed in [blank], and Bigelow's was closed at his death in 1850. Since that time, the Middlesex Hotel has kept no such open bar as formerly. In most of the years the sales have been only in secret and in some entirely suspended.

Condition of Temperance in 1877

Old things have almost entirely passed away. The American population are almost universally abstemious farmers. Now working mechanics [and] laborers have ceased to imagine that alcohol strengthens or protects from cold. People having occasion to use the fire or room at the tavern find other means of paying the host. Men have ceased to gather there for sprees or merry drinking bouts. Or it may be safer to say, that they of the present generation never indulged in these follies. Families have ceased to keep spirits in their houses except very rarely for medicinal purposes. Many of the customs by which the young and the untainted were first beguiled to taste of alcohol and thus take their first steps toward this goal of destruction have passed away and are only known in history, and the people are stronger, healthier, and more able to do their work however hard, and manage their affairs with better wisdom and success than in the former generation. The whole aspect, air, and manner of the town, the people, their houses, without and within their homes, their farms, their gardens, all show a great improvement on the past; more dignity and self-respect, more prosperity, a high tone of life.

This is the pleasant view of the condition of Concord. But it is less gratifying to speak of the increase of the use of wine in some families who imagine the fashionable errors of the great cities or of Europe can be safely transplanted to Concord.

On the opposite social extreme the Irish have multiplied, and they bring a strong appetite for drink which many indulge and some very freely. But not all even of these foreigners are intemperate. Some, and we trust, many, are rigidly abstemious. Others regardless of law, or of their own interest, resolutely keep it for sale in their own houses and invite and urge their fellows, their associates, both male and female, to drink. So among those poor people there are women who drink spirits and beer, some who are occasionally drunken. Nevertheless this class of people drink less in Concord than in some other towns. The moral influence of the rest of the citizens has reached even them and persuaded some of the Irish, many we trust, to touch and taste not, but to be as sober as the best American population. [newspaper clipping:] *Concord Freeman* Aug. 15, 1878, "Illegal Rumselling. It is declared that there are no less than seven places in town where liquors are sold without a license. This the town fathers do not intend to countenance, and so on Monday they brought before the Courts two of the parties suspected, Messrs. A.W. Worcester and S. J. Stone. These gentlemen were put under bonds to appear for trial early in September, quite a cloud of witnesses being relied upon to appear against them then. Worcester is to be defended by ex-Dist. Attorney Morse of Lowell." [newspaper clipping:] *Concord Freeman* [date obliterated], "One hotel and two sixth class liquor licenses granted by the Selectmen." "Lead us not into temptation." The Lord's Prayer. Here are three men authorized to tempt the pure to begin to drink and the practiced drinker to continue his indulgence.

Liquor Selling in 1874 and 1877

Hon. Carroll D. Wright, Chief of Bureau of Statistics of Labor, made inquiry through all the state as to liquor selling in 1874, 1877. He printed the results of his inquiry in the 10th report, Jan. 1879, page 167–180. This does not include the cities but only the towns. I quote the following places.

Places State Counties Town	Number of arrests for drunkenness		Places where liquor was sold illegally in 1874	Licenses of all kinds granted in 1877
	1874	*1877*		
Whole state	3195	2618	1220	877
Middlesex Co.	848	657	227	187
Franklin Co.	18	9	23	61
Concord	0	0	0	0
Stow	0	0	0	0
Lincoln	0	1	0	0
Weston	0	0	0	0
Acton	0	0	0	5
Sudbury	0	0	0	0
Bedford	3	3	2	0
Littleton	0	1	1	0
Carlisle	0	0	1	0
Wayland	0	0	1	0
Waltham	336	169	50	47
Lexington	18	6	0	0
Arlington	11	24	15	10
Hopkinton	20	20	20	0

CHAPTER X

Later prosperity 1815 to 1878. Effect of change of drinking habits on labor,
farmer, and prosperity. New production. Fruit, apples, pears, grapes,
strawberries, rhubarb, asparagus, milk. Prosperity of farmers. Parish fund.
Population. Increase of valuation. Taxation.
School tax. Parish taxes.

After the struggle of life for nearly two hundred years, the hard lot of the people was gradually but slowly ameliorated. The labors of each year had been but little more than sufficient for the year's sustenance and often fell short of that. That little was not invisible substance, but converted into the farm, into clearing forests, removing stones, and draining wet grounds. The farmers had little or no surplus money. Nevertheless there had been a real though slight gain through all this period. Each generation left to its successors better intelligence, better means and opportunities of living than those it had received from those who had gone before them. This progress of improvement was so slow as to be hardly perceptible and acknowledged until fifty or sixty years ago. Then it began to be apparent, and the dawn of better and more comfortable days was visible.

A change was coming over the habits of men, and their means and methods of agriculture. These then promised more return to the cultivation for his labor. Among the prominent and noteworthy changes were the decline of the almost universal faith that spirit was necessary for the working man whether on the farm or elsewhere, and the consequent [change] in habits in this respect.

Effect of Change in Drinking Habits

During the first quarter of the present century, and for several generations previous, the people of Concord, in common with those of other towns of New England, and even of most of the civilized world, had borne the burden of temperate and intemperate use of spirit in accordance with the faith almost universally prevalent, that the natural and healthy human strength was insufficient to sustain man in the hard labors of the farm, the mechanic's shop and elsewhere, but it must be supplemented by alcohol in some form or other; the equally general opinion [was] that this was a necessary element and means of good fellowship and hospitality. Men consumed rum and rum consumed men. In the proportion that it was used and the susceptibility of the consumer to its destructive influence, it impaired and suspended their muscular force and their power to labor. It clouded their brains, their mental faculties and their judgment, or ability, to plan their business and administer their earnings, and in some, it extinguished both and even life.

There were all degrees of impairment of vital force among the consumers of spirit, from him who only felt a slight almost imperceptible exhilaration, down to Breed, who was incapable of any labor, and to those who were prematurely or lately cut off in death by *delirium tremens* or other alcoholic diseases. The sum total of these losses of working power cannot be told, yet it was certainly very great and, in its extent, was so much loss to the productive force of the town. To this extent, it reduced the power of earning, and consequently the aggregate of the annual income of Concord was proportionally diminished.

But about the year 1825, a change began to come over the minds of the people, produced, in some measure, by the temperance advocates. But, in greater part, it was a moral and intellectual epidemic—one of those silent, unrecognized changes in public opinion that creep over a community, [when citizens] occasionally find their views of things, and the motives of action which had governed them, giving way and other [views and motives] taking their places. The farmers and others gradually and imperceptibly found their reasons for drinking losing power over them, and they felt no longer the necessity of spirit for labor; by a similar process, the need of spirit for hospitality vanished. This was a slow but sure process, and ultimately the old customs disappeared; and men labored abroad and in shops more effectively on food alone, than when they added spirit to it. These men came, themselves, to their natural fulness of power. To the extent of their re-establishment of physical and mental and moral force there was an addition to the effective and creative strength of the whole community, and the town was enabled thereby to earn so much more and create a larger income and wealth than it had before. All this gain to the town was without additional cost, for the expense of supporting a strong worker was no greater than that of a weakened drinker. Moreover there was the saving of the cost of deterioration, which was, as shown in the article on intemperance, $11,325 in 1828 and $7,010 in 1833, a greater burden than all the taxes, but probably no greater than it had been for many years before. All this was added to the actual income and capital of the town. This change took place principally in the second quarter of this century and was one of the important elements of, and causes of, the improvement in prosperity from the first to the third quarter of the present century and the great difference in the financial condition of the town in the two periods, the first and third quarters of the present century.

Change in Agricultural Ideas

Sixty years ago, the progress of the world began to be more active and visible especially in agricultural matters. More than before, men began to question the methods of their fathers, which although best in their day, might give way to better.

Philosophers and naturalists gave their attention to these affairs. Observing farmers did the same. Societies had been formed in Massachusetts and elsewhere but with limited influence. Some wealthy gentlemen bought farms and became amateur farmers trying the experiments proposed by the writers. They raised better grain and vegetables and fatted the largest cattle and swine, but at a cost which the market prices would not justify. They were called by the practical agriculturalists *fancy farmers*. [Although they] had no direct influence, yet they showed what could be done in vegetable and animal productions, and possibly at a lower cost and even within the reach of practical cultivation.

Cattle Shows

The average of the exhibitions at cattle shows came more within the means of the ordinary farmers and were therefore more instructive and induced a better following. Here were the best results of skillful culture which spoke for themselves, and the exhibitors explained the ways by which they were obtained. These were offered to all, and all men were invited to read and practice them. These exhibitions have now been held for fifty-eight years and have done great service to the whole county and to Concord, especially whose people necessarily attended more than others more distant.

Agricultural Implements, Machinery etc.

Probably these have been improving from the beginning of civilization, and perhaps this has been the most rapid [development] within sixty years. The cattle shows have taken great pains to exhibit them, and the agricultural warehouses to offer them for public acceptance. Within my knowledge these have all been changed. Cast steel shovels, forks and hoes (bright, and smooth-polished) have taken [the] place of their former heavy and rough iron tools. These pass easily into the beds of earth, manure, compost, hay etc. and are easily handled. With these the laborer can do more work with the same strength than with the iron tools. For ploughs there have been manifold improvements, all making them easier to manage and more effective in dividing and softening the soils; cultivators, better harrows, scythes etc. all came in this time of improvement. The old, clumsy, heavy carts and wagons, with wooden axles, gave place to lighter vehicles with iron axles, more easily moved, with capacity for greater burden. So also hoes, spades and every implement that the farmer used fifty years ago have given way to others of different kind or improved varieties of the same sort. More recently machinery began to be introduced by the farmers—mowing machines, horse rakes, hay tedders and even hay lifters. This shift[ed] the motive power from the men to the animal, which could mow and rake and lift more in one hour than the human muscle could in many hours. With all these means, much more work is done on the farms, and they are better cultivated. A change has taken place in the character of the crops and their use. Such are raised as can be mainly consumed on the place, while that which is sold away is not only in more concentrated form [but also it] produces much larger returns of money.

Habits of Labor Changed

Men too have changed their personal habits within half a century. They labor less intensely and continuously. They make shorter days

187

North Bridge, Concord (1875)

and longer nights, especially in the summer. They work less with their hands and more with their minds. They apply their personal forces more wisely and with better effect. They get more done and that with less exhaustion. They have more thought applied to their business, but less oppressive anxiety. They live more cheerfully and easily. Not much more work is done on the land than in the days of the fathers and grandfathers. As an illustration, the farm now owned and cultivated by Mr. Joseph Derby and Cyrus Jarvis was formerly owned by the late Col. John Buttrick [a fifer at the North Bridge on April 19, 1775] and inherited by him from his ancestors. They had occupied it through several generations. Col. Buttrick, [who was born, lived and died in the same house] sixty to [obliterated] years ago, kept horses, a yoke of oxen, and four or five cows and one or two hogs. He raised fifty bushels of corn yearly and a little more hay than his animals consumed. He and his three sons did all the work. He had a few apple trees on which he had as many russets as the family wanted, and cider apples enough to make the cider they drank. He sold some hay and corn, a few potatoes, and butter and cheese. This is all the farm seemed to require for cultivation and all it would do for the cultivator.

My father, the late Deacon Francis Jarvis, bought it of heirs of Col. Buttrick in [the] winter of 1831–32 and took possession in March following. In 1840 my father died and left the farm to my brother Francis, who died in 1875 and left it to his children, Cyrus H. Jarvis[1] and Mrs. Joseph Derby. Now, under their management with the addition of about 20 more [acres] of arable and mowing land, the farm produces 300 bushels of corn. There were 500 to 600 barrels of apples in 1878, which was a great-bearing year. Of these more than 300 barrels were sent to market and about 200 sold to the cider miller. They sell many bushels of pears and currants. They raise a very large quantity of garden seeds for the market. They keep three horses and find work for all, 30 or more cows, of which 20 were milked through the last winter. The milk is sent daily to Boston. The cultivation required last year the labor of six men through the warm season and two men in the winter.

1. Ed.: Cyrus went to New Orleans to work for his uncles Stephen and Nathan (brothers of Edward), who were in the drug trade. In 1847 he returned to Concord to work on the farm. Blinded in a rock-blasting accident, Cyrus nevertheless learned to care for the cows, help with the haying, and weed the vegetable garden. He died in 1880.

The Growing Market Economy

Change in Marketing

All the heavier produce of the farm—hay, corn, potatoes—is consumed at home, and the land is constantly re-enriched and kept in productive order.

Slow Progress of the Change

This change did not take place suddenly, not in one year, nor even in one generation, but slowly and gradually each year and [each] generation contributed its part to the progress. Looking back one year or even ten years from one point of time, the change may not have been very obvious, but comparing the ideas, habits, and conditions of the farmers of Concord in 1865 to 1878 with those of their father and grandfathers from 1815 to 1825, the difference and the advance is very manifest and gratifying, and apparently the same is going on as rapidly now as ever before. What it will be 50 years hence, no prophet can tell, but as much beyond what we now see as the present is beyond that of 60 years ago.

New Crops

The world now asks for and is willing to pay for matters [food products] which formerly were neither wanted nor produced. This has affected the whole farming interest, within railroad reach of Boston.

New Demands in Market

Fifty to sixty years ago, 1820 to 1830, Boston was a small market for country produce, and the means of transportation then existing limited the supply of perishable articles such as milk, garden vegetables, green peas, beans, cucumbers, and lettuce to a radius of five to ten miles, and in that circle these matters were produced. Some other production: small fruit, strawberries, raspberries, cherries, rhubarb, asparagus, grapes, and some others were then but little known and rarely raised. When I was in college at Cambridge (1822 to 1826) it was considered as an extraordinary fact that a woman living half a mile from the college had a strawberry bed and sold the berries for nine pence a saucer-full, with cream, to the students and others. A few went to her. Probably she sold half a gallon a day. I heard of no other raisers of these at the time. Now the experimental gardeners have produced many and rich varieties of all these matters. The grape, especially, as a northern edible production out-of-doors is entirely new.

The railroads have, by their facilities of quick and easy transportation, extended the radius within which these all can be profitably raised for the Boston market from Lexington to Concord, Groton, and further on every side of the city; the increasing population of that centre, and the still more increased wealth and general taste, has multiplied the sales, and consequently the production is manifold in all the towns in their circle. The intelligent farmers of Concord were rife for their change and adopted it.

Progress of Prosperity: Fruit

In my early days, there were no pears, now and then a peach tree and a cherry tree, no plums, few currants in some gardens which were not much used nor ever sold. There were no smaller berries, no strawberries nor cultivated blackberries. There were apple orchards, but nearly all this fruit was of the poor, sour, hard kind raised for cider only. The only apples for eating were russets and blue pearmains. Farmers put those into their cellars for winter's use; only a few were sold. They were not then considered, as now, an essential element in the household economy. They were given freely to company.

One family in Westford had six sons, all very popular, having many friends. This family had no idea of selling any of their apples. There were no buyers within their reach, but they put into the cellar about 40 barrels of apples and 20 barrels of cider every fall. They had nightly visitors and always entertained them with apples and cider. In this way they consumed all the fruit and cider in each winter. This is one extreme example of this sort of supply and use of the orchard product, plenty for domestic use and hospitality. Yet comparatively few of the apples were cooked for the table.

Applesauce

In the fall, most (probably all) families that could, made a barrel more or less of winter applesauce. For this purpose cider was taken and boiled down to half its quantity and to double its natural strength;

then russet apples were pared, cored, and cut into quarters, and boiled to a pulp in the cider. This was very strong and sour. It could be kept through the winter and spring. This is still used by many farmers, any good apples being used. It is, or was forty years ago when I was in the western country, used and eaten on bread instead of butter by many families and called therefore apple butter. It was kept for sale at the stores and bought by families that did not make it for themselves. I think it was so used in Concord in the last century and previously when butter was not as easily made and obtained as it was afterward.

Progress of Prosperity: Nathan Barrett's Experiment

When the late Deacon Nathan Barrett, son of Nathan, came of age (21) in 1818, as he was the only son and was to live on the farm on Punkatasset Hill in the North East quarter, his father allowed him to follow his own plan of culture. He first bought a very large quantity of young apple trees, of the best improved varieties then known, and planted a large orchard. People generally thought this an unwise investment, and the cautious old farmers foreboded nothing but failure. They said he would never find a market for so much nice fruit. There were no buyers, no consumers, and he could only make cider of his fine apples. His would sell well if carried to market, but for this purpose the old and less expensive kinds of apples were equally good. This proved to be a very profitable investment and still pays a large return for the cost.

About that time, 1818, cultivators had begun to introduce the finer and richer varieties of fruit from abroad and, by culture, to improve their own. The popular taste began to appreciate their productions and to buy them more and more readily. A few years ago my brother, an old farmer and for many years a raiser of fruit, told me that the production of fine eating fruit had increased fifty-fold within his recollection, but such had been the growth of popular taste that this great increase was then sold more readily than the fiftieth part was in his early day. He said, "Poorer people now consider fruit as a needful part of their food."

This is now one of the very important parts of the crops of Concord. Nearly all the farms have their orchards of the best varieties and from this derive no small part of their income. Some have, in good years, many hundred barrels for the market.

Pears

Pears also are now cultivated to considerable extent and pay a large return for the cost and labor.

Smaller Fruits: Strawberries

Strawberries are also cultivated by some very largely. One of the best farmers, Mr. John B. Moore, sends to Boston many thousands of boxes weekly. I was there one day in the summer and counted thirty-six men, women and children picking berries. This, they said, was the usual daily number of pickers. Others raise strawberries in large quantities, though less than Capt. Moore.

Grapes

Another important fruit of comparative late introduction is the grape, and many have gone into the business very largely. Capt. Moore one year raised eight tons. I think Mr. Hurd has raised more than this, and in 1879 he had 14 tons.

Rhubarb, Asparagus

Some garden vegetables are largely [extensively] cultivated. Mr. Moore raises many tons of rhubarb, and several others are also large cultivators of the same. Asparagus also is sent in large quantities from Concord to the market through its season. Many other garden vegetables which were formerly raised only for the families of the cultivators are now grown in large quantities for the market.

[Newspaper clipping:] NOW AND THEN: At this strawberry season, it is of interest to learn about the beginnings of the culture of this fruit in town. The honor of raising the first strawberries in town for the market is claimed by Mr. Charles Bartlett, who put in an acre of strawberries and an acre of asparagus just 36 years ago. He was almost alone in their culture for about eight years, but continued to enlarge his operations until he had six acres in bearing, meanwhile selling thousands of plants a season in various parts of the State. He furnished plants to some of the afterwards leading Dighton raisers. The foremost varieties at the outset were Hovey's seedling and the Early Virginia. For the past eight years has been diminishing production, owing to the low prices prevailing. Last year the average was but 7 cts. a box, and at that price they cannot be raised at profit. First raised strawberries about 38 years ago in Dorchester, and the first he marketed at that time in Boston brought $2 a box. Probably few are aware that there has been so great a fall in the price of the fruit. It is now certainly within the reach of the million, and in that respect low prices are a boon to the public. *Concord Freeman* June 17, 1878.

Note Added June 1880

I am informed that the asparagus ground [has] doubled in the last three years. In 1879 one man had ten acres, and several others had four, five and six acres each. More was set out in 1879 than in any previous year.

Strawberries and Asparagus raised in Concord in 1874
The state census was taken in May 1875. The agricultural facts relate to 1874. I have examined the return of Mr. Warren, who made the inquiry.
His papers are in the state census office, Boston.
I have copied the producers and the quantity they raised.

Producers	Strawberries Qts. or Boxes	Asparagus Bunches
John B. Moore	12,600	6700
G. Brooks	400	1240
G. Donne	150	
G. Lang	300	
Richard Barrett	2400	
C. Hayden	300	
Houghton	3200	4600
Mary Wright	200	
Benj. Clark	2700	880
G. Oliver	280	
G. Miles	4000	
G. F. Wheeler	6000	1000
S. Hall	1350	1000
Heath	320	200
Cynthia Dennis	100	
Henry French	660	6200
Flannery	160	240
Charles Tuttle	4000	2700
Wm. Hunt	1200	
Thos. F. Hunt	200	
Jos. Smith	1236	2000
Gardner Wheeler	4500	300

Producers	Strawberries Qts. or Boxes	Asparagus Bunches
Charles Bartlett	2500	
Francis Wheeler	3600	
G. Wheeler	300	2784
E. Wheeler		2006
Nathan B. Stow	1000	
Franklin Dakin	1333	1080
R. G. Clark	600	
Daniel B. Clark	100	
Enoch Garfield	1600	5000
Mary Ryan	2200	
A. Melvin	200	
M. Caffrey	2000	
G & R. Algeo	2100	
S. C. Paine	2500	150
D. C. Angier	858	
Thomas Burke	220	
Henry Shattuck	700	
Minot Pratt	900	246
G. Rellun	1375	360
W. Smith	4200	
B. Murphy	900	
Sawyer	6667	1200
Paine	600	
E. W. Bull		200
Elijah Wood		2400
J. P. Richardson		100
Lewis Flint		240
John S. Keyes		2400
Wm. D. Brown		50
Hubbard		6000
G. N. Wright		2760
L. Miles		50
Charles Hubbard		4000
[Asa] Calef		276
G. B. Davis		7616
Geo. Pierce		1200
Urban Derby		120
Waldo Flint		2314
The whole town	79,890	73,877

The asparagus of the year was sold for $8,308 and the strawberries for $13,702. All the agricultural products for sale amounted to $296,477. There were 21,915 bushels of apples worth $10,225. Of grapes 52,020 pounds worth $2248.

Present Increase of Fruits

The foregoing account was of the production of 1874, four years ago. Since that time there has been an increase, probably a great increase. When I was in Concord last June (1878), I consulted Capt. John B. Moore and asked him as to the quantities recently raised. Capt. Moore gave his estimates cautiously. There are 100 or more producers of strawberries in Concord. I have before given the names of forty-three who raised the largest quantities in 1874, but there were many small cultivators. Since that time, others have undertaken this work, and now Mr. Chase near Warner's factory, who was not a cultivator four years ago in 1874, is one of the largest. Capt. Moore thinks that more than fifty acres in Concord are devoted to this fruit. Capt. Moore one year raised 25,000 boxes. In one day he sent 3250 boxes to market. He has 3 acres which in one year yielded him $4500 by its strawberries. Probably 200 crates each containing 50 boxes or 10,800 boxes [are] sent to Boston in one day. This is the largest production.

Asparagus

Capt. Moore estimates that 50 acres or more of asparagus are raised in Concord. Judge French, G. Wheeler, Ch. Hubbard are the largest cultivators. One hundred boxes with 44 bunches or 4400 daily [are] sent to market. G. Davis has 4 acres which paid him $1000 last year, 1877. This pays $200 to 400 an acre yearly and some pay much more. I find on Mr. Warner's list 35 who raised it largely in 1874. More have gone into this business since, and there are many who raise small quantities.

Raspberries	Five to ten acres.
Blackberries	Five to ten acres.
Cucumber	[blank]

In former times those who had gardens raised cucumbers for their own use but none for sale. Now many raise them perhaps acres of them for the market.

Milk

Milk is another late addition to the business of the farmer. It always had been provided for family use and perhaps by a few for the neigh-

197

bors in the village and for butter and cheese but not on a large scale for the Boston market until within a few years. Now by their better cultivation the farms produce larger crops of grass, grain and roots etc., and they are enabled to keep more cattle. Besides, they purchase much grain, shorts and other nutriment for their cows. They have greatly increased their number of cows. It is not easy to determine the extent of this increase. The present number is 1204. According to the state reports of the productions of industry, the town sold milk in 1855 for $27,490; in 1865, 21,707 gallons for $38,170; in 1875, 441,000 gallons for $69,014. This branch of industry is almost universal among the farmers, and with many it is their leading business. The contractors or purchasers intervening between the farmers and the consumers take the milk from the farms, and the railroads carry it to Boston.

It is very pleasant to compare the farming interest of the town as it now is and its results with those of former time. Looking at these matters in this way, it appears that there is much more capital invested in this business, and the lands are cultivated at a greater annual cost but manifestly with a much greater profit. It is apparent that the amount of the return from the sales of each one of the important articles herein before mentioned—milk, strawberries, asparagus, rhubarb—is greater than from all the salable articles, hay, grain, potatoes, other roots and vegetables, apples, butter, cheese etc. carried away from the farms to any and all markets in the days of the former generations, adding to these the increased sales of many other articles—apples, pears, currants, grapes, garden seed—and it is plain that the farming interest has very greatly improved, and the cultivators are much more easy in their circumstances than were their fathers. This is plain to every one who has been familiar with the town for forty or fifty years and now travels over it and observes the farms and their accompaniments. It is manifest in the improved and enlarged barns, some of them built at a cost that would [have] bought the whole farms in the first quarter of this century, the improved sheds and other out buildings, vehicles, carts, wagons, carry-alls, buggies, and all sorts of agricultural tools and machinery, the enlarged and more comfortable and tasteful dwellings—pleasant dwellings, pleasant door yards, well fenced, new furnished, and often filled with flowers. Everything in and connected with the farms all indicate an advance in the provincial domestic and social condition of the present generation of the farmers of Concord.

Parish Fund

One proof of this improved condition of the farmers is in the Parish fund. My father was for many years the treasurer. Fifty to sixty years ago, it was loaned almost exclusively to the farmers. They were preferred because they had a substantial basis of credit. They did not pay the principal, it was not wanted, but they paid the interest. This was not then used, but put into the capital, which thus accumulated. The farmers wanted this increase and generally bespoke it, in advance. When I was at home from college in the winter of 1826–27 when teaching the town school, I aided my father in this matter. The fund then was about $11,000. Now the farmers have paid these notes, and many of them have surplus money invested in banks, railroads, U.S. Bonds etc.

Mechanics

There has been no material increase of the mechanics and manufacturers except in and around the woolen factory and Warner's pail factory.

Residents

But there has been a great increase of residents who either do no business or do it elsewhere—probably in Boston or some other place. Charles H. Walcott Esq., assessor, informs me that there are sixty heads of families whose whole business is not in Concord but who have their residence and their families in that town, and about thirty boys and young men whose homes are in Concord but [who] go daily to their business in Boston.

Population

The population of Concord was in

1765	1569
1790	1590
1800	1678
1810	1633
1820	1788
1830	2017
1840	1784

1850	2240
1860	2246
1870	2412
1875	2676

showing a gain of 44% in 35 years, 19% in 25 years, 7.10% in 5 years. This increase is not in the farming population, but it is almost entirely in the factory and the central villages, principally the latter, and these last are mostly of persons who spend their days in Boston, while their families live in Concord. The railroads carry them to their places of business in short time and at very little cost. These have brought some wealth to the town and earn incomes that enable them to contribute much to the support of the town. By all these means, the aggregate wealth of the town has greatly increased within sixteen years. The state reports give us the total valuation of the property of the town in 1861: $1,755,350, and in 1877: $2,765,728. I have no reports older than 1851. It is not easy to determine the true valuation in earlier years. There was a system of reduced valuation in the returns from town to the state government, to avoid what was feared to be an unequal state taxation. But there was no established system in this reduction, so it is impossible to determine how much property was represented by the figures reported. In Mr. Shattuck's history these valuations are given: 1801: $20,362; 1811: $24,554; 1821: $25,860; 1831: $30,681. These can have no relation to the property value of Concord.

Besides their houses, lands etc., the people own stock in banks and railroads. The government taxes all these corporations at the average rate in all the towns of the state but gives to the towns all the tax then paid on the stock owned by their inhabitants. The town report of Concord for 1877 states the town received $3043 from this source. If [the] tax was 1¼ per cent, this represents $290,000 owned by the people in these corporations. Besides this, much of the United States Bonds are owned there. The late Mr. Cheney, cashier of the bank, told me that everybody owned some of this stock, from the servant girl who held a $50 or larger bond to the largest capitalist who had his thousands. The people have manifested a corresponding ability and willingness to tax themselves for public purposes.

Town Expenses

The taxes which the town has paid from time [to time] shows a growing ability and willingness. In 1800 the appropriations were fifty cents per poll for roads to be paid in labor on the highways.

Concord Bank and Printing Office

For schools	883.33
For the poor and other public purposes	1400.00
For schoolhouses extra	200.00
For bridges	270.00
	$2703.33

In 1810 the appropriations were:

For roads (the town record does not mention this)

For schools	1300
Poor etc.	1600
Minister	840
	$3740

In 1820 the appropriations were:

Roads to be paid in labor	1000
Schools	1400
Poor etc.	1800
Other purposes	300
Town debt	200
Minister	850
	$5550

In 1828, the town raised for state, county and town purposes (including highways, which was to be paid in labor) $6,982. In 1877 the whole tax for all purposes including highways was $26,824, all of which was to be paid in money.

The minister tax ceased to be a town matter when the second parish was founded in 1827, but this was paid by the parishes separately.

Church Tax

Before 1825, the town paid $1000 for the support of ministers and other parish purposes. In 1830 and for some years after the formation of the new religious society, and the settlement of Mr. Goodwin as colleague with Dr. Ripley, $2200 was raised. Now over $4000 is raised for the same purpose.

School Tax

When I was chosen member of the school committee in 1832, the town was paying (and for some years had paid) $1400 for support of schools. In 1834 I proposed in the name of the committee that $1800 be granted for schools. This struck some as unreasonable extravagance, and Col. Shattuck, a trader of great sagacity in purchasing, arose and asked if the Doctor would not take a little less. Nevertheless the sum was voted by a large majority. But the next year, 1835, the economists prevailed, and only $1600 was voted for schools. Now $9000 seems to be the established sum to be granted for schools, at least for the present. Fifty years ago the town paid the Common schoolmaster $500. Now the high school master with the same qualifications has $1500 a year as his salary.

CHAPTER XI

Population. Census 1779–1878. Deaths 1779–1878. Rate of mortality
Concord and Massachusetts. In other countries. Ages at death. Average age.
Deaths of children. Causes of death. Ratio of each cause. Diseases most
frequent in Concord. Healthfulness of Concord. Life tables. Survivors by
ages. Foreign populations, effect of, on rate of mortality and average age.
Poor, longevity of. Anglo American population of Concord healthy.

Population

The numbers of the people of Concord were taken by the state authorities in 1765, 1778, 1865 and 1875 and by the national government in 1790 and in every tenth year thereafter, until 1870. There were no enumerations in the intermediate years. In the following table of the annual population of Concord, the state census in 1765, 1865, and 1875 and national census in 1790, 1800, 1810, 1820, 1830,[1] 1850,

---

1. The National Census of 1840 gives only 1784 as the population of that year. This is a falling off of 233 from the numbers in 1830. But with the [obliteration] it necessitates an apparent increase of 465 or 26% in the population from 1840 to 1850. I was familiar with the town during all this period, from 1830 to 1850, and for years previous I neither saw nor did I hear of any evidence of any such decrease in the period, 1830 to 1840, nor of such increase in the succeeding ten years to 1850. There was no perceptible change in any business of the people, no suspension of any factory or manufacturing operations. There were no more houses left vacant in the springs of the first decennial period nor any noticeable increase of business or of dwellings, from 1840 to 1850, more than in any preceding decennial period. The population of the town had a very slow and gradual growth hardly perceptible in all of the first half of this century and no greater in the ten years from 1840 than before. The marshal who took the census in 1840 was not a man of accurate habits or of mental discipline. It is extremely probable that he omitted families and hence comes the apparent decrease. I have therefore omitted this census entirely and calculated the number of the people in each of the years 1831 to 1849, inclusive on the enumerations of 1830 and 1850.

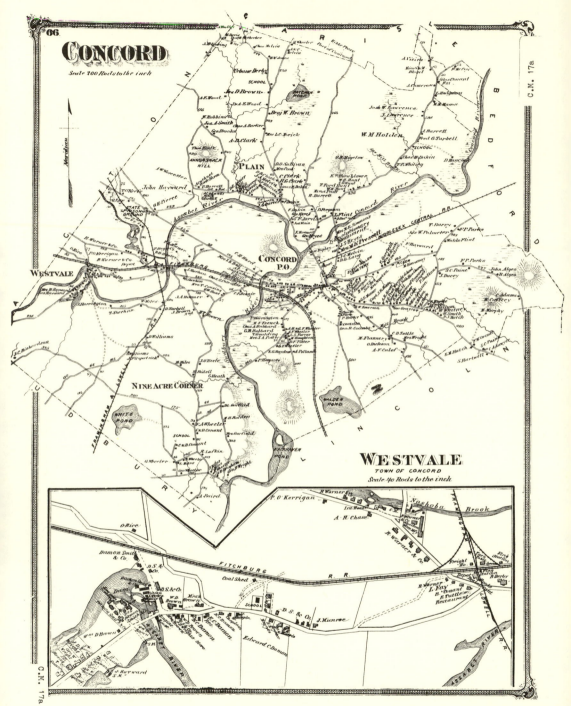

Map of Concord, 1875

1860 and 1870 are assumed for those years. Those of the intermediate years are calculated by algebra and logarithms from these enumerations. They are approximately true and the whole may be considered as the sum of the numbers in each and all of the hundred years, 1779 to 1878 inclusive; and are, with the numbers of deaths in all of these years, a safe basis for the calculation of the rate of mortality of the town in that period and in any part of it. [See Appendix IV]

100 years
Summary of the annual Population in Periods

1779–90	19004	
1791–1800	16379	
1801–1810	16532	
1811–1820	17165	
1821–1828	15104	
1779–1828	[84184]	83184[EJ]
1829–1840	[24781]	22845[EJ]
1841–1850	21942	
1851–1860	22469	
1861–1870	22878	
1871–1878	21209	
1829–1878	[113279]	111343[EJ]
1779–1878	[197463]	194447[EJ]

Mortality

Rev. Dr. Ripley was settled as the minister of the whole town Nov. 7, 1778. He immediately began to keep a record of all the deaths in town, which he continued until the second parish separated from the first in 1827. This record contains the name of the deceased, the date, and cause for the First Parish. This he continued with the aid of his colleague Mr. Goodwin, until the settlement of Mr. Frost, and he did the same down to 1860. This copy is now in the public library of Concord. My brother the late Capt. Francis Jarvis took two copies of these records, one for himself and one for me. He added to the announcement of each death the occupation, location or school district where the deceased had lived. The first of these copies is in my possession. The second is at the farm of my late brother, in the hands of his children, Mrs. Lucy H. Derby and Cyrus H. Jarvis. After the separation of the second parish, the minister or other official kept an imperfect record of their deaths for some of the years. The town clerk kept a similar, though apparently incomplete record, but more full from 1840. This is printed in the selectman's reports from 1850 to the present time. From all these records I have taken the facts in the following tables.

Deaths in Concord in 100 years

Years	Number	Years	Number	
1779	12	1829	29	
1780	12	1830	22	
1781	15	1831	44	
1782	18	1832	28	
1783	24	1833	36	
1784	17	1834	37	
1785	17	1835	22	
1786	19	1836	21	
1787	12	1837	31	
1788	19	1838	33	
1789	17	1839	32	
1790	26	1840	20	
12 yrs.	208	*12 yrs.*	314	[355]
1791	17	1841	31	
1792	27	1842	37	
1793	9	1843	17	
1794	21	1844	34	
1795	22	1845	20	
1796	26	1846	20	
1797	22	1847	35	
1798	23	1848	36	
1799	20	1849	39	
1800	26	1850	26	
10 yrs.	213	*10 yrs.*	294	[295]
1801	35	1851	37	
1802	28	1852	36	
1803	39	1853	39	
1804	34	1854	46	
1805	36	1855	35	
1806	32	1856	39	
1807	34	1857	33	
1808	22	1858	29	
1809	19	1859	17	
1810	40	1860	38	
10 yrs.	319	*10 yrs.*	348	[349]
1811	23	1861	43	
1812	34	1862	25	
1813	30	1863	39	
1814	24	1864	41	

Years	Number	Years	Number
1815	54	1865	47
1816	22	1866	47
1817	22	1867	32
1818	23	1868	37
1819	30	1869	35
1820	30	1870	38
10 yrs.	292	*10 yrs.*	384
1821	59	1871	31
1822	40	1872	29
1823	29	1873	56
1824	36	1874	36
1825	43	1875	47
1826	46	1876	51
1827	19	1877	40
1828	29	1878	39
8 yrs.	301	*8 yrs.*	329

Fifty years 1779–1828

Periods	Deaths	Sum of annual populations	Living to 1 death
1779–90	208	19,004	91.3
1791–1800	213	16,379	76.9
1801–10	319	16,532	51.8
1811–20	292	16,165	55.3
1821–28	301	15,104	50.2
1779–1828	1333	83,184	62.4

Fifty years 1829 to 1878

Periods	Deaths	Sum of annual populations	Living to 1 death
1829–40	314	22,865	72.3
1841–50	294	21,732	78.1
1851–60	348	22,469	64.5
1861–70	384	22,878	59.5
1871–78	329	21,209	64.4
1829–78	1669	111,153	65.7

One Hundred years 1779–1878

Periods	Deaths	Sum of annual populations	Living to 1 death
1779–1878	3002	194,337	64.2

Taking these facts in periods of twenty-five years, we have the following results.

Periods	Deaths	Sum of annual populations	Living to 1 death
1779–1803	523	40,391	77.2
1804–28	810	42,793	52.4
1829–53	720	49,892	69.3
1854–78	949	59,812	63.0
1779–1828	1333	83,184	69.9
1829–78	1669	111,153	65.7
1779–1878	3002	194,337	64.3

The "State" report in 1878 shows the rate in each town for the 13 preceding years 1865–1877 inclusive. In that period, the rate was one in 68 in Concord and in 8 other towns. In 92 other towns the rate was lower, and in 241 towns it was higher, showing that by this rule of measurement Concord was in the healthiest third of towns in Massachusetts. Of the 342 towns and cities 26.9% showed a lower rate, 2.1% the same and 70.4% a higher rate than Concord. In Middlesex County, Belmont, Medford, Watertown, Everett, Melrose, Wayland, Lincoln, Reading, Weston, Malden, Stoneham, Wilmington, Maynard, Tewksbury, Winchester had a lower rate than Concord. Besides these fifteen towns in Middlesex, the other equally healthy towns were in counties of Worcester 14, Hampden 7, Berkshire 16, Suffolk 2, Franklin 8, Barnstable 1, Plymouth 6, Essex 9, Norfolk 5, Dukes 2, Hampshire 2, Bristol 4. All the cities, all the counties, as such and the state in totality showed a higher rate than Concord. The rate in most of the countries in Europe is higher than in Concord. The Registrar General of England in his 39th annual report gives the rates in the following countries. All are drawn from the experience of twenty years 1853 to 1872 except Italy and Spain. Rate in England and Wales one in 44.5,

Scotland one in	44.7
Denmark "	49.2
Sweden	49
Austria	31.3
Prussia	38.99
Netherlands	38.99
France	41.3
Hungary	21.4
Spain 1861, 1870	33.6
Italy 1863, 1872	33.1
Spain 1867*	30

*(calculated from *Annuaria Estadictica España* 1866–67 page 53 of 259.)

Five of the healthier counties of England had in 1876 a rate of mortality one in 60.9, one in 59.9, and one in 59.4 of the living. Some of the country towns and districts had a constant rate for many years not exceeding one in 58.8. These are held up by the Registrar General and other sanitary authorities as models to be imitated as far as possible by all the other districts of the kingdom.

The people of Norway enjoy the longest life and the greatest exemption from death among all the nations of the world of which we have any record. The rate of mortality in the whole kingdom was in periods[2] 1815 to 1825 one in 52.5,

1825–1835	76.9
1835–1845	100.0
1845–1855	90.9
1855–1865	76.9
1866	166.0
1867	200.0

When judging by this standard, the rate of mortality of Concord is healthier than two-thirds of the towns of Massachusetts and healthier than every nation of Europe of which we have the record except Norway.

Number and ages of the deceased

Ages	Periods				
	1779–1828	*1829–58*	*1859–78*	*1829–78*	*1779–1878*
under 1	158	96	155	251	409
1–5	137	90	85	175	312
6–10	52	37	21	58	110
11–20	70	51	45	96	166
21–30	119	72	94	166	285
31–40	101	66	66	132	233
41–50	106	34	46	80	186
51–60	106	55	68	123	229
61–70	112	60	80	140	252
71–80	161	80	144	224	385
81–90	106	56	86	142	248
91–100	28	16	12	28	56
over 100	1	0	0	0	1
		713		1629	2871
Not given		48		48	48

2. *Norge officielle Statistic*, 1870, p. 44.

Ages			Periods		
	1779–1828	*1829–58*	*1859–78*	*1829–78*	*1779–1878*
total	1252	761	916	1677	2923
under 5	290	186	254	440	730
under 20	412	274	320	596	1002
20 to 70	534	287	350	641	1179
under 70	946	561	674	1235	2181
over 70	296	152	242	394	690

Ratios per 1000 of all deaths in the several periods who died
in the ages as named below:

Age	*1779–1828*	*1829–1853*	*1854–78*	*1829–78*	*1779–1878*
−5	243	244	277	263	269
+5	757	756	723	737	751
−20	331	360	344	354	342
+20	669	640	651	646	658
20–70	429	440	382	382	403
−70	761	800	735	736	742
+70	239	200	265	264	258

Comparing the last half century (1829–1878) with the preceding (1779–1828), there was a small increase of mortality under 5 and also under 20. On the contrary, there was an increase of the survivors of 70, and on the whole the life in this respect compares in Concord favorably with that in most of the other towns in Massachusetts. We have no life table of Concord nor of Massachusetts. This would be the best ground for comparing the value of life in the town and state. But the table on the preceding page [now above] offers an approximation to the life table as shown in the preceding pages in respect to Concord.

It is there shown that of all those who died in Concord at known ages within the century ending with 1878, those who had survived their 5th and their 20th years respectively were in slightly larger proportion in the first half than in the last half of the century. But the proportion who survived their 70th year was greater in the last period. And of those who entered full maturity of manhood or womanhood at 20, 35 per cent in the first period and 40 per cent in the second period lived through their working and productive years and entered upon full old age at 71.

Survivors in Massachusetts

The 37th Restoration Report of Massachusetts, page 47, gives the deaths and the ages of the deceased for ten years 1865–1874. The whole number was 287,204 of known ages.

I have condensed these into periods of longevity and calculated the ratios of those who survived the several ages as in the following table:

Number dying in ten years

Under 5	Over 5	Under 20	Over 20	20 to 70	Under 70	Over 70
104,233	183,071	132,567	154,737	114,583	247,150	40,154

Ratio in each period to total in all ages

Under 5	Over 5	Under 20	Over 20	20 to 70	Under 70	Over 70
362	638	461	539	398	860	140

Comparison of Survivorship in Concord and Massachusetts

Comparing these ratios of survivors in Concord with those in the state, it appears that in a thousand persons who had died in all ages in each, 249 in Concord and 362 in the whole state were under five. 658 in the town and 539 in the state had not passed their 20th year. 258 in Concord and 140 had fulfilled their three score and ten years of life.

Mortality: Average Age

In the preceding tables showing the rate of mortality or ratio of the dying to the living, all the deaths are included, and these in the several periods of twenty-five years, of fifty years, and one hundred are compared with the sums of annual population of the same periods. But in determining the average age and in comparing the life in Concord with that in other towns and districts, it is necessary to include only those deaths with which the ages are given; as there are some in the Concord records whose ages are not recorded, the numbers taken for this purpose are less than those taken for the rate of mortality. The average age is thus obtained by dividing the sum of the ages of those who died in the several periods by the number of persons who died in those periods whose ages are given. By this means it is found that the average age of all those whose ages are recorded was in the period:

Average age

1779–1803	40 y.	4 m.	17 d.
1804–1828	43	5	25
1829–1853	37	1	17
1854–1878	38	11	22
1779–1828	42	10	5
1829–1878	38	2	6
1779–1878	39	11	2

The average age is not an exact indication of the value of life in any people. It is materially affected by the composition of the living population. In a newly settled town, where all or most of the families are young, these with their children would have a lower average of age both of the living and the dead than in another and older town, where the old had completed their natural terms of life and the young and middle-aged went to other places to live and have their families.

Nevertheless the average age at death affords an approximation of the value of life in any town or people, and it is here taken as a basis of comparison of Concord with other places.

The 36th Report of Mortality of Massachusetts gives the average age of all who died in 1877. This was in Concord 50.92 years. No other town had exactly this average. 33 towns or 9.6% of the whole had a higher average. 308 towns or 90% had a lower average age.

The 37th report gives these averages for the counties for fourteen years, 1865 to 1878. These are

Nantucket	50.54
Dukes	48.22
Barnstable	40.30
Franklin	40.18
Plymouth	38.86
Hampshire	35.84
Berkshire	33.93
Norfolk	32.55
Worcester	31.43
Bristol	30.83
Essex	29.96
Middlesex	29.07
Hamden	27.20
Suffolk	24.45
Massachusetts	29.82

Average Age in Old Families

Several of the largest families now in Concord have been there from the early periods of its history and some from the beginning of the town. I have copied, from the records, the deaths and ages of the males in eleven of these families from 1779 to 1878.

As a very large portion of the females married and many moved to other places and were thereafter only known by other names, it is impossible to trace them beyond youth and middle age, when most of their deaths have happened. We have then in these Concord records only their deaths in early life. The ages of these give no indications of the average age of the whole or of their vitality or real longevity. Therefore I confine this statement to the males of these families who died in Concord.

There is another difficulty in the fact that some infants are entered in the record without personal names but only as child of the parents as "child of Joseph Buttrick; child of Nathan Barrett" without designation of sex or age. There were fifty of these thus recorded in the eleven families which are herein quoted. I have assumed that one half of them were males, which is very slightly less than the true population. If these were all of one family the difference could be admitted, but it cannot be recognized in the very small numbers that are recorded of the separate families.

Average Age in Old Families Males

Family	Deaths	Sum of ages	Years	Average age Months	Days
Barrett	46	1791	38	5	5
Brown	54	2070	36	9	2
Buttrick	33	1399	41	9	4
Derby	11	345	31	4	11
Flint	13	475	35	2	6
Hosmer	44	1646	37	2	17
Hunt	32	1060	32	7	11
Melvin	17	815	46	6	24
Miles	18	774	43		
Prescott	16	689	43		22
Wheeler	58	2489	43	3	21

Deaths in Childhood

Infancy and childhood are more feeble [times of life and] have less power to resist the course of disease or its destructive force than any part of mature life except extreme old age. Being the most susceptible to the effects of any injurious influence, it is taken by sanitarians as a test of the healthfulness of any place or people, and the ground of comparison of our town with another in this respect.

In the following table the ratio of deaths in infancy (under 1) and in childhood (under 5) is shown for Concord at various periods and for some counties in Massachusetts and also some other counties. These ratios are calculated from the reports of deaths of ages of those several town-counties and counties.

Town county; or country	Period	In 1000 Deaths all under 1	all under 5
Concord	1779–1828	123	233
Concord	1829–1878	162	270
Concord	1779–1878	145	254
Massachusetts[b]	1865–1878	224	358
Suffolk County[b]	1865–1878	252	418
Middlesex Cty[b]	1865–1878	220	360
Berkshire Cty[b]	1865–1878	173	302
Franklin Cty[b]	1865–1878	140	229
Barnstable Cty[b]	1865–1878	129	218
Nantucket Cty[b]	1865–1878	77	130
England[c]	1838–1874	234	402
Scotland[d]	1855–1868	193	379
Ireland[e]	1864–1869	150	266
France[f]	1861–1869	143	329
France[g]	1875	191	285
France[h]	1879	185	285
Spain[i]	1858–1862	175	366
Netherlands[j]	1850–1859	310	464
Norway[k]	1858–1868	193	333
Sweden[l]	1878	174	273
Italy[m]	1868	276	466

b. *37th Registration Report Massachusetts* p. cl & lix.
c. Report of Mortality.
d. Calculated from annual reports.
e. Census of Ireland 1871, Vol. II, p. 274.
f. *Statistique de la France Mouvement de les Population.*
g. *Statistique de la France Mouvement de les Population.*
h. [indecipherable]
i. *Annuario Estadistico de España.*
j. *Statistich Jarhbuch*, 1863.
k. *Norje Officinale Statistik*, 1869.
l. *Statistik Helso och Sjukvarden.*
m. [indecipherable]

In Childhood

It is seen in this table that the smallest proportion die in childhood in Nantucket and Dukes counties; next to them comes Barnstable, and next is Franklin. Concord then follows in the order of health of early life and is more favored in this respect than any other counties and the state at large. Great Britain, Ireland and France all have a higher rate of mortality in infancy and childhood than Concord.

Diseases, Causes of Death

The causes of death are given in most cases both in Dr. Ripley's and in the town records. They are not all stated scientifically, and more than one name is given to the same disease, as "Lung Fever," "Inflammation of the Lungs," and "Pneumonia." All refer to the same conditions of the respiratory organ; some others are given loosely. I have condensed these as far as possible into a scientific morphology, and they are all copied into the manuscript volume of "Mortality in Concord" now or hereafter to be in the town library. In that I have divided them into the two semi-centennial periods ending with 1828 and 1878.

This table is condensed and in the table next following, the proportion which the deaths from each disease to 100,000 living is calculated and given.

This table presents the ratio of deaths caused by each disease to the living population both of Concord and Massachusetts. From this it is easy to see the comparative destructive force of each cause in the town and in the state. In the following table are given several of the most fatal disease and classes of disease, including the proportion of each cause to the whole and also the ratio of each to 100,000 of the living in the town and the Commonwealth. By this it is seen that the mortality is not due always to the same cause in this locality and in the other towns of Massachusetts.

Ratio of Deaths from each Cause

Diseases and Classes of Disease	In 10,000 Deaths		In 100,000 Living	
	Town	State	Town	State
Zymotic disease	2858	2793	411	532
Dis. of children	1788	2096	214	532
Dis. of digestive organs	1279	1374	162	266

Diseases and Classes of Disease	In 10,000 Deaths		In 100,000 Living	
	Town	State	Town	State
Dis. of respiratory organs	2666	2727	383	520
Dis. of brain & nerves	96	89	13	20
Ratio of Deaths from Each Cause				
Consumption	2112	1879	304	324
Typhoid fever	1073	470	149	55
Old Age	959	525	138	98
Pneumonia	438	582	63	144
Cholera Infantum	405	528	57	172
Accident/Negligence	39	71	56	340
Dysentery	391	353	55	29
Scarlet fever	308	404	44	63
Palsy	287	197	41	51
Convulsion	287	181	41	35
Intemperance	129	47	18	4
Croup	96	204	13	35
Whooping cough	39	110	5	20
Teething	32	114	4	16
Rheumatism	25	11	3	4
Measles	25	88	3	10
Diphtheria	17	185	2	115
Diarrhœa	14	122	2	22

Rates of Concord and Massachusetts

[A comparison of] the numbers in the first column in the last table with those in the second shows the difference of the proportion that each disease or class of diseases has born in the mortality of the town and the state. But this does not represent the relative mortality of these causes to the whole number of the living.

Comparing the numbers in the third column with those in the fourth shows the proportion which the destructive power of each cause and class of causes bears to the living in Concord and the Commonwealth and offers a good ground for comparison of their healthfulness.

The *zymotic* diseases are described as *endemic* or arising from local causes, *epidemic* or spreading in the atmosphere, and *contagious* or communicated from one diseased person to a healthy person.[3]

3. Ed: Zymotic is an obsolete term meaning what nowadays is called contagious. It is interesting that Jarvis differentiates between epidemic and contagious diseases, as if their origins derived from different pernicious circumstances.

They are supposed to originate in very great measure from preventable causes either in the condition of the soil or the air, or the habits of the people. They are therefore assumed as a basis of comparison as to healthfulness of one place or the inhabitants with others. Thirteen diseases of this class cause the most deaths of children. They are cholera infantum,[4] dysentery, measles, diarrhœa, croup, teething, whooping cough, quincy [sore throat, tonsillitis], thrush, worms, diphtheria, infantile.

Diseases of Concord and State

On this account I have included these in the class of Diseases of Children in the foregoing table. Several other diseases come within the description of the zymotic class as fever, small pox, erysipelas, rheumatism, influenza, carbuncle[5] etc., but are more common to adults than to children. Looking now to the table and comparing the numbers in the town and the state columns it is seen that the zymotic class—diseases of the brain and nerves, consumption, fevers, old age, dysentery, palsy, convulsions, intemperance, and rheumatism—produced a larger proportion of the mortality in Concord than in the state; and that diseases of children as such diseases of the digestive organs, diseases of the lungs, pneumonia, cholera infantum, scarlet fever, croup, diphtheria, diarrhœa, teething, whooping cough, measles, accident and negligence caused a larger proportion of the mortality in the State than in Concord. But the relations of town and State are different, when the population is assumed as a basis for calculating the ratio of the destructiveness of the various diseases.

Fatality of Various Causes in Concord and Massachusetts

Comparing the numbers in the third and fourth columns of the table it is seen that in proportion to the living, fever, typhoid, old age, convulsions, dysentery, and intemperance were more destructive in the town than in the state; and the zymotic class—scarlet fever, diseases of children, palsy, diseases of the lungs, croup, accident and negligence, diarrhoea, consumption, whooping cough, diseases of the digestive

4. Ed.: Cholera infantum is an obsolete term for an acute intestinal disease, now called intestinal grippe or stomach flu.
5. Ed.: Carbuncle refers to a staphylococcal infection known nowadays as a boil. Before the advent of antibiotics such infections often were fatal.

organs, teething, measles, cholera infantum, rheumatism, pneumonia, and diphtheria—caused more deaths in the state than in Concord in proportion to the population.

The fatality of some of these causes was much greater in the Commonwealth generally than in this town. The proportion of deaths from diseases of childhood, from pneumonia, measles, whooping cough, cholera infantum, teething, accident or negligence as recorded was more than twice as great in the state at large as in Concord. The proportion of diphtheria—115 in the state to 2 in the town—is probably in great measure due to a difference in the name applied to the disease. The term Diphtheria is comparatively new. In the improvements in the medical profession and the more exact diagnosis or distinction of diseases, it is found that many cases that were formerly called cynanche,[6] croup, and malignant sore throat are really a distinct form of disease, to which term diphtheria is now applied. In the table, the column showing the proportion of deaths to population in the state report includes only the last five years (and of course includes the recent improvements in nosology), whereas the town reports include all the deaths for the last hundred years.

Intemperance, Delerium Tremens

Intemperance and delerium tremens seem to have been a much more prevalent cause of death (18 to 9 in 100,000 living) in Concord than in the state. This excess is probably rather apparent in great degree than real and [is] due probably to a difference in the method of reporting. Dr. Ripley in many cases added the word Intemperance to the name of disease, which undoubtedly was true, as one of the causes of the death, whereas in many perhaps most town and cities, this is not given except in manifest cases of delirium tremens. Accident and negligence were much less fatal in Concord than in other places, indicating greater care in the people and less exposure to danger. Old age has been a much more frequent cause of death in Concord, than in the state generally. It is an indication of the healthiness of the town and the habits of the people that so large a proportion survive to the extreme of age. It appears then from this analysis of the prevailing and fatal diseases that

6. Ed.: Cynanche is an old term from a Greek word meaning dog's collar. It refers to acute throat infections, of which diphtheria may be one.

Concord is less subject to those that are most destructive than the whole state generally.

Effect of the Foreign Element on the General Rate of Mortality and Average Age

The introduction of the foreign families and people into Massachusetts materially affects the proportion of death to the living and the average age at death. These immigrants are in very large proportion from Ireland. Taking the national life tables of several counties it is seen that of 10,000 born in each county, there survived:

	20th year	70th year
Norway	7415	3487
Sweden	6698	2557
England	6627	2379
U.S. males	6543	2559
Germany	6121	1607
France	5022	1176
Ireland	4855	861

These tables are based on the census of the whole population and the deaths for many years, with the ages of the living and dead in each nation, and are prepared and published by the national authorities. They must therefore be accepted as evidence of the value of life or the measure of the vital force of their respective peoples. They show that the Irish people have the least vitality and the least longevity. The Irish immigrants are in very large proportion of the marriageable age, 20 to 35, on their arrival in the United States. Nearly all of these, many more than among Americans, are married when they come or may soon be thereafter. Their marriages are more productive than those of other races, of whom we have the records. An examination of the reports of Marriages and Births published by the governments of several nations and states show the following average births to each marriage.

Births to Marriage

Country	Period	Births to Marriage
Mass.[a]	1849, 1878	3,37
England[b]	1846–1879	3,67
France[c]		4,21
Norway[d]	1866, 67, 68	4,57

Country	Period	Births to Marriage
Scotland[e]	1855–1876	4,33
Holland[f]	1860–1869	5,24
Ireland[g]	1868–1877	5,30

a. 37th Report, p. 2 and 23.
b. 39th Report, p. xlviii and lix.
c. *Statistique de la France 1876*, iv to xxvi.
d. Folkmongder in 1856, 57 and 58.
e. 20th Report, XVIII and XIX.
f. *Statistiche Bercheidon.*
g. Report 1878.

This addition of foreigners and their families to the population of Concord has been mostly since 1850. In the census of 1875 there were 2141 native or persons born in the United States and 535 foreigners, about 20%. This number of foreigners includes only those who were born abroad. Their children born here are, in the eye of the law, Americans and are included in the 2141 native. But in a pathological or sanitary point of view they should be included in the class of foreigners, for they inherit the feebler constituency and the low vitality of their parents. These foreigners belong to the class of the poor, among whom as a general law, there is more sickness, more early death, and a lower average longevity. In 1844, I analyzed the bills of mortality of Concord from 1778 to 1842 (65 years), of Dorchester from 1825 to 1842 (17 years), and of Brookline for 40 years. I arranged the deceased according to the classes of occupation, and these again according to age. This enabled me to determine the proportion of death in these classes that fell on infancy and childhood. In 1000 deaths in each class there were in Concord in infancy under two years of age, 119 in the farmers' families and 235 in the laborers' families. This corresponds with the English experience as shown in the Report on the sanitary condition of the laboring classes. Taking into consideration the condition and circumstances of the foreign element and their families and their greater proportion of infancy in the most perishable age, it is manifest that they must increase the mortality in undue proportion and its rate to the whole living population, and also diminish the average age of all at death, while yet the death rate and the average age of the American population of Anglo Saxon origin may remain unchanged or even be more favorable. This must be taken as an explanation of the facts in the table showing that in the whole population of Concord, the ratio of death to the living was less and the average age of the living was greater in the fifty years ending 1828, when the population was almost entirely American or of English origin, than it was in the fifty years ending with 1878, when there was a large admixture of people of Irish origin. The table showing the proportion of early mortality is another proof of this. It is there shown that the deaths of children are in the smallest proportion in the counties of Dukes, Nantucket, Barnstable, and Franklin, where the population is the most purely American, and in the largest proportion in Suffolk and Middlesex, where are the greatest proportions of foreign families. From all these facts it appears that Concord is among the most healthy towns, and it may be assumed that it is now as healthy as and probably more healthy than it has been in the last hundred years.

C H A P T E R   X I I

Battle 19th April 1775. Monument. Legislature asked to aid this and also
Bunker Hill, Concord, in 1835, voted to build on the Battleground.
Inscriptions asked and written, Dr. Ripley, Mr. Emerson, Mr. Shattuck, Dr.
Jarvis. Where was first gun fired? Controversy Concord and Lexington. Dr.
Ripley's, Mr. Phinney's histories. Lendrum's account. Provincial Congress
inquiry. Testimony. Lexington soldiers fired singly not in company nor by
official order. Lexington calls this forcible resistance. Concord fight the
turning point of the war. It produced sudden change in public opinion in
America and England. Dr. Jarvis's inscription. Accepted with change of only
one word the most important of all.

About 1823 or '24 the friends of the Bunker Hill Monument petitioned the Legislature for a grant of $10,000 to aid in its building. At
the same time the people of Concord asked the Legislature for $1,000
to build their monument. Mr. John Keyes was then in the Senate. He
told us in Concord that M. N. P. Russell, the active friend of the
Bunker Hill Monument, came to him and said that the presentation of
the Concord petition would [im]peril both [petitions] in the Legislature, but if the Concord people would withdraw theirs, the Bunker Hill
friends would agree to give $600 to the Concord project, if their
request for $10,000 should be granted. Mr. Keyes thought that this
almost certainty of $600 was better than the uncertain hope of $1000
and so withdrew the Concord petition. The $600 was gained. Concord
then determined to begin a monument in the center near the town
pump where is now a fountain and public watering place. On the 19th
of April, 1825, the cornerstone was laid with all due formality. There

was a procession of the military, Masons and [towns]people. Mr. Everett delivered an oration in the meetinghouse and the Masons did their work. There the matter ended and slept for two years. Some mischievous persons made a large fire on the stone, which was about 4 or 5 feet square and 2 ft. thick. This was cracked and spoiled for the purpose. It was said that the box that was put under it containing mementos of the occasion and the time was stolen. Nothing more was done until 1835, when the town after much discussion voted to build the monument where it now stands. Dr. Ripley gave the land and the avenue that leads to it from the highway. The monument was built in 1836.

Inscription

The monument committee asked for inscriptions from such as were interested in the matter. Several were written. The committee showed these to everyone. Dr. Ripley wrote a long and elaborate one, historical and descriptive of the battle. It was excellent but too long for the tablet on the monument. Mr. Lemuel Shattuck wrote a similar one, but it had the same objection. Mr. R. W. Emerson wrote, I think, the best offered, but this was too long. None of these could be inscribed on that tablet. I took a measure of the tablet that was to be used, ascertained the exact size of the letters to be inscribed. Thus I determined the exact amount of letters and words that would be admitted and constructed my inscription accordingly. In considering what should be written, it was manifest that there was no room for history and details as on the Lexington monument, which had a much larger tablet. No such descriptions could be admitted here. There was only room to indicate the spot, the event, its character and results.

Where Was the First Gun Fired?

At that time there were differences of opinion between the people of Concord and Lexington as to the place where the first armed or forcible resistance was made to the British troops on that day. Mr. Phinney had published a pamphlet account of the matter in Lexington in which he showed that some American did return the fire of the British troops on Lexington Common. Dr. Ripley wrote a rejoinder in which he endeavored to show by negative evidence that no such resistance was made there. This was in 1825, fifty years after the battle.

Revolutionary War Monument at North Bridge, Concord

The witnesses testified that they were present on the occasion but neither saw nor heard any American fire.

Mr. Phinney's witnesses state that after the British Colonel had ordered the Provincial Militia assembled on Lexington Common (whom he called rebels) to disperse and his troops had fired upon them, they broke ranks and went away, but while doing so several fired back on the assailants. This was confirmed by evidence taken by the Provincial Congress at Watertown, three days after the battle. The positive assertion of those who fired their guns and of those who saw and heard the provincial firing could not be denied. But it is not surprising that in the darkness the confusion, the noise and the firing of the British troops, others should neither hear nor see any American fire. Rev. Mr. Clark of

Lexington in his account of the battle makes the same statement as to the firing then by the Provincials.

Lendrum's Account

In my boyhood, I had read Lendrum's *History of the Revolutionary War*, published in Boston in 1795, twenty years after the Battle in Concord. In this he says,

> Maj. Pitcairn who had the advanced corps {at Lexington} rode up to them {the Provincial militia} and called out, "Disperse you rebels. Throw down your arms and disperse." They still continued in a body to fire. This was done with a huzza. A dispersion of the militia was the consequence but the firing of the regulars was nevertheless continued. Individuals finding they were fired upon though dispersing returned the fire. Three or four of the militia were killed on the green, a few more were shot after they began to disperse.

The Testimony before the Provincial Congress

"On the 22nd of April, the Provincial Congress at Watertown appointed a committee to take depositions in perpetuation from which a full account of the transaction of the troops under General Gage in their route to be from Concord etc., on Wednesday last (19th) may be collected to be sent to England by the first ship from Salem."[1] They made their report to Congress on the 22nd of May following. This report was accepted and ordered with the depositions to be printed. In the first paragraph they say the British troops fired and killed eight men on the spot {in Lexington} and wounded several others before any guns were fired upon the {British} troops by our men.[2]

Elijah Sanderson on the 25th, four days after the fight, testified. "The regulars shouted ran and fired on the Lexington company, which did not fire a gun, before the regulars discharged on them."[3] Mr. Sanderson was on the spot at the time. Thomas Rice Willard testified that he was in the house of Mr. Harrington and saw and heard the British officer call upon the Militia to "lay down your arms." But not a gun was fired until the militia were dispersed.[4]

1. Journals of Each Provincial Congress of Massachusetts in 1776 [indecipherable].
2. Provincial Journals, p. 664.
3. Provincial Journals, p. 664.
4. Provincial Journal, p. 666–667.

Simon Winship testified on 25 April that he was seized by the British troops and forced to march with them to Lexington Common. That he heard the British officer order his troops to fire but there was no discharge of arms on either side until the word fire was given by the said officer.

Benjamin Tidd and Joseph Abbott both testified (Ap[ril] 25) that they saw the British troops marching up to the Lexington company and fire just a few guns and then a volley or two before any guns were fired by the Lexington company.

Nathanael Mulliken, Philip Russell and thirty-two others on the 25th all testify that they belonged to the Lexington company and were present on the Lexington green on the morning of the 19th when, "We were fired upon by the troops while our backs were turned upon the troops and a number of our men killed and wounded. Not a gun was fired, by any person in our company on the regulars to our knowledge, before they fired on us."[5] Nathanael Parkhurst and thirteen others on the 25th Ap[ril] testified that they were in the Lexington company on the morning of the 19th upon the green. "The regulars fired on the company before a gun was fired by any of our company."[6]

William Draper Ap[ril] 25 testified "that he was on the parade, at Lexington about half an hour before sunrise on the 19th April. He was within three or four rods of the regular troops and heard the commanding officer give the word "*fire*' and immediately they fired before any of Capt. Parker's company fired."[7]

Timothy Smith, Levi Read and Levi Harrington of Lexington also on the same date, 25 April, testified that they were on the Lexington green and saw and heard the British troops fire on the Lexington company but they said nothing of the firing by the American on the regulars.[8] On the contrary, John Bateman, a soldier of the British regiment, testified on the 23rd of April that he was in Lexington and near the meetinghouse when the troops marched by. He heard the officer order them to fire on the Lexington company and one did fire, and he saw none of the provincials lie dead on the ground near the meetinghouse, but "I never heard any of the inhabitants so much as fire one gun on said troops."[9]

This is negative evidence and is not surprising in that dusky morn-

5. Journal of Prov. Congress, p. 667.
6. Journal of Prov. Congress, p. 668.
7. Prov. Cong. Journal, p. 670.
8. Prov. Cong. Journal, p. 669.
9. Prov. Cong. Journal, p. 671.

ing, half an hour before sunrise in that great noise and confusion and with the firing of the regulars; it is not to be supposed that all could hear the guns so clearly as to determine on which side they were fired or in what part of the field or even in what part of the line they were held. There was a regiment of regulars, and the line extended a considerable distance. The American firing might have been at one end of the line and Bateman on the other beyond reach of eye or of power to hear discriminately.

It must be observed that of the fifty-eight witnesses who testified to the time of the firing by the Lexington company, all used nearly the same language that none of their company fired *until after the regulars had fired on them* and that none of them stated the principal part, that the Americans did fire. They only stated this condition and the relation in order of time to the British fire.

It is plain that this act of firing by the Lexington soldier was so well known and so universally acknowledged that it was not needful to mention but only refer to it as an established fact in reference to its subsequency to the British fire that had provoked it. They had fired, but they were justified in doing so by the preceding British attack on them.

It is also shown by all the witnesses that the firing by the American was not by the organized company nor by order of their officers but after the captain had dismissed them and each on his own responsibility fired while on the retreat. This firing too was by only a few, and it was therefore a very small and ineffectual resistance. Yet, as far as it went, it was a forcible resistance and technically it must be accepted as such.

Moreover the world at large does so accept it and believe that the first forcible resistance to British aggression was made at Lexington. Yet the people of Concord held fast to the faith that the first forcible resistance was at the Concord bridge, and they clung to it as proudly as if in this simple matter of priority of firing lay the great honor of the day and importance of its events.

I had also read the accounts of the British officers who said the same, in their reports to the government at home. All went to confirm the result of the inquiry made on the 22nd of April three days after by our Provincial congress of Massachusetts at Watertown through many witnesses who were at Lexington on the morning of the 19th of April and established the fact that some individuals when they left their ranks turned and fired upon the red coats. I could not then state in my inscription that which Dr. Ripley and almost if not quite all the people of Concord except myself believed and even earnestly contended for as an essential and indisputable fact in the history of that day.

The Effect of the Battle on Public Opinion in America and Britain

But a much more important element in this event presented itself to me. The events of that day had a higher historical interest than the mere question of "who fired the first gun." The effects were broader and more lasting. This was the turning point of the revolution, from the *provincial* to the *national* state of the country. It changed the strife already existing between the British Government and our people from a quarrel of angry words, strengthened sometimes by brick bats, stones or other handy missiles, from individuals or miscellaneous collections of men and boys, to an open war with weapons of death in the hands of organized soldiery.

Americans Then Show Their Real Power

The events of that morning opened the eyes of our own people, and they saw that they were all of one mind and were ready for the struggle for national liberty that they could write and organize and carry on the war.

Before the 19th of April and even on that early morning, the provincials (Americans) had struggled individually and in accidental clusters to resist the oppressions of their acknowledged rulers with only a hope of relief from their excesses of authority. But from that time forth, they fought as a nation to establish their independence of a foreign government.

Change in British Plans and Tactics

Then and there, for the first time, in all these variances, the tactics of the British army were changed from the aggressive to the defensive. More than this, the eyes of the British government and people were opened to see the actual relation they held to the people of the American colonies. The King, Ministers and Parliament saw then that the difficulties were no longer to be met by edicts, threats, and proclamations, and browbeatings of the army, nor by the presence of a few regiments in forts or garrisons in Boston.

The King, George III, had written to Lord North, "The colonies must either triumph or submit. Four regiments will be enough to bring Americans to their senses; they will only be lions while we are lambs. If we take a resolute part they will undoubtedly be very weak."[10] At that time there were about four thousand British troops stationed in Boston. The British Annual Register for 1775[11] says: "By the nearest calculation, there were from eighteen hundred to two thousand of the best troops in the service (being about half the force that was stationed at Boston, engaged upon the expedition" {to Concord}).

Almon's *Remembrances*,[12] says: "The Battle of Concord was a fair fight and the regulars had the worst of it." "Gen. Gage's present force consists of the 27th, 35th and 64th regiments of foot." This had been considered by the British government sufficient to overcome all the resistance that the colonies would offer.

Almon's *Remembrances* continues, "The event {of the Concord expedition} showed how ill informed those were who had so often asserted at home that a regiment or two could force their way through any part of the continent and the very sight of a grenadier cap would be sufficient to put an American army to flight."[13] But immediately, on the receipt of the news of the Battle in Concord and Lexington, all this was changed.

The Annals of George III,[14] says this offer aroused the whole province to arms and a body of militia said to exceed 20,000 men invested the King's troops in Boston. The King and Parliament took new and extraordinary measures to overcome the rebels. They strained their national force to the utmost. The troops in Boston were at once increased to ten thousand men. Fearing this would be insufficient, they sought the loan of twenty regiments from Russia and failing these, the government sought and obtained sixteen regiments from Germany and sent fifty-five regiments to America. Now the Government began to talk of *conquering America* as if it were a separated country and the opposition, Pitt at their head, told the Government they could not conquer America, "however much they might be aided by the other foreign nations."[15]

10. Greene's *History of the English People*.
11. Page 128.
12. English for 1775, page 92.
13. P. 128.
14. Vol. v, p. 165.
15. *General Burgoyne's Opinion*. Gen. Sir John Burgoyne arrived in Boston on the 25th May. [On] June 14, 1775 he wrote to Gen. Hervey, "At my arrival I found the army and town

Here

On the nineteenth of April 1775
was made the first effectual resistance
to British Aggression.

On the opposite bank stood the American Militia
Here stood the invading army.
And on this spot the first of the enemy fell

In the war of the Revolution.

which gave _____
Independence
To the United States.

In gratitude to God
and in the love of Freedom
This monument was erected
A D. 1836.

This is a copy of the final draft given to the committee
in 1836.   It was all accepted by them
excepting the single word *effectual* in the
second line. for which the committee
substituted the word *forcible*.

Edward Jarvis.

*There were other words
made in the later form
I placed them in their
place there only once
received,*

Jarvis's monument inscription

From that time forth until the end in 1783, the King no longer treated the Americans as provincials, his own people in rebellion, but as a foreign nation organized, united, consolidated. Thus the war of the nations began with the battle at the North Bridge. From that time forth, their organized armies stood face to face opposed as hostile nations. With these views I wrote first an outline of the proposed inscription, keeping in short lines to befit the slab on which it was to be engraved. I rewrote this several times, each time improving by better selection of language. I have some of these original drafts and one that was a copy and that which was finally presented.[16] These were preserved among some other papers from the time they were written. When finished, I carried it to the committee. They were apparently much pleased with all except that one word "*effectual*," which to me was the most valuable of all. I had very long discussions with the committee especially with Dr. Ripley and Col. Shattuck, but I failed of convincing them that *effectual* was the true word and *forcible* the wrong one, although they were very kind and cordial as to all the rest of the paper which they accepted. They accepted and adopted my inscription entire with the exception of the word *effectual*, for which they substituted the word *forcible*. In the following pages are my drafts of the inscription as originally written. The last is a copy taken afterward of that which I finally offered to the committee, but which they did not return to me.

Conclusion

Concord began in 1635 with a higher aim, more generous purpose in its people, and a better supply of the means of living than fell to the lot of the average frontier settlements. This nucleus attracted others of

---

unrecovered from the consternation into which they had been thrown by the ill success of April 19th and from the general revolt, which had followed about the same time." p. 140. He wrote to Lord Rockfort, "In all companies whether of officers or inhabitants, men [were] still lost in a sort of stupefaction, which the events of the 19th of April had occasioned, and venting expressions of censure, anger or despondency." *Life and Correspondence of [Field Marshal Sir] John Burgoyne, [bart.]* General, Statesman, Dramatist, p. 143.

16. Ed.: Jarvis may be in error about the provenance of the inscription. See *Houses of Concord, 1810*; annotated with references by Adams Tolman (unpublished manuscript, 1915), and John S. Keyes's memorial essay about Jarvis in the annals of the Social Circle. Keyes argues that Jarvis found a draft of the inscription, believed it was his own creation, and so presented it here, but in fact it was a joint effort in which each member of the committee submitted a line.

similar nature and habit, so that those who joined them from time to time in after ages were of better average worth than those who sought other new places for existence. It is manifest from the history of the town that the present character and condition of its people have been matters of growth from the beginning. The successive generations were in various degrees faithful to their trust for the opportunities and the blessings they here received from their fathers and to their responsibilities for the future. They prepared the seeds of a better and a larger life for those who should come after them, and thus the town has reached its present state of culture and wealth.

APPENDIX I

Mr. Edward Smith, who is a piano teacher by profession in Concord, is probably acquainted with all in town.[1] He sends me the following list of families who own these instruments.

Pianos and melodeons owned in Concord

Mrs. A. Tower	Mr. Jacobs
" Kelly	Miss Emma Barrett
" Geer	Mrs. Sidney Barrett
" LeBrun	" Fuller
" H. Hosmer	" C. O. Richardson
Miss Bean	" L. Eaton
Mrs. Walcott	" Prescott
" Chamberlain	" Jno. Keyes
" Chace	" Jo. Keyes
" G. Reynolds	" Lang
" J. Pratt	" Melvin
" H. Barrett	" Holden
" Cheney	" C. Hosmer
" Mills	Mr. Buttrick
Miss A. Wheildon	Mrs. Staples
Judge Hoar	" Whitcomb
Mrs. Damon	Miss Pratt
The Misses Munroe	Geo. Davis

---

1. Letter of Mr. Smith, pianoforte tuner.

Concord, Mass. Nov. 11, 78

Dr. Jarvis,
  Dear Sir,
  Mrs. Wood of Jamaica Plain sent me one of your envelopes and stating that you would like a list of pianos from this place.
  I am happy to comply with the request. As far as I am able at present. There are probably a good many more in town than I am able to account for, but may do so some future time, if necessary.

Very respectfully,
Yours,
E. W. Smith

233

Henry Smith
Miss Benjamin
Mrs. E. Hoar
C. Brown
Mrs. W. Brown
Misses Whalies
Dr. Cook
W. Todd
G. W. Minns
R. Rice
Judge Brooks
Mr. Collier
" Place
" J. Wood
" J. Wheeler
" Devens
Miss Blaisdel
Prof. Eaton
C. Munroe
Mrs. Grant
" Parker
Mr. Surrette
Miss Hunt
Madam Keyes

Hosmer
Mr. Berry
Mrs. Hallet
Mrs. Webb
Miss Houghton
Mr. N. Bartlett
Miss Calender
" Keef
Miss N. Smith
" B. Brown
M. Pratt
Mr. Tileston
" R. Barrett
Mrs. Geo. Keyes
Miss Katie Byron
Mr. J. Moore
Middlesex Hotel 2 pianos
Town Hall 1
Walden Hall 1
Mrs. C. O. Richardson 1 reed organ
Mr. Bean (melodeon)
3 churches, each having an organ;
and two of them having a melodeon
in addition to the organ.

APPENDIX II

College graduates from Concord, Mass.
From Harvard if not otherwise stated.

| Year | Name | Occupations of | |
		Fathers	Graduates
1642	John Bulkeley	Minister	Medicine
1643	John Jones	Minister	
1645	Samuel Stow		Minister
1655	Gershom Bulkeley	Minister	Minister
1659	Samuel Willard	Merchant	Minister
1660	Peter Bulkeley	Minister	Law
1690	Benjamin Estabrook	Minister	Minister
1695	Joseph Smith		Minister
1696	Samuel Estabrook	Minister	Minister
1709	Benjamin Prescott	Minister	Minister
1718	Timothy Minott	Minister	Minister
1727	Jonathan Miles		
1727	John Prescott	Medicine	Medicine
1730	Peter Prescott	Medicine	Law
1730	Nathaniel Whitaker		Minister
1733	Ephraim Flint		Farmer
1734	Aaron Whittemore		Minister
1740	Jonathan Hoar		Army Offcr
1747	Timothy Minott	Teacher	Teacher
1749	Israel Cheever		Minister
1749	Oliver Merriam		Minister
1749	Samuel Brooks		Reg of Deed
1751	Stephen Minott	Teacher	Minister
1751	George Farrar		Minister
1751	John Monroe		Minister
1755	William H. Wheeler		Minister
1757	Joseph Wheeler		Minister
1760	Daniel Bliss	Minister	Law
1765	Joseph Lee	Physician	Minister
1770	Joseph Hunt	Farmer	Medicine

Year	Name	Occupations of Fathers	Graduates
1772	Nathan Bond	Trader	Merchant
1773	Tilly Merrick	Teacher	Trader
1775	Thomas Whiting	Magistrate	Teacher
1776	Samuel Lee	Physician	Teacher
1777	Peter Clark		Law
1777	Ebenezer Hubbard		Minister
1781	Abiel Haywood	Farmer	Medicine
1781	Timothy Swan		Medicine
1784	Ezra Conant		Minister
1784	Silas Lee	Physician	Law
1784	John Merrick	Trader	Law
1789	William Emerson	Minister	Minister
1793	William Jones	Blacksmith	Law
1793	James Temple (Dart.)	Farmer	Law
1798	Samuel P. P. Fay	Law	Law
1800	Rufus Hosmer	Farmer	Law
1801	Stephen Minott	Farmer	Law
1804	Samuel Ripley	Minister	Minister
1805	Daniel B. Ripley	Minister	Law
1805	Benjamin W. Hildreth	Trader	Medicine
1805	John White	Trader	Minister
1810	Jonas Wheeler		Law
1810	John Barrett (Williams)	Farmer	Minister
1810	Joshua Barrett (Dart.)	Farmer	Minister
1813	John Brown	Farmer	Medicine
1819	Ephraim Buttrick	Farmer	Law
1819	Benjamin Barrett	Farmer	Medicine
1821	Charles Jarvis	Baker/Farmer	Medicine
1821	John M. Cheney	Farmer	Law
1826	George W. Hosmer	Farmer	Minister
1826	Edward Jarvis	Baker/Farmer	Medicine
1829	Reuben Bates	Sea Capt.	Minister
1829	Jonathan Thos. Davis	Trader	Teacher
1829	Horatio C. Merriam	Farmer	Law
1833	Marshall Merriam (Yale)	Farmer	Medicine
1833	William M. Prichard	Trader	Law
1833	William Whiting	Carriagemkr	Law
1834	George Moore	Sheriff	Minister
1835	H. B. Dennis	Farmer	Editor
1835	E. S. Hoar	Law	Law
1836	J. Gardner Davis (Yale)	Trader	Minister
1837	H. D. Thoreau	Pencil Mkr	Author
1841	J. S. Keyes	Law	Law

Year	Name	Occupations of Fathers	Graduates
1844	Edward Hoar	Law	
1844	George M. Brooks	Law	Law
1845	Gorham Bartlett	Medicine	
1845	G. F. Hoar	Law	Law
1848	George Heywood	Medicine	Law
1849	Joseph B. Keyes	Law	Law
1850	Ephraim M. Ball		Trader
1850	Sam Barn (Bowdoin)		Trader
1851	N. H. Barrett	Farmer	Govt Clerk
1851	Francis C. Brown	Merchant	
1851	William Goodwin	Minister	Greek Prof.
1854	Charles Gerrish	Teacher	Merchant
1856	Nehemiah Ball	Trader	
1858	Henry N. Frost	Minister	Lawyer
1862	Charles F. Folsom	Minister	Doctor
1863	William Brown (Amherst)	Farmer	Minister
1864	G. W. Lawrence	Farmer	Law
1864	Charles F. Hildreth	Trader	Law
1866	Edward W. Emerson	Author/Minister	Medicine
1867	Samuel Hoar	Law	Law
1867	George C. Mann	Law	Teacher
1869	William H. Simmons	Minister	Medicine
1870	Charles E. Hoar	Law	Engineer
1870	Charles H. Walcott	Trader	Law
1870	Benj. P. Mann	Law	Naturalist
1871	Henry W. Wheeler	Farmer	Tutor
1871	William Wheeler (Agri. college)	Farmer	Engineer
1873	Francis H. Bigelow	Blacksmith	Minister
1874	Edward E. Simmons	Minister	
1876	Frank W. Barrett	Sec. of Insurance Company	Law
1874	Prescott Keyes	Lawyer	Law
1874	Woodward Hudson	Editor	Law
1882	Sherman Hoar	Lawyer	
	Ivan Parriss		
	Herbert Myrick (Am. Agri)	Teacher	
	Mary B. King (Vassar)	Lawyer	

103 in all from Concord

The desire for education has been diffused through all the classes of society. These 103 graduates (1642 to 1876) belonged to families of all occupations who lived in all the quarters of the town.

Occupation of families sending sons to College

Sons of	Number
Farmers	20
Ministers	17
Traders	14
Lawyers	11
Physicians	7
Mechanics	6
Teachers	3
Sea Captain	1
Sheriff	1
Insurance Sec	1
	80
not stated	23
	103

It is extremely probable that nearly if not quite all of the twenty-three families whose occupation in the first 150 years is not known were farmers. These represent 85 different families in the successive generations. Twelve families sent two sons; three sent three sons each. Ninety-five of these graduated at Harvard, one at the Agricultural college in Amherst, one at Bowdoin, two at Dartmouth, one at Williams, one at Amherst, two at Yale colleges.

Professions of the Concord Graduates

Clergymen	31
Lawyers	30
Teachers	9
Engineers	2
Professors in College	2
Authors	1
Editor	1
Naturalist	1
Reg. Deeds	1
Gov. Officer	1
Merchants	4
Farmer	1
Army Officer	1
None	9
	103

Some of those who are not recorded as having a profession died soon after graduating. Twenty-four of these Concord graduates settled in the town and gave the people the advantage of their educated influence. Each one of these 103 graduates is presumed to have spent four years in college—380 in Harvard, four in Amherst, four in Amherst Agricultural, four in Williams, eight in Yale, eight in Dartmouth and four in Bowdoin. In all, the town was represented 412 years in college by those who have graduated up to this time, 1878.

Add to these Prescott Keyes and Woodward Hudson, who have been three years in Harvard, and will graduate in 1879 and also three others now known to me, Josiah Dudley, who spent three years in Middlebury and Union College; Griffin and Edward Reynolds, each of whom spent two years each in Harvard, all of whom left for various causes; and these will swell the whole representation of Concord to 425 years in college. There may have been others in college for one or more years. These however are all that I have been able to ascertain.

[Jarvis's next three lists are omitted because they present no information beyond what is contained in his list above of college attendees from Concord.]

Graduates of colleges and Professional men living in Concord, March 28, 1878. Graduates of Harvard College

	Profession	Place of Business
R. W. Emerson	Author	
E. Rockwood Hoar	Lawyer	Boston
Edward S. Hoar	Judge of Dist. Court	Concord
John S. Keyes	Lawyer	
George M. Brooks	Judge of Probate	
John B. Tileston	Farmer	Concord
C. Gore Ripley	Lawyer Judge of Sup. Ct of [indecipherable]	
George P. Bradford	Teacher	Boston
A. P. Chamberlain		
George Heywood	Lawyer	Concord
F. B. Sanborn	Editor/Agent of state Board of C[indecipherable]	Boston
George W. Minor		
Edward W. Emerson	Physician	Concord
Samuel Hoar	Lawyer	Boston
Frederic W. Holland	Clergyman	
Charles H. Walcott	Lawyer	Boston
Henry N. Wheeler	Teacher	Harv. College
Frank H. Bigelow	Div. student	
Arthur Mills		
William L. Eaton	Teacher high school	Concord
Samuel Wall	Physician	Concord
Charles Emerson	Teacher	
Grindall Reynolds *Hon*	Clergyman	Concord

Wm Wheeler Agri College	Engineer	Japan
Henry A. Barrett Amherst	Physician	Concord
Henry M. Grout Yale	Clergyman	Concord
Jas. L. Whitney Yale		

Professional Men

George A. King	Lawyer	. Boston
F. W. Griffin	Lawyer	Charlestown
C. H. S. Williams	Homeopath	
James A. Cook	Physician	Concord
E. P. Parker		
Charles Thompson	Lawyer	Concord

Rev. Dr. G. W. Hosmer sent a copy of the preceding tables of graduates and Concord scholars in college to President Eliot of Harvard college. Pres. E., after examining it, returned the papers to Dr. H. with this very gratifying letter.

> Harvard University
> Cambridge, Mass.
> 30 Apr. 1878

My dear Sir:

I have examined with much interest these tables prepared by Dr. Jarvis. They show how good stock tells. Also how a village fed all the learned professions. I thank you for sending them to me.

> Very truly yours,
> Charles W. Eliot

Rev. G. W. Hosmer D.D.

APPENDIX III

Letter of Miss Ellen F. Whitney, Public Library, in respect to the papers and periodicals taken in Concord.

Dr. Jarvis
Dear Sir,
I have been unable to find the item in regard to newspapers which you wished, but have been to Mr. Davis the periodical dealer, from whom the items were obtained before and with this result.
Daily papers taken in Concord
38 journals
50 Heralds
16 Globes
4 Posts
15 Advertisers
6 Travellers
8 Transcripts
These are in addition to those that came through the mail. Hoping this may answer your purpose, I am very respectfully yours, E. F. Whitney

The foregoing papers were sold by Mr. Davis the newspaper dealer. Mr. Edward W. Smith obtained the following from the post office as the list of papers received in Concord through the mail.

List of newspapers, pamphlets, magazines
Received at Concord P. Office, Mass.

Daily	Boston	Post	4
		Globe	5
		Advertiser	7
		Journal	18
		Herald (2 morn 1 eve)	3
		Ev. Traveller	3
		Ev. Transcript	9
		Ev. Journal	3
	Cincinnati	Commercial	1
	N.Y.	Evening Post	1
	Springfield	Republican	3

Weekly	N.Y. Herald	1
	Springfield Republican	3
	Christian Union N.Y.	2
	Catholic Review	2
	Cape Ann Advertiser	2
	The Nation, N.Y.	4
	The Churchman, N.Y.	3
	Boston Weekly Journal	4
	Lowell Weekly Journal	5
	Framingham Gazette	4
	(Lexington) Minute Man	4
	Waltham Free Press	5
	Sat. Eve. Gazette	1
	Advance (Chicago)	2
	Chicago Fields	3
	N.Y. Freeman's Journal (Catholic) [no number recorded]	
	N.Y. Tribune	4
	Boston, The Pilot (Catholic)	18
	" Congregationalist	12
	N.Y. Irish World	10
	" Harper's Bazaar	6
	" Harper's Weekly	10
	" Frank Leslie	
	Boston Banner of Light	2
	" Universalist	2
	" Independent	4
	" Commonwealth	6
	" Agriculturalist	8
	" Youth's Companion	25
	" Weekly Globe	9
	" Christian Register	15
	" New England Farmer	25
	" Massachusetts Ploughman	35
	" Boston Cultivator	15
	Concord Freeman	300
Semi-weekly	Tribune N.Y.	2
"	Journal Boat	1
Weeklies		
	Ayer Turner's Public Spirit	3
	Boston Journal of Education	3
	Chicago Skandinaven	3
	Decorah, Iowa, Decorah Posten	2
	Living Church	1
	Woman's Journal	6
	Weekly Transcript	3
	Turf, Field and Farm	1

Forest and Stream	1
Country Gentleman	2
Record (Philad)	1
Watchman	3
McGees Illinois Weekly	1
Art Interchange	1
Traveller	2
Index	3
Banker and Tradesman	1
Ill, Christian Weekly	3
N.Y. Weekly Witness	2
Sunday School Times	6

Monthlies

Domestic Monthly	5
Appletons	1
Harper's	14
Scribner's	10
St. Nicholas	14
Wide Awake	4
Baby Land	5
Godey's	1
Peterson's	1
Demoreste	2
Fashion Monthly	6
Folio	1
Frank Leslie's Popular Monthly	4
Donahue's Magazine	6
Scientific Farmer	6
Littells Living Age	4
Home Guest	6
Celt Review	1
Life and Light	9
Home Missionary	3
American Missionary	15
Journal of Chemistry [no number recorded]	
Atlantic Monthly [no number recorded]	

Concord Feby 14, 79

Dr. Jarvis
    Dr. Sir,
I have succeeded at last in obtaining the list of papers, delivered by the news agent at Concord Junction. I hope you will find it useful to your collection, if not too late. I suppose you received the other list I sent all right.

   We are all well as usual except Woodward has been suffering somewhat from cold.

Yours respectfully, E. W. Smith.

Boston	Herald	50
	Globe	30
	Journal	20
	Advertiser	5
	Traveller	2
	Post	1
New York	N.Y. Weekly	10
	Sat. Night	15
	N.Y. Ledger	15
	Scientific Am'cn	5
	Harper's Weekly	2

I hope you will be able to read this; am writing in the Post Office with very poor pen and thick Ink. E. W. S.

A P P E N D I X   I V

Concord Population

1765	1564
1766	1565
1767	1566
1768	1567
1769	1568
1770	1569
1771	1570
1772	1571
73	1572
1774	1573
75	1574
76	1575
77	1576
1778	1577

[21987] [omitted by Jarvis]

1779	1578
80	1579
81	1580
82	1581
83	1582
84	1583
85	1584
86	1585
87	1586
88	1587
89	1588
90	1589
	1590

12 yrs. 19004

1791	1598
92	1607
93	1616
94	1624
95	1633
96	1642

97	1651
98	1660
99	1669
1800	1679

10 yrs. 16379

1801	1674
2	1669
3	1665
4	1660
5	1655
6	1651
7	1646
8	1642
9	1637
10	1633

10 yrs. 16532

1811	1647
12	1662
13	1678
14	1693
15	1708
16	1724
17	1739
18	1755
19	1771
20	1788

17165

21	1809
22	1831
23	1853
24	1876
25	1899
26	1922
27	1945
28	1969

8 yrs. 15104

50 yrs.   84184[omitted by Jarvis]

1829	1992
30	2017
31	2028
32	2034
33	2050
34	2061
35	2072
36	2084
37	2095
38	2106
39	2118

40	2124

12 yrs. [24781] 24791 [EJ]

1841	2141
42	2153
43	2164
44	2176
45	2188
46	2200
47	2212
48	2224
49	2235
50	2249

10 yrs. 21942

1851	2248
52	2248
53	2248
54	2247
55	2247
56	2247
57	2246
58	2246
59	2246
1860	2246

10 yrs. 22469

1861	2243
62	2240
63	2237
64	2234
65	2232
66	2266
67	2302
68	2338
69	2374
70	2412

10 yrs. 22878

1871	2462
72	2514
73	2567
74	2621
75	2676
76	2732
77	2789
78	2848

8 yrs. 21209

50 yrs.   [113279] 111343 [EJ]

100 yrs.   197463

I N D E X

References to illustrations are printed in boldface type

DATE DUE

#27432304